Frank H Cunningham

Familiar Sketches of the Phillips Exeter Academy and Surroundings

Frank H Cunningham

Familiar Sketches of the Phillips Exeter Academy and Surroundings

ISBN/EAN: 9783337190675

Printed in Europe, USA, Canada, Australia, Japan

Cover: Foto ©ninafisch / pixelio.de

More available books at **www.hansebooks.com**

FAMILIAR SKETCHES

OF

THE PHILLIPS EXETER ACADEMY.

FAMILIAR SKETCHES

OF

THE PHILLIPS EXETER ACADEMY

AND

SURROUNDINGS.

BY

FRANK H. CUNNINGHAM.

With Illustrations.

BOSTON:
JAMES R. OSGOOD AND COMPANY.
1883.

Copyright, 1883,
BY FRANK H. CUNNINGHAM.

All rights reserved.

UNIVERSITY PRESS:
JOHN WILSON AND SON, CAMBRIDGE.

TO

MY MOTHER,

TO WHOM I OWE MORE THAN I CAN EVER REPAY,

These Sketches

ARE AFFECTIONATELY INSCRIBED.

PREFACE.

A VISIT to some of the great schools of England, one summer, during my student days at Exeter, and a subsequent inquiry into their foundation, endowment, and discipline, led me to study somewhat carefully the history of the school in which I was most interested, — that of the Phillips Exeter Academy. I was surprised to find how meagre were the sources of information. The only available articles were Professor Hoyt's paper, published in 1858, in the North American Review, and Professor Bowen's Preface to the General Catalogue issued by the Academy in 1869. These, although written in a far more scholarly style than I could hope to command, were necessarily brief.

"This institution," I considered, "founded as it was in the days of Washington, of Lafayette, and of Jefferson, possessing as it does such glorious traditions and so many eminent Alumni, deserves, beyond a doubt, a written history." It was suggested that I should write something; but I at first hesitated. A few letters written for the Boston daily and weekly newspapers, during a residence of four years at the South, constituted about all the **work of this nature I had thus far** attempted. Later, however, encouraged by **those whose** advice I value, a series of sketches which should cover the salient points in the Academy's **history was** planned and begun. At the suggestion of the Rev. **John** Langdon Sibley, Harvard's venerable Librarian Emeritus, I at once began an extensive correspondence with the Alumni, young **and** old, and several well-filled **letter-**books attest the interest which all have taken in the project. To these letters, to books, papers, **manu-**scripts, and other letters, found in public and **private** libraries, to the records of **the** Academy, and **to the** information given by the many friends of the **school, I** am indebted for the contents **of** this volume.

It will be observed that, although I have drawn freely on these sources of information, **yet as far as** possible I have endeavored in each case **to give** due credit.

The history of the Academy contained in the **first** seven chapters **is** my own work. The remainder of the volume, owing to the extent of the undertaking and the short time allowed for its completion, is mainly contributed. Of the biographical notices contained in Chapters VIII., IX., X., and XI., the sketch of **Jeremiah** Kingman was written by Prof. Sylvester Waterhouse, of Washington University, St. Louis; **the** sketch of Joseph S. Buckminster, by Mr. George P. **F.** Hobson; that of Benjamin F. Butler, by Mr. P. J. Casey. The sketches **of** Richard Hildreth, A. J. Packard, Nathan Hale, and Theodore Lyman, by Mr. **L.** M. Garrison. The remainder, with the exception of the sketches of Daniel Webster, Edward Everett, Jared Sparks, Robert F. Pennell, and George L. Kittredge, which were written by myself, were supplied by Mr. Thomas Hunt, who, as well as all the above-mentioned contributors, has materially aided in the preparation of this volume. For the chapter of Reminiscences, I am indebted to the gentlemen whose names appear at the end of the articles.

The sketch of the Golden Branch was contributed by Mr. Frank H. Stanyan; that of the G. L. Soule Literary Society, by Mr. John M. Merriam; the history of the Exonian was written by Mr. William N. Needles, of Philadelphia, one of the founders of the paper. The introduction to the sketches of the various societies was written by Mr. Thomas Hunt; and the sketch which appears in the chapter on Sports and Games was written by Mr. L. M. Garrison. The article on Exeter, which was contributed by a friend, is founded mainly on a manuscript sketch of Exeter by the Rev. Jacob Chapman, and on a pamphlet entitled, "Exeter in 1776," by the Hon. Charles H. Bell.

This work, which has greatly outgrown its original proportions, has been prosecuted under unusual difficulties, and in the hours which should have been devoted to study or other work, or to rest. Therefore may the critics be not too critical.

Although no labor or expense has been spared to render the book complete and free from errors, yet omissions will be noticed and mistakes will be found, as in a volume of this nature they are unavoidable. It is to be hoped that revised and enlarged editions of the work may be issued from time to time; and with this in view, the author will esteem it a favor to be notified — through the publishers, Messrs. James R. Osgood & Co. — of any errors that may be discovered. He will also be happy to receive any information or suggestions which will contribute to the completeness of the Academy's history.

Many persons have laid the author under obligations by contributing information or by the loan of documents, books, or photographs. He would here express his deep sense of gratitude for the favors and assistance rendered by that thoroughly unselfish scholar, the Rev. John Langdon Sibley, and also by the Hon. Wendell Phillips and the Rev. Phillips Brooks. Thanks are also due to Dr. Cecil F. P. Bancroft, Principal of the Phillips Academy at Andover; to Rev. William L. Ropes, the Librarian of the Andover Theological Seminary; to the Librarians, and their assistants, of Harvard College Library, the Boston Athenæum Library, the Boston Public Library, and the Library of the Massachusetts Historical Society; to the Trustees of the Phillips Exeter Academy, especially to the Rev. Andrew P. Peabody, the Hon. George S. Hale, and to Dr. Nicholas E. Soule; to the Faculty of the Academy; to Prof. Robert F. Pennell, and to many other gentlemen of Exeter.

CAMBRIDGE, May 31, 1883.

CONTENTS.

CHAPTER		PAGE
I.	Historical Introduction	1
II.	Biographical and Historical: First and Second Periods	15
III.	Biographical and Historical: Third and Fourth Periods	37
IV.	Financial and Chronological	69
V.	The Founder and the Phillips Family	87
VI.	The Buildings	106
VII.	Government	121
VIII.	Biographical Sketches: Alumni	128
IX.	Biographical Sketches: Alumni	151
X.	Biographical Sketches: Instructors, Past and Present	173
XI.	Biographical Sketches: Benefactors and Trustees	203
XII.	Reminiscences and Anecdotes	220
XIII.	Societies	248

CONTENTS.

		PAGE
XIV.	THE EXONIAN,	272
XV.	SPORTS AND GAMES.	281
XVI.	STATISTICAL AND MISCELLANEOUS	287
XVII.	EXETER: ITS PAST AND PRESENT	319

APPENDIX.

ACT OF INCORPORATION 325
CONSTITUTION 330
COMMEMORATIVE POEMS 340
ORDERS OF EXERCISES 346

INDEX 351

LIST OF ILLUSTRATIONS.

	PAGE
ABBOT HALL	116
ACADEMY, FIRST BUILDING	8
" SECOND BUILDING	8
" THIRD BUILDING	59
ACADEMY SEAL	ii
BAPTIST CHURCH	323
EPISCOPAL CHURCH	323
FIRST CONGREGATIONALIST CHURCH	323
G. L. SOULE LITERARY SOCIETY SEAL	263
GORHAM HALL	117
GREAT HALL, OR "CHAPEL"	59
OLD POWDER-HOUSE	321
PHILLIPS FAMILY ARMS	87
PHILLIPS, HON. JOHN, AUTOGRAPH	104
PRINCIPAL'S HOUSE	233
ROOM ON PINE STREET	278
ROOM NO. 12, ABBOT HALL	278

	PAGE
Second Congregationalist Church	323
Tongue of the Old Academy Bell	120
View on Water Street	233

Portraits.

Benjamin Abbot	173
Joseph Gibson Hoyt	"
Woodbridge Odlin	"
Albert Cornelius Perkins	"
Hon. John Phillips (the Founder)	"
John Langdon Sibley	"
Gideon Lane Soule	"

THE PHILLIPS EXETER ACADEMY.

CHAPTER I.

HISTORICAL INTRODUCTION.

EVENTS WHICH LED TO THE ESTABLISHMENT OF THE ACADEMY. — THE FORMAL OPENING OF THE SCHOOL, AND THE INSTALLATION OF THE FIRST PRINCIPAL.

LIKE the waves which roll in upon the neighboring beach at Hampton, their glistening crests following one another in a long line, the first hundred years in the history of the Phillips Exeter Academy have passed. Just as those waves have smiled or frowned under the sunshine or storm of heaven, these hundred years of school life have been made glad or sad by changes which every school must experience. Let us rejoice to-day that, unlike the breakers which strand so many goodly ships, time has made no wreck of the classic halls of Exeter.

The old school, like a tender mother, has smiled and frowned at the tricks of her children: for them she has hidden the gates of the good townsfolk; often has she sneezed at the fumes of burning pepper or tobacco; and once, when she saw an old pupil,[1] done in marble, car-

[1] Hon. Benjamin F. Butler.

ried away in triumph to be hidden for months in some obscure attic, it is said that she heaved a deep sigh.

Many and many a time her bell has proclaimed the victories of her sons at bat and ball, and they have never suffered defeat but she has sorrowed. She has watched, with the satisfaction of a fond parent, the hard work that has made her boys men; and in after years, when they had left her protecting care, and had gone forth, like Don Quixote, to champion the distressed and right the wrongs of humanity, she has been delighted at their successes. If, more happy than the illustrious Don, they won a lady-love, and sent back to their Alma Mater their little Dons, she has indeed been proud.

So the years have passed, until to-day, looking over this broad land, we see these former students, these Exeter graduates, engaged in every honorable employment, and "bearing their part well in every State and Territory of the Union, and in every civilized nation of the world."

Let us take a hasty look at the events that led to the establishment of this Academy.

This school had its origin in no royal grant. No bishop framed its charter. It was the work of neither State nor Church. Only the kingly Christian hand of a native of Massachusetts, the State that has bred so many noble-hearted Yankees, only a humble citizen of New Hampshire, wrote its constitution and devoted his whole fortune to the endowment of this and kindred institutions. Let us ever venerate the name of the founder, and let the honorable Board of Trustees set apart some day in each year as Founder's Day, to be appropriately celebrated by literary and athletic exercises.

Just as the origin of our first town-meeting, an institution dear to every American heart, was the signing of the compact in the cabin of the "Mayflower" by our Puritan fathers, so also the covenant signed by John Winthrop and his companions was the germ from which sprung the educational and religious movement that has made our land so remarkable for its Christian civilization. Winthrop's followers landed at Salem in 1630. A few remained at Salem, others of them founded Boston, while still others settled Watertown on the royal river Charles. Among the last were Sir Richard Saltonstall, and his friend and pastor, the Rev. George Phillips. From this Phillips was descended the founder of the Phillips Exeter Academy.

This was a remarkable colony. Unlike the settlers of Jamestown, they brought with them their wives and children, their schools and churches; and even while their good ship "Arbella" was ploughing and plunging through mid-ocean, they "taught and catechised." Immediately after landing they provided homes for themselves and their ministers; then they built the log-church. Five years after they landed we learn that they had "free schools." Here we see them progressing towards The Phillips Exeter Academy. The next year we read that the General Court of Massachusetts Bay "agreed to give £400 toward a school or college."

A year later the College was ordered to be established at "Newetowne," a name soon changed to Cambridge, — the college town of George Phillips in dear Old England. Observe how they strive to reproduce in the New England the schools, the churches, the colleges, the names even, that they enjoyed and loved in the mother country. The next year the College received the name and bequest of John Harvard.

In 1639 the first printing-press in America was set up at Cambridge, and on it the first Bible ever translated into a heathen tongue by an Englishman was printed. In 1647, just a hundred years before the founder of this Academy gave up a professional for a business life, it was ordered that every township of fifty householders should appoint a teacher for its children. Soon schools, open to all, were established in Roxbury, in Jamaica Plain, and in the adjoining hamlets. From this time the colony grew, its schools multiplied, and its influence extended.

In the early part of the next century, however, things received a check. Immigration stopped, and emigration began. Learning suffered. To be sure, they had grammar schools and a college; but, if progress was to be made, they must have a school to prepare their young men for the college and to provide their schools with teachers. They thought of England and their school days at Harrow or Eton, and straightway set up the Dummer Academy at Byfield. Here, again, we trace the beginning of The Phillips Exeter Academy.

To this school, in 1765, comes a thoughtful, sober boy, fonder of stories of the French and Indian wars than of play; slow to learn, but sure to remember; one destined to be alike the friend of education and of Washington,— both a statesman and a patriot. To-day we can look back to that boy, and truly give him the honor of originating our American academy system.

In the third generation from George Phillips of Watertown was Samuel Phillips, for sixty years pastor of the Second Church at Andover.

His son Samuel received a liberal education, and, making his home at North Andover, became a merchant and filled many offices of honor. His son was Judge Samuel Phillips, the boy of the Dummer Academy.

Let the lad who desires a grand model, who loves the memory of the "boys of '76," the smell of powder, and the virtues of our Puritan fathers, read the story of this life, which has been told so well.[1]

A lad named Eliphalet Pearson (when a child he always said his name was "Elephant Pearson") was his friend and schoolmate. Together they roamed the Byfield woods, roused the deer, chased the squirrels, and, in addition, planned for the future. Leaving Harvard in 1771, at the age of nineteen, young Phillips soon married, and his home life forms one of the sweetest and best pages in American history.

[1] Memoir of Judge Phillips, by Rev. John L. Taylor.

He plunged into the struggle for independence, and in the midst of revolution was one of the foremost of the rebels. Now he is town clerk and treasurer, now member of the Provincial Congress, now hiding the valuables of Harvard College from the British soldiery, — now here, now there, now everywhere. In answer to Putnam's cry, "Ye gods, give us powder!" he gallops home, summons his neighbors, and, relating the facts, says that on themselves the fate of the young nation depends. Then in his coarse, rustic frock he sets to work; and the result is powder, followed by the evacuation of Boston.

It has been said that his life was full of great purposes. True. And now, although he himself has but little fortune, and although he is the heir to his father's wealth and that of his childless Uncle John, of Exeter, still this generous youth unfolds to them his plan for an academy, and urges them to endow such a school with the wealth that would otherwise descend to him.

This is the result of the "catechizing" on board the "Arbella"; this is the result of the college, the church, and the printing-press; this is the result of the plans made in the woods of Byfield.

The father and uncle are wise, far-seeing men, both graduates of Harvard College; John Phillips himself was formerly a preacher and schoolmaster. They eagerly enter into the young man's plan, — a plan as broad and Christian as it could well be made; and the result is the Phillips Academy at Andover. Projected by young Phillips, the scheme was developed by his friend Pearson; and together these young men wrote the constitution, signed by the joint founders, Samuel and John Phillips, on the 21st of April, 1778.

To this John Phillips and his kindred, and the motives that led him to establish and endow the Academy at Exeter, we shall devote an entire chapter.

We have thus reviewed the historical points which led to the founding of the Phillips Exeter Academy.

The act of incorporation [1] obtained by Dr. Phillips was signed by the President of New Hampshire, as the Governor was formerly called, on the 3d of April, 1781, just six months, lacking one day, subsequent to the incorporation of the Phillips Academy at Andover. It is thus the oldest educational institution established by the State legislature.[2]

By this act,[3] gentlemen selected by the founder were appointed trustees of the fund, with full powers to erect a building, appoint a Preceptor and instructors, and to nominate their successors forever. He reserved the right to preside over the Board of Trustees during his own life, and to appoint his successor. It is mainly through the wise plans of the founder, during these years, that the school was so firmly and successfully established. The first meeting of the Board of Trus-

[1] See Appendix.
[2] Dartmouth College was established by royal grant in 1769.
[3] For an analysis of this remarkable document, see the chapter on Government.

tees was held on December 18, 1781. The opening of the school, however, was delayed by the difficulty the Trustees experienced in obtaining land for the Academy building. It was the same old story; the most eligible land was held at double its real value. Dr. Phillips wrote several letters to his nephew on this subject. Later he writes: —

DEAR KINSMAN, — Having a favorable opportunity by Mr. Thurston, I write, hoping he will more freely communicate matters respecting himself and the school here. . . . The building is erected where the builders pleased; and suppose one room may be furnished this month. But whether it would be best to desire a gentleman so out of health as Mr. Thurston really is to enter for so short a time, or to wait till spring in order to procure an instructor who might be employed and settled to his own and others' advantage, is the question.

Your sentiments herein would lay a fresh obligation upon your loving uncle,

JOHN PHILLIPS.

This, then, was the building in which was heard the first Latin lesson. Mr. Benjamin Thurston was named as the first Preceptor,[1] but he was not appointed to fill that office on account of his uncertain health.

The school is said to have been opened on Thursday, the 20th of February, 1783, with a discourse by the Rev. David McClure, A. M., pastor of the church at North Hampton, and a Trustee of the Academy. On that day Mr. Thurston, as temporary instructor, probably

---

[1] See letter, Chapter V. p. 100.

FIRST ACADEMY BUILDING.

SECOND ACADEMY BUILDING.

heard the first lesson ever recited in the Phillips Exeter Academy.

The formal dedication of the building and the installation of William Woodbridge as the first Preceptor did not take place until "two P. M." on Thursday, May 1, 1783. An oration on the "Advantages of Learning" was delivered by the Rev. David McClure, after which the Rev. Benjamin Thurston, a Trustee of the Academy, addressed the Preceptor as follows: —

"You, sir, being invited by the honorable Founder of this institution, with the universal approbation of the Board of Trustees, to take upon you, as Preceptor, the charge of this Academy, and having accepted the invitation, I, in behalf and in the name of the Board, in this public manner welcome you to this literary function. The business, sir, you are entering upon is arduous and weighty; but, from your distinguished character, we presume you will make it agreeable, honorable, and useful: nothing, we trust, will be wanting to render it so from the public, the end of this institution being the general good of society. The citizens of this town, we presume, will join their endeavors with their approbation to facilitate your undertaking; and you may, sir, at all times, in the line of duty, depend on our confidence, approbation, and support. The theatre before you is large, the field of your instruction extending, as occasion requires, to all those sciences and arts commonly taught in academical institutions; every state, town, and family having equal right by the constitution to all the privileges of the seminary, and none wanting encouragement to apply for entrance who are suitably qualified for admission. .You will therefore, sir, make no discrimination in favor of any particular state, town, or family, on account of parentage, age, wealth, sentiments of religion, &c. The institution is founded on principles of the most extensive liberality. The constitution and laws of the institution you will adopt as your guide in the government and instruction of the seminary, and in the exercise of all those powers and rights vested in you by the constitution, which I now present you; that is our warrant in these public transactions, and your encouragement in this solemn induction; governing yourself in your public capacity by that, without prejudice or fear, will recommend you to the approbation and esteem of all good men, and place you under the patronage of that God whose blessing will crown your endeavors with success. The time, sir, is at hand when you will actually enter on the business of your appointment; the academical edifice erected for that purpose in this place, and wholly devoted to the public by some generous friends to literature, we now commit to your immediate care and possession for carrying into execution the design of this institution; in evidence of which, and as your warrant in taking possession, I now, sir, present you the keys. You will then enter on the business of your appointment with assurance of our affection and sincere friendship, as a token of which I now give you my hand; at the same time wishing you a blessing from Him, in the improvement of your gifts, who giveth to all their talents, with confident expectation of seeing virtue and literature adding a crown to your labors."

To which the Preceptor replied as follows: —

"DEAR AND RESPECTED SIR, — The cordiality and politeness of such a friendly welcome to this institution merit a return of my sincere thanks. Decency and propriety require that reply which the sensibility of a grateful mind would dictate. Great, inexpressibly weighty, are the duties of that important station to which I am now invited; and singular the exercise of that labor and self-denial, of that wisdom and patience, absolutely necessary to a faithful discharge.

"Without the assured expectation of aid from Heaven and from you, nothing could induce me to accept the charge; but with full confidence of your fidelity and honor to discharge the duties of your trust in granting every necessary and proper support, both for maintenance and authority, with raised expectations that the generous founder will continue his smiles, that those gentlemen whose generosity has furnished a building will yet be friends, that the town which has so worthily promoted its welfare by their influence with the General Court will persevere in their endeavors to establish its reputation and promote its usefulness, I am confident in my hopes of its prosperity and success.

"With a due sense of the importance of the charge, where minds are to be formed for immortality, and furnished for the duties of a useful life; with a becoming sense of deficiency in that wisdom, those virtues and accomplishments, that finish the character of a complete instructor; and with constant dependence upon the aid of Providence (without which every attempt is vain), — I would readily obey the providential call, and step forth thus publicly to manifest my acceptance of it; and, as I would humbly hope, with solemn sincerity, to devote myself to the service of this institution, and, being thus supported, pledge my character and sacred honor conscientiously and faithfully to discharge the station while Providence may continue me there.

"Kindly aid me, **O ye** friends of virtue, of piety, and **of** learning! **ever support** me by your friendship **and your candor! 'T is the interest of yourselves and your children, of society and virtue, that demands your aid.** As the speaker asks nothing for **himself, unconnected with this institution, he** hopes his wishes may be granted. He **would modestly** hope the interest **of** virtue and a useful **life** were not among the least **of** his motives **to** forsake his tender friends, bid adieu **to the** prospect **of affluence** and the pleasing hopes of more leisure life.

"**As** Providence has determined my residence **among you, I** hope **to be** excused if, upon this occasion, **I deliver my** sentiments with unusual freedom; and more especially when I can **sincerely add that I** wish for your **friendship and** support, that my labors **may be** beneficial to *you*, to *society*, and to your *sons*.

" I congratulate myself upon the prospect of becoming **a** friendly member of **your** societies, ardently wishing to merit your approbation and friendship.

" I congratulate the honorable and benevolent Founder of this institution upon the **happy prospect of its proving a** valuable and extensive blessing to society **while time** endures. May unborn thousands of this rising empire meet him in glory, and hail him as the benefactor of piety and virtue, while both pay their united adoration to Him whose bounty bestowed the gift and whose goodness first excited the generous purpose!

" I congratulate this honorable Trust in the opportunity they have to **serve** the interests **of** learning and virtue; **and** upon these singular motives now presented to perse**vere** in their endeavors to **render** this institution an **extensive** blessing. Its success greatly, very greatly, **depends** upon the liberality and fidelity with which they discharge **the trust.**

HISTORICAL INTRODUCTION. 13

"I congratulate you all, my affectionate friends, upon the arrival of this happy day which opens the Exeter Academy; and at a time when every patriotic heart dilates with unusual joy at the delightful sound of peace.

"While the glories of this rising empire dawn upon us, let us unitedly exert every effort to cherish the institutions of *knowledge*, which is the *stability* of these *glorious* times when the voice of *liberty* and *peace* is heard.

"*So* shall *that* science and virtue which have seated America in the throne of empires, and made her revered among the nations, be extensively spread to form the minds and virtues of her illustrious sons.

"So shall they be formed for usefulness and famed for wisdom, for virtue, and for glory.

"And so, my friends, shall we offer a grateful return for the blessings we now enjoy, to the wonderful Counsellor, the mighty God, the everlasting Father, and the Prince of Peace."

A newspaper published the succeeding week contained the following interesting account of these exercises: —

"Thursday, the 1st instant, being appointed for the dedication of the building for the use of the Phillips Exeter Academy, in this town, and for the inauguration of the Preceptor, accordingly in the afternoon the honorable Founder and Trustees, with many other gentlemen and a respectable auditory, attended in one of the meeting-houses in this town. The exercises began with singing; a prayer succeeded, by the Rev. Mr. Rogers; and an oration on the 'Advantages of Learning and its Happy Tendency to promote Virtue and Piety' was delivered by the Rev. Mr. McCluer, with an address to the Founder,

Trustees, and Preceptor. The inaugurating ceremonies were performed by Mr. Thurston, a gentleman of the Trust, with a particular address and a charge to the Preceptor. Mr. Woodbridge, the Preceptor, publicly manifested his acceptance of the important charge, and pronounced an affectionate address to the Trustees and auditory. A prayer was made by the Rev. Mr. Mansfield, and the whole was concluded by singing. Each part was performed with propriety, and a solemnity suitable to the occasion, — the whole to universal acceptance.

"Thus we behold with pleasing satisfaction the birth of a new institution, founded on noble principles, for promoting learning, virtue, and piety; and we have raised expectations that this institution will speedily flourish." [1]

Having thus referred to the events which preceded and led to the establishment of the Academy, and having noticed at length the opening ceremony, it seems proper, in discussing its subsequent history, to divide it into periods corresponding to the respective administration of its four Principals. And we shall say more about the men themselves than of the incidents of their terms of service, believing that the story of their lives will present to our readers the most salient and pleasing characteristics of the Academy's history.

[1] *New Hampshire Gazette*, May 10, 1783.

CHAPTER II.

BIOGRAPHICAL AND HISTORICAL.

THE LIVES AND ADMINISTRATIONS OF WILLIAM WOODBRIDGE AND BENJAMIN ABBOT.

FIRST PERIOD.—1783-1788.

WILLIAM WOODBRIDGE, A. B., the first Principal of the Phillips Exeter Academy, was the son of Rev. Ashbel Woodbridge, a resident of Glastenbury, Connecticut. He received his education at Yale College, under the learned and venerable President Stiles. His labors at Exeter extended over a period of but five years, at the end of which he was obliged to resign on account of ill health. Afterwards, with his sister, he kept a private school in Medford, Massachusetts, and preached at Jamaica Plain and other places. His salary as Preceptor of the Academy was one hundred pounds sterling per annum. The Trustees accepted his resignation, October 8, 1788. At the same time they thanked him for his "faithful services and unwearied exertions," and expressed the hope that, " in whatever sphere he may hereafter move, his efforts may be crowned with distinguished success.".

Summary.— While Mr. Woodbridge was Preceptor, little progress was made, and at the date of his resignation there were but two students in the classical department of the Academy.

SECOND PERIOD. — 1788–1838.

"He was a scholar, and a ripe and good one;
Exceeding wise, fair-spoken, and persuading."
KING HENRY VIII., Act IV. Sc. 2.

BENJAMIN ABBOT, LL. D., was the second Principal of the Phillips Exeter Academy, and with him was its real beginning. He found a school "few in numbers and backward in scholarship," but soon new students could not be accommodated. The life he infused made the Academy celebrated.

Most of the Abbots in America are descendants of George Abbot, who, leaving Yorkshire County, England, about the year 1640, became one of the first settlers of Andover, Massachusetts.

His farm was literally carved from the then unbroken forest, and the trees thus felled were used to build his house, the garrison house of the settlement. This ancestor is described as a man of heroic courage, who, with his wife, endured with Christian fortitude the many privations and hardships incident to a frontier life.

The eldest son of each of the following five generations was born and died on this same farm. Each bore the name of John. All were men of ability and sound piety: all lived long, useful lives. The average of their ages is nearly eighty-two years. Each of the first three served the town many years as "selectman," and was a deacon of the parish church. The fourth was an enterprising farmer, fond of reading, energetic, and of sound judgment. He was constant in attendance upon divine service, and had daily family worship. On Sunday morning and evening the family sung a psalm or hymn before prayers: this old custom of the Abbot family was observed through many generations. The wife of this John Abbot was a woman of discretion and ability, loved both for her Christian character and active benevolence. Both parents appreciated a liberal education, and consequently three of their sons received the advantages of Harvard College.

John, the eldest, for fourteen years was a Professor, and for twenty-four years was the Librarian, at Bowdoin College. He was also Treasurer and Fellow of the same College. After a life of great usefulness, he retired to the old homestead, at Andover. This was the property of his brother Ezra, who, like his ancestors, was a sturdy farmer.

Abiel Abbot, another son, was an assistant instructor in the Phillips Exeter Academy; he afterwards became a successful preacher.

The third son was Benjamin Abbot, the subject of this sketch.

Little is known of his boyhood, but one may easily imagine that, having such parents, he grew up obedient, trusty, and brave, fond of play, but sure first to perform his allotted task. Indeed, one might almost have anticipated the future years, and, judging from his ancestors, have delineated the character of the mature man. No one, however, could have assigned to him a life so full of rare service, nor have imagined that he was to mould the minds of so many who would later become great men.

Young Abbot was working on his father's farm when the Phillips Academy at Andover began its career; but he soon left the plough, and, although twenty-one years of age, began the study of the Latin grammar. No doubt, according to the method of that day, he repeated the pages of his Latin grammar *memoriter*, and took ten pages of Cheever's Accidence for a lesson. One of his schoolmates at Andover was John T. Kirkland; another was Josiah Quincy; each of these afterwards became President of Harvard College.

Mr. Quincy thus describes their teacher's method of communicating knowledge: "I was called upon to give the principal parts of the Latin verb *noceo*. Unfortunately, I gave to the *c* a hard sound. I said, 'nokeo, nokere, nokui.' The next thing I knew *I* was *knocked*." This reminds one of the story told of Dr. Johnson, who, when asked how he came to have such an exact knowledge of Latin, said, "My master whipped me very well. Without that I should have done nothing." And all the while this master was flogging his boys so unmercifully he used to say, "And this I do to save you from the gallows." Truly, this was a hard method of education.

Mr. Abbot's teachers at this time were Eliphalet Pearson and Jeremiah Smith. Under them young

Abbot must have made rapid progress, for in 1788 he was graduated from Harvard with the Salutatory Oration. He was at once engaged by the Trustees as an instructor in the Phillips Exeter Academy, and although not regularly chosen Preceptor until October 15, 1790, yet he discharged the duties of that office from the first.

Under his guidance the school prospered. In six years the little schoolhouse became too small, and a new building was erected just in front of the present structure. His salary, at first fixed at "one hundred and thirty-three pounds six shillings and eightpence, lawful money," was soon increased to one hundred and fifty pounds, per annum. An assistant was then engaged at about one half the Preceptor's salary, and, August 23, 1803, the Trustees voted "that there be established in the Academy a permanent instructor, to be denominated the Mathematical Instructor," a title soon changed to "Professor of Mathematics and Natural Philosophy." This chair was first filled by Ebenezer Adams.

Dr. Abbot proved a model teacher. He was a scholar, and knew how to impart what he had learned. His studies did not end with his graduation, but he stepped into the procession, and marched on with the age. He loved his work, and no calls from colleges or other schools, although accompanied with offers of larger salary, could tempt him to leave the school into which he had determined to put the work of his whole life.

His rare presence was fitted to command the respect of his neighbors and the obedience and **love of his pupils**. It has been said that "he never **met the** youngest Academy scholar in the street **without lifting his hat** entirely from his head, as in courteous recognition of an equal; and an abashed and awkward attempt to return the compliment was the urchin's first **lesson in** good manners and respect for his teacher."[1]

Look at him **now, old men, who,** as boys, **saw him** so often; look at him coming toward the old Academy! How grand **he is,** and how dignified! His **is a figure** fit for the sculptor. Tall, broad-shouldered, and fine-looking, his graceful movements render it impossible for one soon to forget him. **Sweetness and** gentleness beam from his very eyes. Now he **lifts his** hat to this boy, and now to that, and now pats the four-year-old upon the head. Now he turns into the broad path which leads through the long rows of seedy poplars to the Academy. All play is instantly stopped, the football is respectfully held, while each boy returns the good man's salutation.

At times he would visit the newly established manufactories **of** machinery, of hats and caps, and of carriages, and as he left, with his well-remembered bow, and his "Very creditable to the industry of the town," the proprietors **felt as though** they had **an** approval equal to a sale.

[1] Prefatory notice, Catalogue **of the** Phillips Exeter Academy, 1783–1869.

Thus he walked about the village, repelling none by his dignity, but winning the esteem of every one by his genuine kindness. Dr. Abbot met all kinds of boys; and the spoiled child of fortune, the awkward son of the farmer, and the proud heir of the rich West India planter alike quaked under the *ominous shake of that long forefinger.* He knew the "science of boys." He showed this by seldom lecturing them on their behavior. And what need, since they had a daily and instructive lecture in his own admirable example of the true gentleman? As has been well said, "the pupils of Dr. Abbot got their ethics mainly by absorption." But when he had occasion to censure, his reproof cut like a cimeter, and when he rose up to judgment, he did not say, "Please be good"; he did not labor with the offender; he punished him. There was no quarrel, no discussion. The boy heard his sentence and took his punishment. There was no thought of resistance or escape from Dr. Abbot's decree.

"In the process of discipline for a specific offence, the culprit was treated as having forfeited all respect. But the discipline once finished, there were no lingering revenges, no remembrance of sins. After the thunder, came the smile of Jupiter through the clouds."[1]

Judge H. C. Whitman, of Cincinnati, once told a story that illustrates this point. He said: —

"One day, at the close of school, the Doctor called me to the desk, and said, 'Come to my house to-morrow

[1] Letter of John B. L. Soule to writer, Dec. 29, 1882.

morning at eight o'clock.' The stern tone left no doubt in my mind as to the nature of the summons. At the hour appointed, I promptly reported myself by rapping loudly on the front door with the great iron knocker. With equal promptness the door was opened an inch or two, and I was met with the stern command, 'Go round to the back door, sir!' To the back door I went; and, after an interview in the library, the Doctor, with his *usual politeness*, bowed me out of the front door."

One of the old students relates the following: —

"One day I was arranging an elaborate plaything behind my book. I felt sure that the Doctor, who was walking back and forth across the room, had taken no notice of my waste of time. Suddenly, however, he stopped, and began to snap my forehead with his long forefinger, and I assure you he did not pause until I cried aloud for mercy."

Usually, however, the Doctor's rebukes were of the mildest nature. This is illustrated by the following incident.

One winter night there was a heavy fall of snow, followed by rain and a sharp frost. This made the walking somewhat difficult, and several of the boys did not appear the next day. When one of the absentees, who lived but a short distance away, came the following morning, the Doctor said to him, "You were not at school yesterday?" "No, sir." "Why not?" "Could not get here, sir," said the shrinking youth, who now felt that he had committed a deadly sin. The

Doctor knew how near to the school the boy lived, and, turning to young Lyford, who *had* been present the day before, said, " Lyford, how far from here do you live ? " " Rather more than a mile, sir." Nothing more was said, but as the boy took his seat he resolved that no storm should keep him from Dr. Abbot's school in the future.

It was a common remark among the boys that it was a shame to deceive Dr. Abbot, or to tell him a lie, and the boy who did always felt guilty and shamefaced.

" Dr. Abbot, in his intercourse with pupils, never laughed. He seldom smiled. But we often noticed flashes of electric humor, like 'heat-lightning,' playing around the corners of his mouth. I shall never forget the struggles of his countenance to suppress a threatening merriment, when a big-headed Newburyport boy, famous for his volubility and fondness for large words, translated *inscius Æneas* 'the unsophisticated Æneas.' With a comical expression, and a rapid glance at each face in the class, the Doctor instantly sobered, saying, 'How 's that, sir ? how 's that ? ' "

The above we have from a former pupil of Dr. Abbot,[1] who also says : —

" I never but once heard from him anything approaching a joke. Our written exercises in Latin he examined, not by classes, but individually. In preparing mine, one day, I was very desirous of using a certain word, but was rather doubtful of its classical purity. So I hunted up, in various authors, instances of its use that seemed to

[1] J. B. L. Soule, D. D., Ph. D.

warrant mine, and marched to his desk, fortified with an armful of books, still half convinced that I was **wrong**. With a quill pen in readiness, **he** ran his eye along the lines till it caught the intrusive word, and, dashing a blot under it, he looked up for explanation. With a faint heart, but ready to retreat by a substituted word, I opened upon him my battery of authorities. He listened so calmly and patiently to my argument, I began to hope for victory; when **he** raised his spectacles to the top of his head, and, with a gentle wave of his hand, said, 'Catch an old bird with chaff!'"

The **same** gentleman further says: —

"At **one time I** was appointed as chairman of a band of six 'inspectors,' whose **duty it was** to **notice** and report infraction of rules, among which **was a rule** against smoking. After receiving instructions, **and** being in doubt as to the extent of the smoking rule, I was deputed to return and inquire if it applied to the Academy premises only, or was to be observed everywhere. 'What,' said he, 'would you confine *virtue* **to** the Academy yard?'"

Dr. Abbot was proud of the Academy, **and** never liked to hear it spoken of with disparagement; his ideas of **the** propriety and dignity of things did not permit this. A lad, afterwards well known as a brave and skilful navigator, was one day leaving the schoolroom with the other boys of **his** section, when the Doctor, beckoning, called him **to the desk.**

There he stood, his knees trembling more than they **ever did** when, later, he paced the quarter-deck. In his most urbane tone the Doctor said, "I understand that you have been speaking disrespectfully of the Academy." "No, sir, I have n't." "But I am credibly informed that such is the case." Chadwick hung his head, and, with flushed face, said in a faint voice, "I only called it a schoolhouse, sir." The Doctor, bowing, said, "Remember that in the future it is not a schoolhouse, but an Academy."

A summary of the characteristics of this great man from one who knew him during his last and best years, will give our readers an impression impossible for us to create. He writes: —

"Dr. Abbot, in his time, was foremost among scholars, as he was a primate among teachers. His high position in college was but the foundation on which he was rearing a superstructure, story after story, all his life. He knew that, among regal minds, progress is the supreme law; and he was not content to sit by the roadside, a wondering spectator, while the grand procession moved on. He did not, like some men, merely mark time, but he fell into line and marched. New books and new educational systems did not come and go without his knowledge. By his request, his brother-in-law, James Perkins, Esq., who visited Europe in 1802, examined the methods of instruction in Eton and other prominent schools in England, and transmitted the fruits of his observations to him. He made the Academy the centre of his efforts and his thoughts. Everything else he compelled to pay tribute to this. Invitations to the Boston Latin School and to other positions, though offering larger rewards for less labor, he resolutely declined. Prevented by his con-

tinuous duties from **seeing** much **of the** great world, he
was nevertheless emphatically **a** *live* man. His **mind**
was a fountain, not a reservoir. His knowledge **came**
gushing up from the overflowing depths of his own being;
it was not drawn up with rope and bucket from the moss-
grown wells **of** antiquity alone. He breathed his own
spirit into the worn text-books of the recitation-room,
and the mystic page glowed with his inspiration. The
Latin of Cicero and Horace, his favorite authors, when
pronounced by him, seemed instinct with new life and
meaning. The denunciations against Catiline **sounded**
to his electrified pupils as terrific as when they **were first**
uttered **in the** old Roman senate-chamber; **while the**
rhythm of **the** *Carmen* ***Sæculare*** was as musical **as when**,
two thousand years ago, it won the 'friendly ear' **of**
Diana. He was a scholar **of** breadth **as** well as depth,
knowing something more **than the mere** routine of
daily study. **Modern** literature, politics, and theology,
as well as the ancient classics, found a place in the circle
of his reading. Few men were so deeply versed as he in
that most abstruse of all studies, *the human nature* **of**
boys. He had striven to **obey** the precept **emblazoned**
on the Delphic temple; **and, as a natural consequence**
of his self-knowledge, he **had** an intuitive perception of
the modes of thought **and** springs of **action**. He had
the faculty of making his classes believe that the particular subject on which they were engaged was the
most important and attractive branch of study in the
world. They caught fire from him, and teacher and pupils
alike glowed with the same enthusiasm. He knew how
to put himself **in** communication with youthful minds.
Age did not make him morose; but he was always fresh
in his feelings and sympathies, and his heart was young

to the last in all its pulsations. It is fitting to add, that
the light of a Christian faith irradiated all his intellectual attainments, giving them a brighter lustre, just
as a lamp in an alabaster vase brings out into bolder
relief and clearer expression the beautiful figures sculptured upon it." [1]

His successor, Dr. Soule, spoke of him as "the
second founder of the institution, not *scriptis legibus*, but by the wisdom and consistency of his government. His dignity was unsurpassed; but it was
always adorned and rendered attractive by his sweet
affability. He was always a gentleman, even to the
youngest of his pupils, inspiring them with high-mindedness and courage to do right. Indeed, the whole
history of his connection with the Academy is a comment on the necessity of good manners, not only for the
proper government of the school, but for the best
development and culture of the youthful mind." [2]

THE ABBOT FESTIVAL.

In 1838, when Dr. Abbot had completed a term of
fifty years' service, and had passed beyond the allotted
threescore years and ten, he resigned his position as
Principal, to take effect the twenty-third of the following August. Arrangements were immediately made
for a reunion, on that day, of his old pupils. It was

[1] J. G. Hoyt, LL. D., in *North American Review*, July, 1858.
[2] Letter of G. L. Soule, LL. D., to Dr. A. P. Peabody, D. D.,
June, 1872.

meant to be a day when old friends might renew the sacred tie of friendship, and again sit at the feet of their beloved master.

The morning's sun was still in the horizon when the guests began to assemble. It was, as you will remember, two years before the staid and sober Boston and Maine Railroad reached Exeter, and on this morning the streets were noisy with the rattle of the stage-coaches and the crack of the drivers' whips as they urged on their steaming horses. At the Swamscot all was bustle and confusion, and the stable-yard presented as animated a picture as ever did the courtyard of the old and famous White Horse Inn at Edinburgh. The streets were thronged with people.

Soon it was found that no building in the village would contain the gathering crowd, and a hasty arrangement was made by extending an awning from the piazza of the east wing of the Academy. The ladies took possession of the English room, corresponding to room number three of the present building, and the vast audience, seated on benches and chairs, extended to the street. Mr. Saltonstall, of Salem, Massachusetts, called the meeting to order, and then Daniel Webster, as President of the Day, took the chair. After the invocation of the Divine blessing, by Dr. John G. Palfrey, a brief business meeting was held, in which the President read the letters of Lewis Cass, Dr. Dana, and others, regretting their inability to be present. This was immediately followed by the speeches of Leverett Saltonstall, Edward Everett, Dr. Henry Ware, Jr., Jonathan Chapman, Judge Thacher, Dr. John G. Palfrey, and many others, whose names add lustre to the fame of the Academy and do honor to Dr. Abbot; after which the alumni adjourned to the Academy Hall, and spent a happy hour with their former teacher. At half past one a procession was formed by Chief Marshal Nathaniel Gilman, Jr., and his aids, and then, headed by a band of music, the company proceeded to the vestry of the First Congregational Church, where over three hundred persons sat down to a dinner, prepared by Major Blake, of the Swamscot. An eloquent speech by Daniel Webster, who presided, followed the dinner. He alluded to the annals of the school, then to the nature of boys, and to the methods of teaching them. "Boys," he remarked, "must be taught to feel, as well as to act well. To expect pupils to be free from feelings of emulation, in boyhood and youth, is as unnatural as to expect to find them with bald heads and beards." He then addressed more particularly the venerable Preceptor.

"You see around you, sir, pupils who have been instructed by you. We have come together to-day, to offer you the tributes of our hearts. We have all been here, sir, at different years, — we have all, sir, been called up to your chair to be examined in our various studies. We remember, sir, when we were brought here by our parents. We remember well the kind looks with which you received us.

"You governed us, sir, by a steady and even temper,

but you governed us with that **kindness which won our** hearts.

"We have here, sir, formed a little republic; we have had **a** public opinion; but, sir, there **never** was yet **an** Exeter boy who could obtain respect **or** countenance **by** setting himself **up** against your will.

. . . . .

"We do not regret, sir, that **you** have arrived at that age when you must retire **from** your trust. You, no doubt, have desired it, and be assured, sir, that we have prayed for it; for you have all that makes old age **desirable**, the reverence and respect of all around you.

"And now, sir, I present you with this token[1] of **our** remembrance. We greet **you with** the best feelings, and with hearts full of hope **for** your welfare and happiness."

A reply, full of emotion, by Dr. Abbot, was followed **by** toasts, songs,[2] and other speeches.

Mr. Webster offered as a toast, "Good health and long life to Preceptor Abbot," which, as may well **be** supposed, **was** received with loud and continued applause.

Alexander H. Everett, at the close of an eloquent speech, proposed as a sentiment, "Our venerable friend and his works."

One of the most **impressive of** the after-dinner speeches was that of the aged **Jeremiah** Smith. This white-haired **man** arose and claimed a distinction which, **he** said, "could belong to **no** other man living. You

---

[1] A massive silver vase. [2] See Appendix.

were his scholars, I was his teacher. It was little that I had to impart, but that little was most cheerfully given. I well remember the promise he then gave; and Providence has been kind in placing him in just that position where his life could be most usefully and honorably spent."

A letter from **Josiah Quincy**, President of Harvard University, was read. In concluding, he offered the following toast: "The Abbot Festival, at which Harvard rejoices with the joy of a mother over the success and honor of a favorite son."

Among the other speakers were Judge Emery, Dr. Gilman of York, Mr. Page of New Bedford, Prentiss Mellen, John P. Hale, the Hon. Edward Everett, Dr. Charles Burroughs, and Caleb Cushing.

Two of the most notable speeches were those of Jonathan Chapman, Mayor of Boston, and Dr. Palfrey of Cambridge. Mr. Chapman spoke, in an eloquent vein, of the old Academy, — how, since his day, it had been enlarged by the addition of wings, — and closed with this sentiment: "The Old Academy, — although she has taken wings, thank God she has not flown away!"

Dr. Palfrey told how he had spent the afternoon before in endeavoring to find Cuffey and Dinah, two old darkies who used to sell cake and ale to the boys. He said he had found the spot, the remains of the house; but, alas! Cuffey and Dinah were no more. He said that he had called at a house near by, had regaled himself upon **cake** and **ale,** in memory of **the aged couple** and he recommended these people to the boys of **to-day** as worthy successors to Cuffey and **Dinah.**

The speakers' minds, throughout the whole day, seemed full of the most vivid recollections of their **school** days, and their tongues **spoke with a** simplicity which was eloquence itself. They spoke of the trees they had planted, of the streams on whose **banks they** had wandered and on whose bosoms they had sailed, of the hills they had climbed, and of the **groves in whose** shade **they** had delighted to wander ; **of Jada** Hill, the String Bridge, the Governor's Farm, the Old Powder-House ; of their **sports and** games, foot-ball and bat-ball, marbles, hop-scotch, and hare-and-hounds ; of the rooms **they** had **occupied, and of the** families they remembered so well.

One of the **most** pleasing events **of** the day was the presentation of **the** portrait of Dr. **Abbot,** which **had** been **secured** for the occasion, to the Academy.

Besides this, and the **vase** already referred **to, the sum of two** thousand dollars was subscribed for the establishment **of** the ABBOT SCHOLARSHIP at Cambridge. This has **now an** income of **one** hundred **and** twenty dollars, which is paid to such needy undergraduate as may **be** selected by **the College** Faculty for scholarship and good character ; **the** descendants and other relatives **of** Dr. Abbot, and the best scholars from the Phillips Exeter Academy, are preferred, in the order named.

When at length the venerable teacher was about to retire from the room, the entire company rose, as they did of old when he retired from the school-room, and cheer after cheer made the arches of the old church ring as they had never done before.

Inquiry was soon made for Mr. Soule, the newly-elected successor to Dr. Abbot, and he was forced to his feet by loud calls and hearty applause. In a happy but modest address, he expressed the diffidence he should feel in assuming the duties and the position of Dr. Abbot, whose place, he said, "I can never fill."

Thus ended the Abbot Festival, the most notable occasion in the history of the Phillips Exeter Academy. With the fading of the evening sun, the company reluctantly departed.

A contemporary, writing of the occasion, says: —

"Latin and Greek were as common, if not so well understood, as 'household words.' Poetry became almost our 'mother tongue,' and common, every-day prose was as little accounted of as silver in the days of Solomon. All was harmony, all was poetry. But what most distinguished the Festival was this: *it was a festival of the heart.* The intellect was feasted, but *the heart rioted* in *the fulness of its joy.*"[1]

Dr. Abbot lived more than ten years after this semi-centennial celebration, surrounded by loving friends and kindly remembered by grateful pupils, whose

[1] *Exeter News Letter,* Aug. 28, 1838.

"kindly visits made many a green spot in the winter scenery of his life." His was the

"Old age serene and bright,
And lovely as a Lapland night,"

which comes to but few. On October 25, 1849, at the age of eighty-seven, he "fell asleep." The angel Death gently closed his eyes only to re-open them in a land fitted for such Christian scholars as was Dr. Abbot.

Dr. Abbot was twice married. His first wife, Hannah Tracy Emery, whom he married in 1791, died at the early age of twenty-two, exactly four months after the birth of John Emery Abbot, their only child.[1]

In May, 1798, Mr. Abbot married Mary, daughter of James and Elizabeth (Peck) Perkins, of Boston. She proved a worthy companion, and the marriage was eminently happy. Two children blessed this union, Elizabeth Perkins Abbot,[2] and Charles Benjamin Abbot.[3]

[1] This son, born August 6, 1798, became a young man of much promise, and his death at the age of twenty-six was a severe blow to the fond hopes of his loving father. Graduating from Bowdoin College in 1810, he applied himself to the study of theology, and succeeded Dr Barnard at the North Church, Salem, Mass., where his abilities were quickly recognized and his manly Christian character highly esteemed. He was much admired as a preacher, and a volume of his sermons, prefaced by a brief memoir of his life by Dr. Henry Ware, Jr., has been published.

[2] Elizabeth P. Abbot, b. Nov. 14, 1801; m. 1826, David W. Gorham, M.D., of Exeter; d. Aug. 10, 1873; children, William Henry, Mary Abbot, and Emma Forbes.

[3] Charles B. Abbot, b. Jan. 19, 1805; m. Harriet Thurston (daughter of Rev. Benjamin Thurston); d. Bangor, Me., March 8, 1874; only child, Francis Peabody.

This wife, surviving him, was for many years "a cherished remembrancer of the past." She died in 1863, at the advanced age of ninety-three years, nine months.

Dr. Abbot's grave may be found in the new cemetery at Exeter, near the tomb of his friend, the "Founder." The simple inscription, from the classic pen of Nathaniel A. Haven, sums up the life work of America's Dr. Arnold as follows: —

BENJAMIN ABBOT, LL. D.
Born
September 17, 1762,
Died
October 25, 1849,
Aged 87 years.
Appointed by the
Founder and
For fifty years
Principal
of
PHILLIPS EXETER
ACADEMY.

Boys and gray-haired men, new and "old scholars" of Exeter, let not his grave be neglected. Go to it as to that of a hero; care for it as for that of a nobleman; venerate it as that of a saint. Above all, remember the life and work of Dr. Abbot.

Summary. — The administration of Benjamin Abbot was eminently successful. At the time he assumed the management of the Academy, the membership had been reduced to thirteen or fourteen new students a year, but during the following **decade the average** exceeded forty-one. This was uniformly maintained.

During his principalship, a new academy building was erected, and later enlarged ; the Golden Branch Society was founded, and a high standard of scholarship was established and maintained.

Dr. Abbot gathered about him instructors as interested in the work of education as himself. A large proportion **of** these were **men of** unusual **ability,** — men who have **since** become justly eminent. **Among** them **were Hosea** Hildreth, John P. Cleveland, **Francis** Bowen, Daniel Dana, **Peter O. Thacher,** Nicholas Emery, Joseph **S.** Buckminster, Ashur Ware, Nathan Hale, Alexander Hill Everett, **Henry Ware, Jr.,** Nathan Lord, Alpheus S. Packard, and James Walker.

Among his pupils he numbered **such men** as Lewis Cass, Joseph Stevens Buckminster, Daniel Webster, Leverett Saltonstall, John Langdon **Sibley,** Jeffries Wyman, Nathaniel A. Haven, Joseph **G.** Cogswell, Theodore Lyman, Edward Everett, the twin Peabodys, John A. Dix, John G. Palfrey, Jared Sparks, **George** Bancroft, Jonathan Chapman, and Ephraim **Peabody.**

CHAPTER III.

BIOGRAPHICAL AND HISTORICAL.

GIDEON LANE SOULE: HIS LIFE AND SERVICE. — ADMINISTRATION OF ALBERT CORNELIUS PERKINS.

THIRD PERIOD. — 1838-1873.

"It has been said that he is a public benefactor who makes one blade of grass grow where it did not grow before. How much greater the benefactor who makes a scholar!" — CHARLES SUMNER, *in a letter to President Quincy*, Feb. 12, 1841.

DOCTOR ABBOT was fortunate in surrounding himself with able instructors. In the early years of his administration he had always about him some young man, fresh from college, who came to teach for a year at Exeter just before entering upon the study of his chosen profession. Many of these afterwards became distinguished as jurists, clergymen, historians, etc. No name in this long and brilliant list is to-day more respected and venerated than that of GIDEON LANE SOULE, the third Principal of the Phillips Exeter Academy. He came of good old Puritan stock, and his ancestors were noted for their upright dealings and their intelligence.

George Soule, who came to this country in the "Mayflower," was a devoted friend of Miles Standish,[1] and one of the most efficient men of the Colony.

[1] *Harper's Magazine:* "Standish House in Duxbury."

His eldest son, John, and his grandson, Moses, were prominent citizens of Duxbury, Massachusetts. Barnabas, the son of the latter, who moved to North Yarmouth, Maine, was a devoted Christian. He married [1] the great-granddaughter of that noted divine, John Wheelwright, founder of the town of Exeter.

Moses, the son, and Moses, the grandson of Barnabas, were both deacons of the parish church in Freeport, Maine. The latter, the father of Gideon Lane Soule, is described as a tall, strong, fine-looking man, whose commanding person and dignified bearing are still well remembered. In his domestic relations he was most happy. He was a calker by trade, and tradition reports him to have been a leader among men of his craft. You will remember that the shores of Maine were busy shipyards in those days; and although he loved and cultivated his acres, yet he often worked among the "columns of smoke" which

> " Rose from the boiling, bubbling, seething
> Caldron, that glowed
> And overflowed
> With the black tar, heated for the sheathing"

of the vessel's lofty sides.

He was also somewhat of a scholar, and during the winter months often taught school in the neighboring villages. Much interested in military affairs, in early life he served as first lieutenant of artillery in the militia, while later he was frequently one of the select-

[1] *The Soule Family*, page 10.

men in his native town. Although somewhat diffident, leadership seems to have been his most prominent characteristic; this his sons inherited in a marked degree.

His proximity to Brunswick — only six miles away — enabled him the more easily to give to these sons the best educational advantages. In the catalogue of the Phillips Exeter Academy, as well as that of Bowdoin College, one may find the names of the four brothers, Charles, Gideon, Moses, and John. Of these, Charles Soule spent a long life in the good work, and is affectionately referred to as a gifted and beloved pastor; Moses Soule, and John Babson Lane Soule, now living in the West, have given their most active years to journalism and teaching, and are noted scholars; Gideon Lane Soule, the subject of this sketch, was one of the best known and most successful schoolmasters that America has ever produced.

Born in Freeport, Maine, July 25, 1796, he spent his earliest years on his father's farm, almost within sound of the great ocean which beats upon the rocky shores of Maine. "Pleasant Hill Farm," his birthplace, is skirted by the old stage road, which, at that time, connected the mercantile towns of Boston and Portland with the college town of Brunswick, and the long line of sea-coast which lay beyond. To-day the stage-coach, drawn by the powerful steam horse of the Maine Central Railroad, rushes along the brook which, with dark, unruffled surface, quietly winds through a dense growth of alder bushes.

These alders form a background for the beautiful meadows which extend, like a vast green lawn, from the quaint old farmhouse above. The place now belongs to Dr. Soule's favorite nephew,[1] and, owing to his loving care, the old house is in an excellent state of preservation. Within its hospitable walls several rooms are arranged as in the days of Deacon Moses Soule. The panelled room, used only on rare occasions, is still hung with the family portraits, and furnished with the old fittings. Here, as in the other rooms, there is a spacious fireplace, built in a huge chimney which fills the whole centre of the house.

On these hearths bright fires are kept ablaze throughout the fall, winter, and spring, as in the old days, and by the ruddy glow of the flames the visitor may discover many a relic, among them a picture of the Academy at Exeter, where Dr. Soule spent the greater part of his life.

The household of Deacon Soule must have formed a happy family circle, for in it was all that is conducive to happiness, — a noble Christian father, a tender mother, brave, obedient children, peace, contentment, and prosperity.

Gideon Lane Soule, who in the family was always called " Lane," — his mother's maiden name, — was the second of eleven children. Young Soule was bright and active, but not over-strong, and to his fondness for play, which kept him much out of doors, perhaps may

---

[1] Robert F. Pennell, A. B.

be attributed his strength and health in later years. During his early youth he is said to have been slender, lithe, and frail, but at the same time full of activity, and of hard muscle. Heavier boys grappling with him in the ring, formed for a friendly contest, were not always sure of the advantage.

In school he was quick of apprehension, studious, and obedient. These qualities gave him easy pre-eminence in scholarship. Thus the first scholar was also the best wrestler. His mates loved to make him their leader, and with him roam the woods and neighboring shores. In throwing stones he excelled both in range and in accuracy. In the winter, when squadrons were marshalled for snowballing, he could not always join in the play, both sides stipulating that Lane Soule should not fight against them. We have heard this anecdote: —

One day a large, coarse fellow was harassing a squad of young boys returning from school by shouting and throwing snowballs at them from the rear. Lane, scooping a little wet snow, and forming it into an iceball, unexpectedly wheeled and threw it at their pursuer. We can assure you that the noise of the bully was suddenly and effectively stopped; for, looking over their shoulders, they saw him clawing furiously at his face, and, taking in the situation at a glance, ran back and cut the ball out of his mouth with a jackknife.

Mr. Soule was of a nervous temperament, and very sensitive to changes in the atmosphere. If he was working in the hay-field with the other boys, **as soon as** a storm cloud appeared in the west, and **the mutterings** of distant thunder **were heard, he was at once excused** from work, and, trembling and half exhausted, made **his** way to the house.

In his early youth his opportunities for obtaining an education were limited. Until he was seventeen, he was able to attend the district school only a small portion of the year; the rest of the time he worked on **his** father's farm. In his seventeenth year **he began his** classical studies under the Rev. Reuben Nason (Harv. 1802), his minister, and a man of superior scholarship for that day.

In 1813 Mr. Soule entered the **Phillips** Exeter Academy. Here he remained **two years, having** for instructors such men as James Walker, who afterwards became President of Harvard College, **and the** saintly Henry **Ware, Jr. Under** Hosea Hildreth, that strong, noble-minded Christian, he became a lover of the **exact sciences**, while with Dr. Abbot as instructor he made rapid strides in the study of the ancient languages.

In September, 1815, Mr. Soule entered the Sophomore class at Bowdoin College. His preparation at Exeter had been so thorough that at Brunswick he became at once distinguished for the high rank which he maintained. Of his superior scholarship, Professor **A. S.** Packard, of Bowdoin College, who became acquainted with him at that time, and who boarded at the **same table** with him during the two years they were together in college, bears the following honorable testimony. "In the classics," writes this venerable librarian, "Mr. Soule had no superior in his class, the largest and ablest of that day."

By his classmates he was respected for his excellent character, and loved for his strong friendship. His was a nature to make friends, and he had for his companions the first men in his class.

In 1818 Mr. Soule was graduated from college. Although not the first in his class, the "Intermediate Latin" was assigned to him at Commencement; this indicated that he had made a special study of the Latin language, and that in it he had ranked well. He at once became an assistant instructor in the Phillips Exeter Academy, under Dr. Benjamin Abbot, but, according to the custom of those days, remained but one year.

In 1819 Mr. Soule entered the Andover Theological Seminary, but shortly after left to take charge of a private school in Amherst, New Hampshire. Later we find him, for a few months, again at Brunswick, reading, attending lectures, and rooming with his old friend, Alpheus Packard, at that time a tutor in the College. His reading here was of a miscellaneous character, but he made a special study of the Greek language, in order that he might be better fitted for the position which, induced by the earnest and repeated solicitations of Dr. Abbot, the counsel of President Appleton, and the advice of his father, he had finally decided to accept.

In 1822 Mr. Soule was appointed Professor of Ancient Languages in the Phillips Exeter Academy. Although at the outset his modesty caused him to fear that he was not equal to the requirements of this position, yet he soon attained a high rank, both as a teacher and as a disciplinarian. The ability he displayed as a disciplinarian, and the success that crowned his efforts as a teacher, made it only a matter of course that, upon the resignation of Dr. Abbot, he should be elevated to the more responsible station which had been so dignified by his eminent predecessor.

Thus, August 22, 1838, Mr. Soule became the Principal of the Phillips Exeter Academy.

Mr. Soule made Exeter the scene of his life-work, and his connection with the Academy covers a period of over fifty years.

August 26, 1822, he married Elizabeth Phillips, daughter of Noah Emery, Esq., of Exeter. The issue of this marriage was a family of five children, three sons and two daughters. The daughters died almost in their infancy, " leaving always the light of a tender and holy memory in the home which they had gladdened for a little while." Of the sons, one is a lawyer in New York; Nicholas — the young Dr. Soule — resides in Exeter, and is a Trustee of the Academy, while the third is a prosperous attorney in Boston, and until lately a judge of the Supreme Court of Massachusetts.

In July, 1856, the degree of Doctor of Laws was conferred upon Mr. Soule by Harvard College.

June 19, 1872, a semi-centennial festival was celebrated in his honor, by the alumni and friends of the Academy. This was a grand and fitting tribute to the great teacher, who for half a century had been doing so much for the intellectual and moral development of the young. On this occasion Dr. Soule tendered his resignation to the Trustees, and begged to be relieved from the duties of his position, but he was pressed to remain a little longer. In the words of Dr. Peabody, the President of the Board, they said : —

" We accept not his proffered resignation. We will not let him go. A few weeks earlier, he would have stood before you with 'his eye not dim, nor his natural force abated'; and though he is now enfeebled by recent illness, . . . we trust that the kind Providence which has restored him thus far has yet in reserve for him a season of precious service, in which, with diminished labor, he shall inaugurate the new era for our Academy."

On July 1, 1873, warned by the failing health of the venerable teacher, the Trustees felt forced to give way, and to accept his resignation. They conferred upon him the title " Principal Emeritus," and voted him a pension and the free use of his house during the remainder of his life.

After Dr. Soule was relieved from the care and anxiety of the position so long held by him, he lived contentedly and happily, surrounded by loving and attentive friends and relatives.

In these last years of his life, the Doctor took unceasing delight in watching the students, as they went to or from the Academy. He would stand by his window with watch in hand, and count the minutes until it was time for "my boys," as he still called them, to come from their recitations, and as they came romping from the school yard his face would become radiant with pleasure.

His strength, however, gradually failed, and after a time the walks about town, which he had enjoyed so much, were given up, and his exercise was confined to the more immediate neighborhood of his house. His mental powers also failed, but he remained cheerful to the last, and until within a few days of his death was able to walk abroad.

On Tuesday, May 27, 1879, he appeared to have taken cold. The next day he grew weaker, and apparently unconscious, and passed away very peacefully at half past eleven o'clock in the evening, at the age of eighty-two years, ten months, and three days.

The funeral services took place on the following Saturday. Among the mourners appeared the students of the Academy; who, forming a long procession, accompanied the mortal remains of Dr. Soule to their last resting-place. No monument yet marks the spot, but we understand that his former pupils are now making arrangements to place above his grave a fitting memorial stone.

Dr. Soule was rather tall, but well-proportioned. He had a finely-shaped head, an ample brow, and dark, searching eyes, which, as one of his pupils once said, "took a boy in at a glance, from his boots up." The high, white forehead, snowy hair and beard, the heavy eyebrows, and the deepened facial lines of his later years, are all well remembered by those who knew him. These changes only added new glory to his already venerated form. In a large assembly one would note his dignified, stately bearing, and would instinctively select him as a leader. His elastic step and his business-like ways taught many a lad to be prompt and accurate. One incident will serve to illustrate this. When a certain boy, on entering the school, went to register his name, the Doctor asked, "How old are you." The boy began to answer, "I shall be —" But the old gentleman, interrupting him, said, "No! I wish to know how old you are *now*."

It was a mere accident which drew him from the agricultural life of his father and grandfather, and led him to the Academy and college, and to his subsequent career of usefulness and honor. How this was brought about may be best learned from the following incidents, which are given, substantially, in Dr. Soule's own words : —

"My elder brother Charles and I were accustomed, in the intervals of farm work, to catch up the old family musket, and hie to the neighboring woods in pursuit of the partridge and the squirrel. We took turns in possessing the gun. One afternoon, in the midst of our hunt, Charles said, 'Now it is my turn; and if you will cut across to the bars yonder, where the line fence crosses the logging road, and wait for me, I will sweep around through this point of woods and meet you there.' This road was a narrow one, cut across lots through a thick growth of young trees, and was used in winter for sledding, but was grass-grown in summer. The tall, luxuriant saplings crowded on each side, and, mingling their thick boughs overhead, subdued the light. The scene was still and sombre; and as I sat perched on the fence, gazing through the narrowing vista of green leaves, heavy-dipped in gloom, I was quickly lost in abstraction, — absorbed in a vision of imaginings spread out before me, not clearly defined in particulars, but somehow, as a whole, most real. I was impressed with the idea that some notable chapter of my future was ready to burst upon me. My spell was suddenly broken by the exclamation, 'Why, Lane, what are you doing here?' It was the voice of our aged neighbor, John Adderton, who was crossing from his end of the road. 'I am going over to your house,' continued he, 'to invite your father and you boys to my husking this evening.' And to the husking we all went. As the two fathers sat by the heap of corn, in friendly chat, Mr. Adderton said: 'I have an idea. Esquire Abbot, at whose store in Brunswick I do my trading, wants to get a young boy to be about him in his store and family; advanced in years, he needs such help for errands and other small matters. You have two little fellows, and if you would spare Lane, the younger, and he would be willing to go, I think he would just suit the Esquire. He is a fine old gentleman, and the position might open up something for the boy.' Esquire Abbot was Jacob Abbot, a wealthy, solid, indispensable patriarch of Brunswick, foremost in every good work, and especially a patron of learning. He was an Overseer of

Bowdoin College, at which institution he educated his five sons, among them the well-known authors, Jacob and John S. C. In a few days the matter was arranged as suggested. The good Esquire found plenty of business for me by day; and by the hearth, in evenings, he amused himself by talking with me, and drawing me out by questions suited to my years. I seemed to gain his favor. One evening he proposed to me a rather tangling question in arithmetic; which, placing my face between my hands on my knees, I quickly solved. He seemed surprised and pleased at the rapid and correct solution. After some further acquaintance he said to Mr. Adderton, 'That boy ought to be educated; and, with his father's consent, I will write to my cousin Benjamin at Exeter, and have him admitted to the Phillips Academy.' In due time this was settled; and, after a short preparation under the noted teacher and disciplinarian, Rev. Reuben Nason, then pastor of our church in Freeport, I took my seat at the feet of the renowned Dr. Benjamin Abbot, Preceptor of the Phillips Exeter Academy. From Exeter I entered Bowdoin College, under the presidency of the venerated Dr. Jesse Appleton."

Professor Moses Soule says: —

"My brother, in after years, retained a vivid impression of the vision in the grove, seeming to regard it as a sort of second-sight or prophecy of the future to him, instantly followed, as it was, by a marked change in his condition, succeeded by link after link of that unforeseen chain of Providence (which led him directly to his great life-work): the vision; the meeting with Adderton; the husking; the sojourn with Esquire Abbot; the solution of the question; the training under Nason; the course under Dr. Abbot; and, through college, the precept and example of President Appleton. It may be added that Dr. Soule opened the way for the education of his three brothers in the same institutions."

Mr. Soule is said to have been of a happy, joyous disposition, a fine singer, and a profound laugher. Throwing back his head, and displaying a wealth of teeth, there would gush forth, *ab imo pectore*, a burst of honest, happy laughter.

One day, soon after graduation, he called at the Foreign Mission Rooms to see his classmate, Rufus Anderson, who was at that time engaged in preparing for the press an edition of the Christian Almanac, of which he was the projector.

While waiting for his friend, who was then busy, he took up a book and soon became absorbed in its contents. Suddenly Mr. Anderson was electrified by a peal of old-fashioned college laughter, and, looking up from a manuscript page of the calendar, he said, "There, Soule, this is July; I will enter in this column, '*Thunder about this time.*'" "So, I suppose," added the friend who told me this, "a peal of the Doctor's laughter is floating along the ages in the chronicles of thunder."

The influence for good of Dr. Soule's strong personality can neither be estimated nor exaggerated. The constant presence of such a model of the scholarly Christian gentleman did not fail to have the happiest effects upon the students as individuals, and the school as a whole. Dr. Soule honored his calling, and his pupils honored him. His popularity among the students was wonderful. They scorned to do even a petty meanness, and to lie to Dr. Soule was most remote from their thoughts. It is said that the only time the Doctor was ever known to be angry was when he caught one of his pupils in a lie.

Who does not remember his famous speech at the beginning of each term, when he always said, " Whoever crosses the threshold of a *saloon* crosses the threshold of the Academy for the last time." At these times he told the students what he should expect of them, recited the few rules by which they were to be governed, — all summed up in the injunction that they were to behave as gentlemen, — and then added that he should trust to their honor, and that the honor of a gentleman was inviolable.

His reliance in the uprightness and honor of his " boys " made men of them, in that they seldom abused his confidence. This then, more than anything else, was the secret of his success. In the words of another,[1] —

"He believed and he rejoiced in boys. No eye of suspicion was needlessly turned upon them. Because he believed in them, they believed in him, and strove not to disappoint him. Nearly twenty years ago, one night, many of the gates in the village disappeared. It was not an act that required much originality or wit. But boys have a keen appetite for fun, and probably they got, or at

[1] Rev. John H. Morison, D. D.

least expected to get, some enjoyment out of it. But the town's people whose gates had been stolen did not see it exactly in that light. They regarded it as a public outrage, and were very indignant. Some of them angrily remonstrated with Dr. Soule, and insisted upon it that the police should be called in, and summary punishment inflicted on the culprits who had taken part in this highhanded proceeding. Dr. Soule calmly listened to them, and told them they had better wait.

"That evening, after prayers, he made a little address to the students on the conduct which a nice sense of honor requires of gentlemen towards those whom they have injured. Precisely what redress should be made, must depend upon the relation of the parties to one another, and on other circumstances. He instanced the case of a friend of his who had spoken harshly to his man, for bringing his horse to the door a quarter of an hour after the time, and who afterwards learned that it was not the man's fault, and therefore made him a small present of money as an acknowledgment. But from one gentleman to another this could not be done. 'There *are* cases, however,' he said, 'where immediate and entire reparation can be made.' His object was to impress them with the idea that a gentleman owes it to himself to repair as soon as possible any injury that he has done to another. He then dismissed the school, and was himself detained a short time in his place. When he went out, it was raining and just at nightfall. But he saw in the Academy yard students moving in little groups, each with a gate on his shoulder; and thus every gate found its way back to the place where it had belonged."

" He loved his boys, for in them he saw, not only the possible law-makers, judges, rulers, the great merchants, physicians, divines, who were to mould the coming age, but, more and greater than all this, he saw before him children of God intrusted to him that they might grow up to be a joy and blessing to themselves and to all around them. In them, with his prophetic eye, he saw men of large hearts, of well-trained minds, of just views, of sterling integrity, — men who, in the breadth and loftiness of their attainments and the severity of their moral convictions, would one day sit in judgment on him and the work which he was doing."

Dr. Soule was eminently distinguished as a disciplinarian. Active but gentle, helpful and sympathetic, he was never underhanded, but always vigilant. While always kind and approachable, he never allowed the least infringement of his dignity. He rigidly enforced every deference due to his office. It is well known how he always maintained the custom established by Dr. Abbot, that no ball should be moved on the playground in front of the Academy while the Preceptor or any of the teachers were crossing. From the moment he entered the gate, the football lay quiet in the midst of the panting crowd, and there it remained until he disappeared through the Academy door.

A friend[1] sends us the following amusing account of his own experience, when, through ignorance, on the first day of his school life in Exeter, he disregarded this rule.

"It was in September, 1862, I think, when I entered the Senior class, coming from a high school in the cen-

[1] George T. Tilden, Esq.

tral part of Massachusetts. As this was my **first experi**ence of academy life, I had all the pride which a thorough consciousness of the added dignity could bestow. **I** was especially anxious to appear to the best advantage before my newly-adopted comrades.

Throughout **that memorable first** forenoon and afternoon all had gone well, and **when** the last recitation was over the boys had gathered in the campus in front of the Academy for their usual sports. We had just paired off, the 'Juniors and Middlers' against the 'Seniors and **Advance,**' for a game of foot-ball, and Hunnewell was **to** give the 'warning kick.' He had just **started towards** the ball when, for some reason which at **the time I could not comprehend, he suddenly** checked himself, turned **on** his heel **in** his light, **graceful way, and was** about to take his position again **to start the** game, when I thought it a grand opportunity **to** show **the** boys what I could do in the **way** of flying a football. So I rushed in ahead of Hunnewell, whose quick eye had caught sight of Dr. Soule as he emerged from the Academy building and started to cross the yard. By **the** time **I had reached** the ball **the** good Doctor was nearly **in** line **with it,** and all **the** other boys, who **knew** what **was** expected of them, stood quietly and respectfully waiting until he should **have** passed beyond the limits of the grounds. But all this hesitancy on the part of the others only gave me the greater confidence to go ahead, for I was far from being one of the big boys, and seldom found it worth while to **get into** the 'rush.' So now was my time, and **I gave that ball** such a kick as to send it whizzing just above the Doctor's head. **Not** one of the **boys** 'made for it,' as I expected they would do; but instead **of** that each one remained where he stood, and

the dignified form of the Doctor halted, turned towards
me, straightening up to his full height as he extended
his long arm, and with his long, slim finger beckoned me
to him. He was calm and dignified, and seemed to me
very tall as I came near and looked up at him, while I,
feeling myself in disgrace, seemed to lessen and dwindle
proportionately. Very calmly, but without severity, he
asked me if I was not a new pupil. I said that I was.
Then he said, 'Take the ball and come home with me.'
With all the meekness imaginable I picked up the ball,
and followed the worthy Principal to his house, opposite
the Academy grounds. What an interminable distance
those few rods seemed to me! It is said that a drowning
person in two minutes can live over again every incident
in a long and checkered career; and you will not doubt
the possibility of such a phenomenon if you have ever
walked ten rods with a football under your arm, a new
schoolmaster ten feet ahead, and the consciousness in
your palpitating heart that you have committed a heinous crime against that glorious institution with which
for a year you had been longing to be identified.

"I thought of all the mishaps of Tom Brown at Rugby,
of the wretched Smike, and Oliver Twist, and by the
time we had reached the Doctor's house, although I was
not visibly black and blue from the rattan, I was inwardly
black and blue from my harassing reflections. Once inside the door, however, the Doctor was most pleasant and
affable. He assured me that he needed no explanation;
that he saw just how the case stood; that he was sure I
had intended no disrespect; that I was probably not
aware that it was customary at the Academy for the
pupils to check their sport for the minute or two required
for the instructors to pass through the yard. This was

all he said on that subject; then, with a pleasant word or two on academy life in general, he with a knowing smile bade me take the ball back to the rest of the boys, and have as good a time as I knew how. With a lightened heart I hastened to rejoin my companions; and when I sent that ball back among them with the very highest kick that I could give, it did not even then rise to the level of my exalted opinion of the PHILLIPS EXETER ACADEMY and its gentlemanly way of disciplining its pupils."

His methods of government were judicious, calm, and decided. During the troubles of the Rebellion, a worthy colored student was a member of the Academy. Exeter knew no color line. Four students coming from Kentucky were full of indignation, and, after talking the matter over among themselves, called upon the Principal in his study, and said, "Doctor, we see that you have a colored student in the Academy, and we have called to say that if he stays we must leave." Said the Doctor, "The colored student will stay; you can do as you please." The Southrons left.

For the shirk he had no sympathy, but the good man was always a friend of those who tried. Sometimes a lad who had become so interested in sports and games as to neglect his studies would receive the awful summons to call at the Doctor's house; where, after listening to a reasonable talk, he would go away feeling as though he never could neglect his books again. If, perchance, one was so careless as to forget again, the noted "three hundred lines of Virgil" would bring him quickly to his senses, and perhaps mar the pleasures of the next holiday.

In the school-room he was at his best. When he entered his recitation-room (number five of the new building), the class rose and remained standing until he bowed for it to sit. This was not mere form; it was genuine respect for the good doctor, whom all so loved and reverenced.

"As a teacher he devoted himself chiefly to the Latin language and literature, and in that department he has left his brilliant record in all our colleges. Those who have attended his examinations for many years bear witness to his critical accuracy, his pure taste, his keen appreciation of the classic authors, the thoroughness of his drill, the measured stages by which he has raised his successive classes to a level of attainment which has commanded always our warm approval, often our surprised admiration. We who have been most conversant with his class-work, and have seen much of the same elsewhere, have known none better, — were it not invidious, we might be tempted to say, none so good."[1]

He had a "lottery" system of calling up his pupils, in which there seemed to be as little chance as in those of which we read. Hon. Robert T. Lincoln writes: —
"I shall never forget his lottery system of calling up a boy in recitation. The little tickets were carefully faced downward in a tin box, and delicately picked out, one by one, with the moistened tip of his finger, and —

[1] Rev. A. P. Peabody, D. D., in his address delivered at the "Soule Festival."

laid aside until the name of the fellow he was after was reached."

One of the pleasantest remembrances that his pupils have of him is his after-school talks. In those days, in addition to the morning exercises, the school closed with afternoon prayers, always conducted by Dr. Soule. At the end of this service he frequently told the school some anecdote, generally amusing, and always pointing to some moral which never failed to impress itself upon his hearers. The Doctor's mind was well-stored with anecdotes and he had the reputation of being a wonderfully good story-teller. He seemed to enjoy his own stories quite as much as his privileged hearers. Even after he retired from active work, and in those last sad days when it was plain that his powers were waning, he would occasionally tell an anecdote with the same old vivacity and with as good an effect as ever.

On the street he always met his pupils with a gracious smile and bow, and at his house he often received them with cordial hospitality.

Mr. Soule took part in the various interests of Exeter, and identified himself with its citizens. He was a strong advocate of all improvements and the welfare of his fellow-townsmen was very near his heart. In town meetings his dignified yet unassuming manner won universal respect, and gained for him a ready hearing.

Mr. Soule was a sincere Christian. Throughout his life he sought to be a co-worker with the Great Teacher,

THIRD ACADEMY BUILDING.

whose blessing he so frequently sought. It was thus that he gained the power to fit his pupils for the highest and noblest duties of this life. At the same time he taught them to look forward to life eternal.

His pupils rise up and bless his memory.

THE SOULE FESTIVAL.

The semi-centennial celebration in honor of Gideon Lane Soule, LL. D., and of the dedication of the new Academy building, was held on June 19, 1872.

This day marked the close of the second epoch in the history of the Academy, and although no extraordinary pains had been taken to secure the attendance of friends and former pupils of the school, yet the long trains brought crowds of guests eager to be present at the dedication of the new Academy building, erected by the generosity of the friends of the school, and to do honor to the venerable Dr. Soule, who thirty-four years ago had succeeded to the charge of the institution, and who, like Dr. Abbot at that time, had now completed his half-century of service as an instructor in the Academy.

The occasion was memorable. By eleven o'clock the lecture-room of the new building was crowded. The walls of the room were adorned with portraits, which were collected through the efforts of one of the Academy's best-loved sons.[1] Wendell Phillips, the most

---
[1] Hon. Benjamin F. Prescott.

prominent gentleman present, sat on the platform under the portrait of his benevolent kinsman, the Founder, while among the other eminent men present were Dr. John G. Palfrey and Prof. Francis Bowen of Harvard University, Prof. A. S. Packard of Bowdoin College, President Paul A. Chadbourne of Williams College, Judge Jeremiah Smith of Dover, Hon. George S. Hale of Boston, Prof. Jeffries Wyman of Cambridge, and Rev. R. D. Hitchcock of New York. After a prayer by the Rev. John H. Morison, the Rev. Andrew P. Peabody, President of the Board of Trustees, delivered a finished and interesting address. This has since been published. The tribute which Dr. Peabody paid to the Principal, Dr. Soule, was received with rounds of applause.

The exercises of the morning were closed with the singing of the ode written for the occasion by C. H. B. Snow, who more than thirty years before had been a pupil in the Academy. About two o'clock, Chief Marshal James C. Davis of Boston formed the Alumni and invited guests into a procession, and, enlivened by the strains of the United States Marine Band of Portsmouth, which furnished the music throughout the day, all moved toward the Town Hall, where a tempting repast had been spread.

In an easy speech, after alluding to the use of wines at festivals, the Chairman, Dr. Palfrey, said that they proposed to maintain this feast with pure water, and announced the first toast, "John Phillips," which all drank standing. The Chairman exhibited several interesting relics of Dr. Phillips, among which were the diploma received from Dartmouth College, conferring upon him the degree of Doctor of Laws; several memorandum-books, bound in the wrappers of the sugar-loaves in which he dealt; his marriage certificate, pocket-book, and watch. He then called upon the oldest graduate present. John Swasey, an old gentleman of eighty-five, who was in the Academy seventy years before, arose, and in response to this toast gave his youthful recollections of the Founder. He closed by proposing a toast to Dr. Abbot, his own teacher.

Dr. Palfrey then called upon Wendell Phillips; and as the graceful orator stood up to speak, he was welcomed with a hearty burst of applause, which the band caught up with the strains, "Hail to the Chief." Mr. Phillips was to speak, he said, to the toast in honor of the Phillips family, and especially of the Founder of the school; and he began by saying that his relationship was so distant that he could speak of his kinsman's endowment without a pang, and of his virtues as if they had adorned some other name. He told several anecdotes of the Founder, and then went on to say that it was to the credit of the Phillips family, who founded the twin academies at Exeter and Andover, that they set the fashion in New England of munificent gifts to the cause of education. None before them had given so much; but since the days of John Phillips it had been the **custom to hold** wealth as a trust, and **make it** subservient to the public welfare.

"But," continued Mr. Phillips, "as **much as I praise** the munificence of your Founder, **I** admire still more **the** faithfulness **of** your Trustees. You will find in **the** second century of your **school** many liberal givers, but you will hardly find such a self-denying and frugal Board of Trustees. But, to use an Irish bull, we should never be as good as our predecessors, unless we are better than they; we are not to copy **them, but** to be as good as they in our circumstances. **This school is to** be cherished, to be maintained and augmented. The need of our day is for an education in work as well as in books. In the days of John Phillips and Dr. Abbot, the rule was half the year at school and half the year at work; and when the scholar had graduated he could earn his bread with his hands, if need be. Nowadays the book education is continued and increased, **and we** turn out scholars who cannot give a dose of catnip tea without using the Greek phrase for it; but the industrial education is dropped down, and must be restored in some way."

One word he would address to the scholars before him, — men of high scholarship and very many of them engaged in the work of education. He could not echo the speech **of** Walter Savage Landor, who said there was a spice of the scoundrel in every English scholar, but he did find **in** too many **of** the American scholars a spice of cowardly indifference. They no longer led the people, but followed or were dragged by them. "In our dealings with slavery, if the scholars had done their duty, the Civil War with its enormous debt might have been avoided. Let the lesson avail, and may the scholars of this generation welcome every new question, throw it open to the light of discussion, and lead the attack on the evils of the present time, so that the future reformer, when he wins his next victory, may not say to the American scholar, as Henry IV. said to Coillon, after one of his great battles, '*Tu n'y étais pas!*' Such a day as we had, and thou not there!" This sentiment was loudly applauded, and Mr. Phillips sat down amid hearty cheers.

The Chairman then said that, having done honor to the great benefactors of the Academy who were dead, it now became their duty to do honor to its greatest living friend, Principal Soule; and thereupon the company gave three hearty cheers. Dr. Soule, whose feeble health had kept him from hearing Dr. Peabody in the morning, made a short but happy speech, and then withdrew, followed by the cheers of hundreds of his admirers.

Speeches were also made by President Chadbourne, Hon. Amos Tuck, Hon. George S. Hale, Prof. Francis Bowen, Judge Jeremiah Smith, Rev. R. D. Hitchcock, of New York, and Mr. Tilden, the successor to Dr. Taylor at Andover. Mr. Hale[1] read a poem recalling reminiscences of his school life at Exeter, and

[1] Mr. Hale's poem may be found in the Appendix.

Judge **Smith** alluded **to the** plans **his father had of** endowing **the Academy,** which **were** "frustrated **by an** event which he did not then foresee," meaning the birth **of a son** and heir in his old **age.**

But the most notable speech of the occasion was that **made** by John Langdon Sibley, **the** venerable librarian of Harvard College, who was revealed **to the** Alumni as having endowed the Academy from his small estate with fifteen thousand dollars to increase the charity scholarships. **For ten years** Mr. Sibley had guarded **his secret, as if he had done a** base rather than a noble **deed ; but** now, urged **by the** persistency of the Trustees, he had reluctantly consented to **make it** known at this gathering. **The** storm of applause which greeted the announcement of this gift could scarcely be resisted, even by a gentleman as hale and stout as Mr. Sibley; and though at first the gray head was bowed, he was soon forced to his feet by the continued applause of the audience. After a moment of silence, which, indeed, seemed eloquence itself, he told the story of the gift in a speech full of touching pathos, and thronging with tender memories.

He disclaimed any credit for the gift, which, he said, was first suggested by his father, a hard-working farmer in Maine, who had no advantages for obtaining an education, but **who early** felt the want of it, and determined that his **son should** not suffer in a like respect. Riding through Exeter **in 1797, his** father had seen the Academy, and the **boys** at play in the school yard, **and had** resolved **that his** own son should be entered there. "So," said Mr. Sibley, "in 1819 I was sent to Dr. Abbot's school, while my father continued to toil on his rough farm in the woods of Maine. Never shall I forget the day when I was admitted to the benefits of the foundation fund of the Academy. My clothes were of the rough homespun of the backwoods, and I was as green as the grass on the village common. I was very poor, but by rigid economy, and by teaching during the winter months, I managed to keep body and soul together. It was a hard struggle, and had it not been for the little aid my father gave me, I could not have succeeded. Now and then there came from the farm one dollar, or perhaps two, — never more than three, — which the utmost self-denial alone enabled my father to send me." Mr. Sibley then referred to the Academy as it was in his day, and spoke of his classmates, his delight in his studies, and the joy with which his father heard of his progress.

"Years after," continued Mr. Sibley, "when all our family except my father had died, wishing to dispose of the little property that his extreme frugality had enabled him to acquire, he said, 'Exeter must be remembered,' and gave me one hundred dollars to take to the Trustees. Then he asked what he should do with the remainder of his property, and spoke about bequeathing it to me. 'Will you give it to Exeter Academy?' 'Take it, John,' said he, 'and do what you think best with it.' I received from him five thousand dollars, the earnings of his life, and have made over to your Trustees the sacred **trust. Five** thousand more I have gladly given, though it leaves me with scarcely as **much.** Still I will add **yet another five** thousand to the 'Sibley Charity **Fund**' if, before the new **year,** there be subscribed a generous sum for our Alma Mater."

None **who** were present **will** ever forget that brief half-hour. **The** minds of all were deeply stirred by the **tenderest emotions, and before** Mr. Sibley **had** finished there was scarcely a **dry** eye in the audience.

The festival closed with a promenade concert and ball in the **Town Hall, at which hundreds of the alumni were present.**

"**The impressions of this meeting,**" an alumnus writes, "**will not** easily **be effaced. The old** place and its memories, **renewed by** meeting **again** those who were our fellow-students **and** playmates, **the** noble address **of Dr.** Peabody, **the** words of **those renowned** as scholars, statesmen, **and jurists, as well as** the music and song, combined to gladden our hearts, and **make** us prouder than **ever of our** '**dear mother.**'"

Summary. — The administration of Dr. Soule was **one** of uniform prosperity. It could scarcely have been otherwise, since he followed closely in the footsteps of **Dr.** Abbot. The changes made **by Dr.** Soule were all for the **better. Under his** direction the school was classified, Abbot **Hall and** the new Academy building were erected, Gorham **Hall** purchased, and the Christian **Fraternity founded.**

Among the instructors whom he associated with himself were Joseph G. Hoyt, Paul A. Chadbourne, George A. Wentworth, and Bradbury L. Cilley.

Among his pupils were Paul A. Chadbourne, George S. Hale, Benjamin F. Prescott, Robert T. Lincoln, Christopher C. Langdell, and Sylvester Waterhouse, as well as many of those already named as pupils of Dr. Abbot.

FOURTH PERIOD.—1873-1883.

ALBERT CORNELIUS PERKINS, son of Nehemiah P. and Lydia Bradstreet (the latter a descendant of Governor Bradstreet of Massachusetts), was born in Topsfield, Massachusetts, on December 18, 1833, and there spent his boyhood and early youth. In 1852 he entered the Phillips Academy at Andover, and after three years spent there entered Dartmouth College, where he was graduated in 1859. After graduation Mr. Perkins taught for two years in the Phillips Academy at Andover, and afterwards in the High School at Peabody, Massachusetts. In 1863 he became a lecturer in the High School at Lawrence, Massachusetts, part of the time acting as Principal. In May, 1873, Mr. Perkins was elected Principal and Odlin Professor of English in the Phillips Exeter Academy, and entered upon the duties of the position in September, 1873.

In May, 1883, Dr. Perkins resigned his post at Exeter, in order to accept the Principalship of the Adelphi Academy at Brooklyn, N. Y.

Summary. — With the advent of Mr. Perkins **as** Principal, a new epoch in the history of the Phillips Exeter Academy began.

Dr. Perkins's administration, which thus covered a period of ten years, was not one of retrogression. **The** English department **was** re-established, the school **was** re-classified, the funds were increased thirty **per** cent, **and a** second literary society **was** founded.

If some hold that at times mistakes were made, still all must acknowledge that **the** enviable reputation for superior scholarship, which **the** Academy has always borne, was jealously guarded **and maintained by** him.

CHAPTER IV.

FINANCIAL AND CHRONOLOGICAL.

Financial History. — Chronological Summary of the most important Events in the History of the Phillips Exeter Academy.

FINANCIAL.

WE have already given an account of the founding of the Phillips Exeter Academy by John Phillips. It now becomes us to refer more particularly to its endowment, and to its subsequent financial history.

1782–1818. — The property for the purpose of establishing the Academy was given by legal conveyances, dated respectively January 9, 1782, March 29, 1787, and November 25, 1789; and by a will approved and allowed April 28, 1795. It is impossible after the lapse of nearly a century to ascertain the exact value of the Founder's benefactions. Indeed, the property was of such a nature that we hardly think its value could be more than approximated, even in the Founder's lifetime. However, an article [1] written a short time before

---

[1] Topographical Description of Exeter, New Hampshire, by Dr. Samuel Tenney, Corresponding Member of the Historical Society, Mass. Hist. Coll., Vol. IV.

the death of Mr. Phillips fixes the amounts as follows: —

First gift, wild lands in several townships . . £2,000
Second gift, specie notes, bearing interest . . £4,000
Third gift, specie notes, bearing interest . . . £2,000

From this statement it appears that the Founder gave to the Academy eight thousand pounds during his lifetime, which with the amount received at his death makes a total endowment of about twelve thousand pounds. The article from which we have just quoted states that the income of the gift of 1789 is appropriated for paying the board of "poor scholars."

From another authority it seems that the notes and mortgages given in 1787 amounted to "£4,167, lawful money," while the gift of 1789 was of uncertain value. It is probable that the round numbers given by the former writer are approximately correct.

At his death, Mr. Phillips, after making a few trifling bequests, left the remainder of his property, valued at about thirty thousand dollars, to the Phillips Academy at Andover and the Phillips Exeter Academy, one third to the former, and two thirds to the latter institution.

Five years later it is known that these various gifts amounted to $58,880.37. This was in addition to the late residence of Mr. Phillips, and the school building and grounds. We append here an inventory of the property belonging to the Academy at that time, which we have taken from the first financial report found upon the records of the Trustees. It will be noticed that it is signed by the Treasurer, John Taylor Gilman, and countersigned by three gentlemen of the trust. It is as follows: —

"*Memorandum of Property belonging to the Phillips Exeter Academy, July* 1, 1800, *viz.:* —

Notes of hand, and stock in Merrimack Bank,	$26,471.21
Sundry notes unremitted	1,695.00
Funded stock on hand and a note for same, specific value about	900.00
500 acres of land in Sandwich, valued at . .	700.00
850 " " Gilmantown, " . .	1,700.00
40 " " Epping, " . .	400.00
Sundry tracts of land in various towns, worth perhaps	700.00
	$32,566.21

"The above property belongs to the 'General Fund.'

Notes on hand and stock in the New Hampshire Bank	$25,268.16	
Notes unsettled, about	180.00	
10 acres of land in Exeter . . .	166.00	
Part of house and land in Exeter, bought of Samuel Odlin . . .	700.00	
		26,314.16

"This sum appertains to the 'Charity Fund.'

$58,880.37

"Also late mansion-house of the Hon. John Phillips, and some other notes, and about fifty notes considered of no value.

J. T. GILMAN.

"Sam'l Phillips.
Paine Wingate.
Oliver Peabody."

It also appears from this same report, that "all these sums have arisen from the benevolent gifts of the Founder." It is therefore evident that the entire amount of the original endowment could not have been far from sixty-five thousand dollars. And here let the generosity of Elizabeth, the wife of John Phillips, be recorded. She relinquished "freely and voluntarily . . . all rights of dower and power of thirds," in order to share with her husband in this pious and glorious undertaking, reserving for herself only "one thousand silver dollars," and beef and pork and clothing to the amount of fifty dollars a year, as long as she should live. Truly the widow bestowed her mite, and therefore should receive due honor. Some of the friends of Madam Phillips, thinking she had reserved for herself too small a portion of the good things of this world, induced the Trustees of the Academy to give her fifty pounds in lawful money, a cow, and the use of a house and garden. We doubt not that this cow took in the situation, and did her utmost to remunerate the worthy widow for her self-sacrificing generosity.

By the report of the Treasurer rendered July 1, 1818, we find the property to be valued as follows: —

General Fund	$41,765.30
Charity Fund	26,701.35
House and land occupied by Benjamin Abbot, also another house	5,000.00
"Musical Fund"	1,000.00
	$74,466.65

1818-1858. — There was but little change in the financial condition of the Academy during the succeeding forty years. At the end of that period, by judicious investments and the general appreciation of values, the funds had been almost doubled. It was then (1858) valued, in round numbers, as follows: —

Real Estate, including six or seven acres of
land in the village, the Academy building,
Abbot Hall, and the Principal's house . . $ 35,000.00
Productive fund in notes and stocks . . . 100,000.00

$135,000.00

It was at this period that the Phillips Charity Fund was merged into the general fund of the Academy. There may have been good reasons for making this change, but, as the Founder gave a specific sum for this special purpose, we hardly think it was a wise policy to confound the two. This act of the Trustees, however, did not affect the interests of the "foundation scholars," who continued to receive aid as before.

Up to this time the Academy was indebted to the Founder for all its funds, with the exception of a bequest of one thousand dollars by Hon. Nicholas Gilman, the income of which was to be expended for instruction in music, and one hundred dollars given by Hon. Leverett Saltonstall for the library.

1858-1883. — During the last twenty-five years the funds, through the generosity of the Alumni and friends of the Academy have been largely increased.[1] Among these benefactors may be mentioned Rev. John Langdon Sibley, of Cambridge; Jeremiah Kingman, Esq., of Barrington, N. H.; Woodbridge Odlin, Esq., of Exeter; Henry Winkley, Esq., of Philadelphia, whose generosity to the cause of education has been so often manifested; a gentleman whose name we are not allowed to publish, but who has contributed five thousand dollars; and William Phillips, Esq., of Boston, a kinsman of the Founder, who contributed ten thousand dollars toward the Rebuilding Fund in 1871.

"These and other gifts of less magnitude have been faithfully applied to the specific purposes for which they were bestowed, and with results which have secured to this Academy no second place among the educational institutions of the land. The extensive charities which the Academy has been able to dispense have doubtless led to the impression that its endowment for all other purposes was equally ample. But this is not the fact." Although, during the last twenty-five years, the amount appropriated for charity scholarships and kindred purposes has been increased nearly if not quite four hundred per cent, and although the Academy has acquired

---

[1] A record of these various benefactions will be found in the Chronological Summary contained in this chapter. The subscriptions to the Rebuilding Fund, received just after the destruction of the Academy in 1870, are not included in this list. They were very numerous, and came from all parts of the country. See also sketches of Rev. John L. Sibley and Jeremiah Kingman, Esq., and the account of Mr. Sibley's speech at the "Soule Festival."

new and more commodious buildings and ampler playgrounds, yet the general fund has been increased only about thirty per cent.

From the last report of the Treasurer, rendered June 7, 1882, we see that the productive funds of the Academy (exclusive of grounds, buildings, etc.) amount to $203,125. Of this amount $102,801.43 are restricted as follows: —

Kingman Fund; income only to be used in aid
  of indigent meritorious students $42,421.43
Sibley Fund; income to be limited to same,
  and not yet available $32,380.00
Odlin Fund; to endow professorship of English $20,000.00
Gilman Fund; for instruction in sacred music $1,000.00
Bancroft, Burroughs, Hale, and Gordon Funds;
  to found special scholarships $7,000.00

Thus there remains but $100,323.57. Of this amount about $20,000 belongs to the Phillips Charity Fund; while the remainder constitutes what is called the General Fund. It is from the income of this fund, together with the amount received from tuition fees, that the salaries of the instructors, expense of fuel, new furnishings, new reference books, and all other ordinary and extraordinary expenses, are paid. Now in order that the Academy may be enabled to hold its own in competition with recent munificently endowed schools, this fund should be largely increased. The history of the Academy warrants it; the future of our country demands it.

The funds of this institution, from its establishment in 1781 to the present day, have "been managed at a minimum cost, — sometimes gratuitously, sometimes for a mere pittance, never for an adequate compensation, — by a series of Exeter gentlemen of the highest position and character, who have borne the charge of the treasury as a philanthropic service."

The eminent reputation and distinguished usefulness of the Academy during the last century is due, in no small degree, to the skilful financial management of its treasurers.

In conclusion, we will add that the funds of the Academy are invested safely and well. We would suggest, however, that it would not be unwise for the Trustees to publish, each year, the Treasurer's report. This is a custom which has proved beneficial to similar institutions; and we feel sure that such a policy would greatly increase the interest which so many have in the financial welfare of the Academy.

CHRONOLOGICAL SUMMARY.

EARLY HISTORY. — 1781-1788.

1781, April 3. The Academy incorporated.
1781, Dec. 18. The Constitution adopted.
[By this document John and Elizabeth Phillips conveyed to the Academy over 3,200 acres of land, and other property, and also made the rules by which the school and its officers are governed.]

1781-82. The first Academy building erected.

1783, **Feb. 20.** The school opened by the Rev. Benjamin Thurston.

ADMINISTRATION OF MR. WOODBRIDGE.—1783-1788.

1783, May 1. **The first Academy building dedicated,** and William Woodbridge installed Principal.

1784. Colonel Henry **Dearborn and** other gentlemen of Exeter presented the Academy with a bell.

1787, **Oct. 11. The Trustees vote** thanks to **John Phillips for** his large and liberal donation of March 29, **1787.** This second **gift to the** Academy amounted to about $20,000.

1788, June 11. William Woodbridge, the **first Principal,** resigns.

1788, Oct. 8. The resignation of William **Woodbridge** accepted, and Benjamin **Abbot engaged as an** instructor.

ADMINISTRATION OF BENJAMIN ABBOT.—1788-1838.

1790, Oct. **15. Benjamin Abbot becomes the second** Principal.

The Rev. **Joseph Buckminster elected** " Professor of Divinity in the Phillips **Exeter** Academy, and **joyn't** instructor with the Preceptor thereof."

[Although he was voted a salary **of "one hundred and thirty-three pounds** six shillings **and eight-pence, lawful** money, per annum," **it does not appear that he** accepted **this position.**]

1793, Nov. 13. The Trustees vote to erect a new Academy building.

1794. The second Academy building erected.

1795, April 21. Death of John Phillips, LL. D., the founder.

1798, Oct. 10. The Board of Trustees voted, " That after the vacation in April next no student in the Academy shall wear silk of any kind as a part of his dress, and that it be recommended to the students after that time to discontinue the use of gowns, and that it would be pleasing to the Trustees to see the dress of the students less expensive, and in all instances, when consistent, composed of the manufactures of your own country." Rigid economy in all other respects also recommended.

1799, Aug. 8. The Preceptor's salary fixed at $700. This is in addition to the free use of a dwelling-house.

1801, July 9. The records of the Trustees refer, for the first time, to the annual school exhibitions, afterwards so famous.

1803, Aug. 23. The Trustees appropriate $200 for the support of divinity students. They also vote to employ a mathematical instructor at a salary not to exceed $500.

1804, Aug. 22. The Trustees appropriate $500 for books for the use of divinity students.

[About this time the Trustees seem to have made vigorous efforts to carry out the Founder's wishes in regard to religious instruction, but they soon found it impossible to combine a theological seminary with a college preparatory school, and consequently relaxed their efforts in this direction.]

1809. The first tuition fee levied.

[This amounted to $2.00 per year, and was remitted to "foundationers." Previous to this the Phillips Exeter Academy had been a free school. In many cases the board as well as tuition had been free.]

1814, Aug. 29. By the will of Nicholas Gilman the Trustees receive one thousand dollars, the income of which is to pay for instruction in "solemn musick."

1817, June 16. The Rev. Isaac C. Hurd, pastor of the Second Parish, is elected "Theological Instructor," at a salary of $250 per year.

1818, June 3. It is voted to have an English department consisting of a three-years course.

1818, July 16. The "Golden Branch Society" is founded.

1822, April 30. Gideon Lane Soule is appointed "permanent instructor."

1822, June 27. It is voted to enlarge the Academy building by the addition of wings, and also to employ Nathaniel Connor to build the same.

1827, Aug. 21. Hon. John Taylor Gilman, the successor of the Founder as President of the Board of Trustees, in resigning this position, declined to appoint his successor, as he had the right to do. Consequently the Founder's successor in this office is now elected in the same manner as the other members of the Board.

[At this time the **funds were** unequal to **the necessary** expenses **of** this growing institution, and Governor **Gilman concludes his letter of** resignation by expressing regret **that one** sixth **of the** funds had not been set **apart, at** the founding of the school, as an accumulative fund. For in that case, **he says, "we** would have an amount double **our** present **endowment."** A few years later (1832), **when Dr.** Abbot **wished to be** relieved from some **of the** duties of his office (for the Trustees would **not hear of** his resignation) it was decided that, **owing to the want of** funds, there was no **other way** than **to reduce the** number of pupils to **sixty. From this** has arisen the seemingly mistaken idea that the number of pupils **in the school is necessarily** limited. It is our desire **that the school may some time** number **five** hundred students.]

1835, **Aug. 20.** Daniel Webster elected a Trustee **of the Academy.** His letter of acceptance, addressed to **Dr. Abbot, ends as** follows:—

"I cannot close this **letter,** sir, without signifying **to** you the uncommon pleasure I feel in having received the communication which **I am** now answering, from your own **hand.** I pray **you** to be assured of the consistent and sincere attachment and **regard** of your affectionate pupil and friend,

"DANIEL WEBSTER."

1838, Aug. 22. **The resignation of** Benjamin **Abbot as** Principal accepted.

1838, **Aug.** 23. "Abbot Festival" **celebrated.**

ADMINISTRATION OF DR. SOULE. — 1838-1873.

1838, Aug. 22. Gideon Lane Soule becomes the third Principal of the Academy.

1841, Aug. 19. The Trustees vote that " the Golden Branch Society shall be merely a private one, with no secret or secrecy in their exercises or proceedings."

1849, Oct. 25. Death of Benjamin Abbot.

1849, Oct. 27. The Trustees adopt the following resolution : —

" The undersigned, having been appointed a committee to draft appropriate resolutions, submitted the following, which was then adopted by the Board.

"*Resolved*, That we, the Trustees of Phillips Exeter Academy, holding in very high appreciation the distinguished services of Dr. Abbot, while he was, for half a century, the Principal of this seminary; his untiring devotion to its interests; the eminent reputation with which he has adorned it, and the good learning and morals which he has ably and diligently labored to impart to those under his charge; his discreet zeal and judicious counsel while a member of the Board of Trustees; his faith and virtues as a Christian; his dignity and courtesy as a gentleman; his classical accomplishments as a scholar; his fidelity, generosity, and warmth as a friend; his delightful and endearing traits in all his domestic relations; and his intelligence, usefulness, example, and liberality as a citizen, — do now express to his family our high veneration of his name, our desire ever to cherish a remembrance of his worth, and our most grateful sense of the numerous and various excellences of his life; and we would also now express our most tender sympathies with his bereaved widow and his family; and we most earnestly and devoutly implore for them the Divine blessing, support, sanctification, and solace.

[Signed,]   "CHARLES BURROUGHS, *President* } *of the*
               G. L. SOULE, *Clerk*   } *Board.*"

1854, July 31. Adopting the plan of Professor Hoyt, the school is divided into Junior, Middle, and Senior Classes. There is also a Preparatory and an Advanced Class. But while the former is to be kept as small as possible, every effort is to be made to increase the size of the latter which corresponds to the Freshman Class in college.

From this time until 1874, foundationers received aid as follows: those of the Advanced Class, $1.75; of the Senior Class, $1.50; and of the other Classes, $1.25 each per week.

1855, Aug. 13. The Trustees vote that the use of intoxicating liquors by any student shall cause them to sever his connection with the Academy.

1855, Nov. 27. The room rent in the new dormitory, "Abbot Hall," is fixed at $1.00 per year for each student.

1856, April 23. The "Christian Fraternity" is founded.

1858, July 13. The students are excused from attendance at the Academy except during recitation hours and prayers.

1859, July 12. A committee is appointed to ascertain the necessary expense of building a Gymnasium.

1860, Nov. 26. The Trustees receive the gift of Dr. Jonathan Sibley, M. D., of Union, Maine.

[From this gentleman, the Trustees received the sum of one hundred dollars in grateful remembrance of the favors which his son, John Langdon Sibley, had received at the Phillips Exeter Academy; this sum was increased to three hundred dollars by the Rev. J. L. Sibley, the son, and constitutes the "Sibley Book Fund," the income of which is expended in purchasing text-books for students who are in straitened circumstances. No one, however, is to have any part of it if he uses opium, ardent spirits, or tobacco in any form.]

1862, Nov. 25. The Trustees receive the nucleus of the munificent "Sibley Charity Fund" from the Rev. John Langdon Sibley, the librarian of Harvard College.

1863, Nov. 24. Tuition increased to ten dollars per term.

1867, July 2. Jeremiah Kingman, of Barrington, N. H., gives five hundred dollars to increase the Charity Fund. [At the death of Mr. Kingman, in 1873, the Academy received $42,421.43 for the same fund.]

1870, Dec. 18. Second Academy building destroyed by fire.

The Trustees receive two thousand dollars from George Bancroft to endow the Bancroft Scholarship. Mr. Bancroft writes: "I desire to repeat for others that come after me, what was done for me."

Tuition increased to fifteen dollars per term.

Dec. 24. The Alumni determine **to raise** $100,000 **to rebuild the Academy,** and for other purposes.

1871–72. — **Third Academy** building erected.

1872, June 19. The "Soule Festival" celebrated, and the new building dedicated.

1872, Sept. 28. Tuition **fees are** increased to twenty dollars per **term.**

1872, Oct. 26. Nathaniel Gordon gives one thousand dollars, afterwards doubled, to found **the** Gordon **Scholarship.**

The Trustees vote thanks to William Phillips, **who gave ten** thousand dollars to the Building Fund.

They also vote Principal **Soule a** pension of twelve hundred dollars per year, and the free use of a house, whenever it shall be necessary for him to retire.

1872, Dec. 17. The Trustees **arrange to** purchase the **Swamscot** House for a school dormitory. [This building **was** renamed Gorham Hall.]

They also receive from Miss Martha Hale two thousand dollars to found the Samuel Hale Scholarship.

1873, Feb. 1. The resignation of Gideon Lane Soule, **third** Principal of **the** Academy, accepted, and he retires from office at the end of the school year.

ADMINISTRATION OF DR. PERKINS. — 1873–1883.

1873, May 22. Albert Cornelius Perkins is elected fourth Principal of **the** Academy.

Dec. 22. Prof. George A. Wentworth appointed **supervisor** of dormitory buildings.

1875, March 13. Woodbridge Odlin re-establishes the English department, and founds the Odlin Professorship of English, by giving twenty thousand dollars to the Academy.

1878, Oct. 12. Henry Winkley, of Philadelphia, increases the "general fund" of the Academy by the gift of five thousand dollars. [He later sends another gift of the same amount.]

1878, March. The "Exonian" founded.

1879, May 28. The death of Gideon Lane Soule. The Trustees caused the following entry to be made upon the school records: —

"The death of Gideon Lane Soule, LL. D., for more than forty years a teacher in the Academy, and for twenty-five years the Principal, occurred on the 28th of May, 1879. In view of this event, it is

"*Resolved*, That the Trustees place upon the record some expression of their regard for the character of the deceased and for the services he rendered to the Academy. His devotion to the interests of the school was unwavering, he brought to the work of instruction and government earnest zeal, fine literary culture, love for young men, a nice sense of honor and integrity, dignity and courtesy of a high order, fidelity and generosity; these traits he applied with wisdom and success to the interests of the young men under his care. His love for the Academy, and his concern for the welfare of it, ended only with his life. His name is cherished with affectionate veneration, and the reputation which the school acquired under his management is his fitting monument. The Trustees desire to express their sympathy with the widow and family of the deceased, and to join with them in loving respect for his memory.

"A. C. PERKINS, *Clerk*."

1880, December. The Burroughs Scholarship Fund becomes available.

1881, April 3. One hundredth anniversary of the incorporation of the Phillips Exeter Academy.

1881. The "G. L. Soule Literary Society" founded.

1883, May 1. One hundredth anniversary of the formal opening of the Phillips Exeter Academy.

1883, May 8. The Trustees accept the resignation of A. C. Perkins, as Principal of the Academy. [This resignation took effect at the end of the school year.]

1883, June 20. Reunion dinners of the various classes, followed by a general reunion of the Alumni of the Academy in the evening.

1883, June 21. The Phillips Exeter Academy celebrates its Centennial. The order of exercises is as follows : —

Centennial Oration, by Rev. Horatio Stebbins, D. D., of San Francisco, Cal., (Class of 1844,) at 10.30 A. M.
Poem, by Edward Hale, A. B., of Boston, Mass., (Class of 1875,) immediately after the Oration.
Meeting of Classes from 12 M. to 2 P. M.
Dinner in a tent at 2 P. M., after which speeches by distinguished Alumni, George Bancroft the historian (Class of 1813) presiding.
Promenade Concert in tent, floored for the occasion, at 7.30 P. M.

CHAPTER V.

THE FOUNDER AND THE PHILLIPS FAMILY.

Rev. George Phillips. — The Three Samuel Phillipses. — Hon. John Phillips, the Founder. — Genealogical Table.

IN these days, when the courts are crowded by the crimes of our increasing population, when the corrupt state of our civil service turns our Capitol into a lottery office, and brings an honored President to a woful death, it is refreshing to look back to the early days of the republic, and to review such noble characters as this truly remarkable family presents.

On the 12th day of June, 1630, the ship "Arbella" sailed into Salem harbor, bearing the royal charter and the first Governor and Deputy-Governor of the now prosperous Commonwealth of Massachusetts. Among the foremost of this noted company was the Rev. George Phillips, the ancestor of the Phillips family in America.

To understand why this company of yeomen and noble-

PHILLIPS.

men, scholars and clergymen, — men prominent both in state and church, — left the comforts of home for the "deserts of America," one must recall the history of England at that time. The Church was divided into two great parties, the Arminian or High-Church party, and the Nonconformists; the former representing the King and court, the latter the commons and people.

Burdened as they were by the extravagant and absolute rule of Charles I., sickened by the horrors of La Rochelle, is it any wonder that they determined to secure that civil and religious liberty which they could not obtain in England, by emigrating to America?

We cannot rightly understand the principles which governed the family of the Founder of the Phillips Academies unless we know something of his English ancestor, George Phillips.[1]

Entering Gonville and Caius College, Cambridge, April 20, 1610, he was graduated B. A. in 1613, and M. A. in 1617. Soon after, he settled in Bosted (or Boxted) and began to preach. But his views were too simple and puritan for the Established Church, then leaning towards "Popery" and Rome. Driven from England by the extreme violence of the spirit of persecution, this young man, already "mighty in the Scripture," came, with his wife, his son and daughter, his neighbors and friends, to found an American home.

---

[1] George Phillips was the son of Christopher Phillips of Rainham (or Raymund) St. Martins, near Rougham, Hundred of Gallows, Norfolk County, England, *mediocris fortunæ*.

He settled in Watertown, and for fourteen years was a devoted pastor and a leader in the Colony. He is represented as having been "the earliest advocate of the Congregational order and discipline,"[1] and was among the first in the Colonies to resist taxation laid without the people's consent. He was "a godly man," says his intimate friend, Governor John Winthrop, "specially gifted and very peaceful."[2] Cotton Mather[3] speaks of him as "among the first saints of New England, *a good man full of faith and of the Holy Ghost*," and refers to his son Samuel in the following quaint epitaph:—

Epitaphium.
Hic jacet GEORGIUS PHILLIPPI,
Vir incomparabilis, nisi SAMUELEM genuisset.[4]

This son Samuel was the first of the Phillips family to be graduated at Harvard (1650). He settled in Rowley, "where he served God and his generation faithfully forty-five years."[5] We can imagine what the temper of this fearless patriot was, when we learn that he suffered imprisonment for having denounced Governor Randolph in one of his sermons.[6] About Samuel, the son of this Rowley preacher, not much is known, except that he was a successful goldsmith at Salem, and that he transmitted the virtues of his ancestors and

---

[1] Cong. Coll., Vol. I. p. 334.   [2] Winthrop's Journal.
[3] Mather's Magnalia, Book III. p. 85.
[4] "Here lies George Phillips, a man to be compared to none, had he not begotten Samuel."
[5] From the Phillips Monument at Rowley.
[6] Washburn's Judicial History of Massachusetts.

their favorite prænomen to his eldest son, Samuel, the first minister of the Old South Church at Andover.

The latter was the father of the Founder of this Academy, and deserves special mention, as he was considered one of the most eminent divines of his day, and as pastor endeared himself to his people during a period of over sixty years. In every way he seems to have been an excellent man. At least once a year he called at every house in his parish, and is said to have had much influence in maintaining household worship throughout the town. All these good habits he taught his children, and thus the virtues of the parent were inherited by the children.

He says in his will: "And now my desire and prayer is, yt. my sd. three Sons . . . make their care to be found in Christ, and to serve their Generation according to the Will of God by doing good as they shall have opportunity unto all men, and especially to ye Household of Faith, as knowing it is more blessed to give than to receive."

His son, John Phillips, was born in Andover on "Lord's Day," December 27, 1719. As a boy he loved books. Indeed, he made such progress in his Latin and Greek, as to enter Harvard University at the early age of eleven, and receive the honors of a degree in the fifteenth year of his age. After leaving college he studied divinity and the sciences with his father, and also taught in the public schools of Andover and the neighboring towns. Soon after this he came to Exeter and opened a private classical school, still studying for the ministry.

In Exeter he connected himself with the New Parish and was made Ruling Elder. He soon began to preach both in Exeter and the surrounding towns, and "was esteemed a zealous, pathetic, and animated preacher." We have before us his "preaching Bible," a quaint, much-worn pocket edition of the Scriptures, published in 1727. The names of the books are lettered on the edge, and within, written in a firm hand, is his signature, "John Phillips," and below are the Phillips arms curiously printed.

On the 25th of May, 1747, he was invited to become the pastor of the Second Church in Exeter. Soon after he received a most urgent call from Portsmouth, and invitations from other places. He refused them all. He had heard Whitefield, the mighty Methodist, and the eloquence that could cause the tears to roll down the cheeks of the sooty collier, and draw together an audience of thirty thousand persons, seemed so unattainable that he at once abandoned his profession and turned his attention to business, especially the lumber trade. Those habits of regularity, carefulness, and accuracy to which he had accustomed himself, combined with his native energy and sagacity, quickened as it was by a liberal education, enabled him to accomplish much more than most men. He had a keen sense of the value of time, and if he had anything to do, he did it, believing a pitched battle to be better than a continued skirmish. In his business dealings, he practised exactly what he had preached, and he grew rich, not by grinding the poor, but by industry and economy.

In these days we see some men become millionnaires by forming gigantic combinations to construct railroads and to operate telegraph lines. Sometimes even the mere sound of the "ticker," or a glance at the "tape," will indicate that a fortune has been won. In John Phillips's time, however, fortunes were *worked*, **not won, and it** was a good thing, no doubt, that **in those** early days **the people knew** nothing of construction companies **or of the paraphernalia** of the Stock **Exchange.**

If you will but call **to mind the period in** which he lived, — if you will remember that **it was** during the dark days of **the** Revolution, before the remarkable prosperity of the present century had set in, — you will perhaps understand how necessary it was that one who wished to **lay** by a competency should practise the strictest kind of economy.

We honor the Founder's thrift, and wish there was more of it at the present day. It is his savings that have made possible these hundred years of school work at Exeter, and that have sent abroad over the face of this earth more than five thousand intelligent workers. Sometimes the stories told of **this good** man's economy appear somewhat laughable, and then the ludicrous side **of** the picture **is the stronger.**

You of course know that, **in the days of** which we

write, the houses were all heated by wood-fires kept burning against a huge backlog in open fireplaces. In the Phillips house the backlogs were soaked in water for several hours before they were placed in the fireplace. This caused them to burn slowly, — this was economy. Imagine the grim old Founder of "Phillips Exeter" bringing in a dripping log for the fire! Tradition further affirms that when the household was assembled for evening prayers, and the chapter had been read, the good man always extinguished the light before the long prayer. This was to save the candle, which could be readily relighted at the open fire after the prayer was ended.

Many of his account-books he made himself. The original lists of his various gifts to the Academy are still preserved. They are in books of his own manufacture, mere pieces of paper sewed together, but in the "neatest possible manner," as our Professor of Latin used to say.

The humble home of this great man, in which he both lived and "kept store," stood on the present site of John Getchell's hardware store. (Water Street has since been widened, and taken in both the little dooryard, five feet deep, and eighteen inches of the land on which the Phillips house itself stood.) Measuring happiness by the amount of good done, he spent the best days of his life in this house. Here he entertained the clergy, the royal Governors and strangers of high and low degree. A few days ago, Wendell Phillips, that venerable hero, who in our time so fitly represents the Founder's noble family, related to me the following, which he said he had from his "goody" when in college.

This "goody" had been a servant in Exeter, and had known Dr. Phillips and his household. She said that it was customary for the Doctor to entertain the clergy when they met in Exeter, and that on such occasions he gave to each of them a glass of ordinary table wine; but to the one who was to preach the sermon of the day he gave a glass of rich mulled drink, a sort of cherry-bounce, in order, perhaps, to excite in him a proper amount of enthusiasm. He was, as has been well said, a rigorous old Puritan, a trifle sombre perhaps in his exterior, but with his friends always genial and warm-hearted, always greatly respected; in later years he became the object of affection and reverence. Indeed, he was a man to command respect. In his youth he had been carefully trained; he had seen his father and relatives, all patterns of old-time politeness, revered by neighbors, old and young; and it was only natural that he should have their same fine manners, and both expect and receive the love and honor of all. No boy dared scale his orchard wall, nor cry at him, "Say, Mister, gimme a cent!" but a low bow and a reverent tone would open this good man's purse, and at the same time fill the boy's pockets with cherries from his tree. Although a prodigy of activity, books and business did not occupy all his time. He was a patriot, and interested in the welfare of his country. He raised a corps of cadets, and the same method and discipline displayed in his business affairs made this the best-drilled body of militia in the State.

His commission has lately been found, signed by Governor John Wentworth, and dated "the 15th day of May, 1771, and the eleventh year of his Majesty's reign," appointing him "the commander of the Corps of Cadets, with rank of Colonel of Foot in the militia of said Province." The whole family took the patriotic side in the Revolution, and a story which illustrates the ardor of the family in the good cause is told of his brother William, who was a member of the Committee of Safety. It had been announced to the friends of the cause and to the members of the Committee, that a meeting was to be held in the loft of one of the stores on Long Wharf, Boston. The night proved stormy and cold, and a cutting sleet fell thick and fast. It was just the night to conceal their movements, but a rough night for the members coming in from out of town. About eleven o'clock Mr. Phillips appeared. He had come on horseback all the way from Andover, and when he threw off his outside coat it was frozen so stiff as to stand alone. These were indeed Revolutionary times, — times that not only "tried men's souls," but wet their skins and froze their ears. This same brother is said to have been one of the famous tea-party which took Boston harbor for a teapot.

Retiring from active business at the beginning of

the war, **Dr.** Phillips devoted himself **to the care of his** large estate, and **to** the execution of long-cherished plans for the advancement of education and the spirit **of the** Christian religion **which he** loved so well. He **was** a trustee of Dartmouth College (1773-1793), and founded and endowed the Phillips Professorship of Theology. From this college he received his honorary degree of Doctor of Laws. To Nassau Hall (now Princeton College) he also gave liberally, but the work by which **he** will be longest remembered was the **founding** of the two academies which bear his name. **It is** certain that the plan **of** founding the Academy at Andover originated with his favorite nephew, Samuel Phillips, Jr.; but it is quite as certain that this nephew depended upon the practical advice and mature wisdom **of** his uncle to put into execution his own incomplete plans. Thus we name the nephew "the projector," and his father and uncle "the founders," of the Phillips Academy at Andover. In January, 1777, they began to carry their plans into execution by the purchase of land. **On** the 21st of April, 1778, the constitution was signed, and seven days later the first meeting of the Trustees was held. Two days after this the school opened with thirteen students, and at the time of incorporation (October 4, 1780) the number had increased to sixty.

Dr. Phillips was one **of** the two original signers of **the** constitution of the Academy. He served most efficiently as one **of** its Trustees, from the origin of the school till his death, and during the last five years of his life he was President of the Board. "For its endowment he did more than any other man. He gave to it at the outset, in equal shares with Samuel Phillips, senior, three hundred and forty-one acres of land, and the sum of £1614 sterling. His interest in it continued through life, and his contributions to it were not less than $31,000." His last gift to the Academy at Andover amounted to over twenty thousand dollars. On receiving which the Trustees immediately " Voted, That the Honorable Samuel Phillips, Jr., Rev. Mr. Tappan, and Mr. Pearson, be a committee to draft a vote of thanks to the Honorable John Phillips, Esq., for his very generous donation to the Academy." Their report, which was adopted and recorded, was in these words : —

"The Board, having been made acquainted by a legal instrument, bearing date the 16th day of October, 1789, this day communicated, that the Hon. John Phillips, Esq., of Exeter, one of the founders of this Academy, 'for and in consideration of further promoting the virtuous and pious education of youth, (poor children of genius, and of serious disposition especially,) in Phillips Academy, founded in Andover, in the State of Massachusetts,' has given and granted to the Trustees of said Academy and their successors, or their order, certain notes of hand, therein described, to a very large amount, under certain reservations, therein mentioned, —

" *Voted*, That the thanks of the Board be presented to the Hon. John Phillips, Esq., for his before-cited pious and liberal donation, whereby he has still **further manifested his generous and** ardent zeal **for the promotion of** knowledge, virtue, and piety, and **conferred** an additional and lasting obligation upon **the** Academy.

"Upon this occasion the **Trustees** cannot but add their fervent wish and prayer, that the DONOR, **the** distinguished *Friend* and *Patron* of science and religion, may live to behold, with increasing joy and satisfaction, the happy fruits **of this, and of** all his other pious liberalities; and at a very remote period, his numerous acts of benevolence **may** receive that reward which original and infinite **goodness can** bestow."[1]

The generous spirit manifested by Samuel Phillips, **Jr.,** in inducing his father and uncle **to give** to charity and education the fortune that he himself would otherwise **have inherited, has been** deservingly eulogized by **his** biographer.[2] Indeed, every **act and** word **of this** glorious man seems worthy of imitation. The Phillips Exeter Academy, however, was originally conceived by Dr. Phillips alone, and its creation and endowment **were his** own work. He had no children, and what better use, therefore, could he make of his wealth than **to** devote it to learning, to humanity, and to God? **Thinking thus, he writes to** his nephew, and shortly after receives the following: —

"HONORED SIR: —

". . . Since receiving your last **favor, I** have been chiefly from home, and when at home have been so unfor-

---

[1] Academy Records, pp. 77, 78.
[2] Rev. John L. Taylor.

tunate as not to obtain Messrs. French's and Pearson's opinion of the dimensions of a building that would be most convenient for an Academy: this I hope for speedily, and shall with great pleasure transmit it. The joy I felt, on finding that you had it in contemplation to lay the foundation of another Academy, was great indeed: so great, that I hardly know of anything within human reach that could have given me more satisfaction, save the intelligence that your purpose was executed. May my honored uncle *long* enjoy the fruits of his pious cares and projections, in seeing those who are furnished with the best principles filling the most important places in Church and State, and doing worthily for the kingdom of our glorious Saviour. The impatience of the bearer forbids my adding more than my dutiful addresses to my honored aunt, and that I am, with the warmest sentiments of gratitude and respect,

"Your very dutiful nephew,
"S. PHILLIPS, JR."

To this his uncle replies:—

"EXETER, April 27, 1781.

"DEAR SIR:—

"... Your concurring sentiments and warm expressions respecting another Academy are very refreshing and highly animating; and will greatly endear you to my friends here, who were encouraged to expect the help of your advice, and such assistance as might, in a course of time, when you shall have more leisure especially, greatly increase the benefit of such an institution. The motion was exceedingly agreeable to the General Court, who have incorporated the Academy, by the name of the Phillips Exeter Academy, for the purposes mentioned in yours; **and** the Trustees nominated and appointed (besides myself) are Daniel Tilton and Thomas Odiorne, Esquires, of this town, John Pickering, Esq., of Portsmouth, David M'Clure, of Northampton, Clerk, the Hon. S. Phillips, **Jr.**, Esq., Andover, and the Preceptor, Mr. Benjamin Thurston — the estate **allowed the same with** yours — and might have been twice so much (I doubt not) had it been asked; and the Act concludes thus: 'And whereas the said Institution may be of very great and general advantage to **this** State, and deserves every encouragement, be it therefore enacted, by the authority aforesaid, **that all the lands,** tenements, and personal estate, that **shall be given to** the said Trustees for the use of said **Academy** shall be and hereby are forever exempted from all taxes whatsoever'; which very encouraging clause concludes me.

"**Most** affectionately yours,
"J. PHILLIPS.
"HON. S. PHILLIPS, JR., ESQ."

Thus the grand purpose of John Phillips was at last accomplished. The Academy was incorporated on the 3d of April, 1781, and **officially** opened, as we have before stated, on the **1st of May, 1783.** During his life he was the Chairman of the Board of Trustees, and the later growth of the school has been largely influenced by the fostering care that it received **from** Dr Phillips during the first fourteen years of its existence. He it **was** who **met** and solved the difficult questions constantly arising, and it was his mind that gave scope to **the** liberal **views** upon which the school was founded. **Living** in a humble country town, where frugality is wont to become meanness, at a time when such ideas of philanthropy and benevolence were unknown, it was most remarkable that he should have become the most liberal public benefactor among our countrymen of the last century. He was no example of the story of the five peas, who, sitting in their little pod, and seeing that they were green and that their pod was green, thought that the whole world must be of the same complexion. No, instead of keeping his wealth to bestow upon humanity when he could no longer use it himself, he gave it in the years of his activity, and had the satisfaction of seeing his own noble project carried into execution with the brightest prospect of future growth and increase.

He was twice married. His first wife, Sarah, widow of Nathaniel Gilman, Esq., and daughter of Rev. Mr. Emery of Wells, died in October, 1765. Two years later he married Elizabeth Hale, widow of the village physician, and daughter of Hon. E. Dennett of Portland. In connection with this second marriage, we have found the quaint congratulation of Governor John Wentworth enclosing their marriage license. Mr. Phillips was one of George Benning Wentworth's Council (1767–1775),[1] a justice of the peace (and this office was of some importance in his day), and a Judge in special cases of the Supreme Court.

He died, April 21, 1795, at the advanced age of seventy-five years and four months.

[1] New Hampshire State Papers, Vol. VII.

The peace and comfort of his last hours will be best understood by a quotation from the memorial sermon preached by Rev. John French, in Andover, the next Sunday. Having dilated upon his many virtues, this gentleman says: "He was seized with a kind of fainting fit on Monday morning, from which he in part recovered, so as to walk about the house, and was perfectly sensible and apprised of his approaching dissolution, and spoke of it to his friends with calmness and serenity and fervent pleasure; and according to information expressed himself in words to this effect: 'My work is done. I have settled all my affairs, and have now nothing to do but to die, it is no matter how soon.' And, retaining his reason to the last, the next morning he died, . . . of whom it might be said, as was said of David, 'After he had served his generation according to the will of God, he fell asleep.'"

In Exeter a eulogy upon the deceased was delivered in the parish meeting-house by the Rev. Benjamin Thurston, on October 14, 1795, the day of the annual meeting of the Trustees, but we regret to state that no copy of this tribute of friendship has been preserved.

As we have said, he had no children. All his fortune except a few legacies went to his beloved academies,— two thirds to the Phillips Exeter Academy, and one third to the Phillips Academy at Andover. Truly, "without natural issue, he made posterity his heir." His portrait by Stuart hangs in the chapel of the Phillips Exeter Academy; another is at Andover;

while still a third, presented by Hon. Josiah Quincy, may be found among the "distinguished laymen" in the hall of the Massachusetts Historical Society.

His grave may be found in the new cemetery, marked by a tablet bearing the following simple epitaph : —

JOHN PHILLIPS, LL. D.,
Founder
Of the Phillips Exeter Academy;
an
Associate Founder
of the Phillips Academy in Andover,
and
a liberal benefactor of Dartmouth College
Died April 21,
1795,
Aged 75 years.
Actuated by his ardent attachment to the
cause of Christianity, he devoted his
wealth to the advancement
of
Letters and Religion.
His appropriate monuments are the institutions
which bear his name.

We will close this sketch by quoting from a letter to Dr. Soule, the late Principal of the Academy, written by the venerable Josiah Quincy in 1855, when the writer was already more than eighty-three years of age. Referring to the Phillips family and to Dr. Phillips himself, Mr. Quincy said, with his characteristic earnestness, " Would to Heaven I could express all that I feel, and all that I owe, and all that the country owes, to that name and family! John Phillips, your Founder, I knew well, — that is, as well as a boy of fourteen could be expected to know and realize the worth of a man of perhaps sixty. About the year 1785 I visited him at Exeter in his family, with my mother, who was his niece. I spent three or four days there, and partook of his simple meals. I heard him at his family devotions. I shall never forget the patriarchal sweetness of his countenance, or the somewhat stern, yet not unattractive manner, in which he greeted and responded. He had an austere faith, softened by natural temperament and inherent kindliness of spirit. I rejoice that the spirit of his benevolence still lives and breathes in the spot he selected for its abode, and that it bears the Phillips name upward from its foundation to its height."

Your most cordial Friend,
John Phillips

[Fac-simile of the Founder's handwriting.]

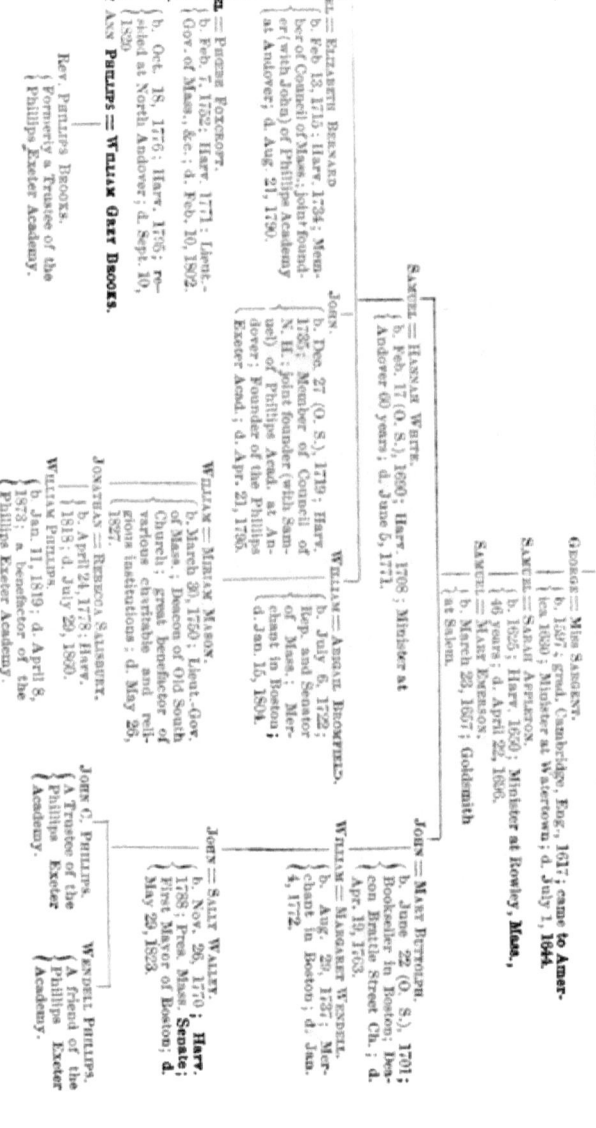

CHAPTER VI.

THE BUILDINGS.

ORIGINAL BUILDING. — SECOND ACADEMY BUILDING. — NEW BUILDING. — ABBOT HALL. — GORHAM HALL. — PORTRAITS AND BUSTS.

THE original schoolhouse, erected in the autumn of 1781, stood on the rise of ground, a few rods west of Tan Lane, since named Academy Street. This land is now owned by the Julian heirs. It was a modest frame building, and will be chiefly remembered as the one in which the first Latin lesson was recited, and in which Dr. Abbot began his administration. Afterwards this building was moved to the Kingston road, about a mile away, where, remodelled into a farm-house, it was for many years occupied by John T. Gordon, Esq. Some years ago, in re-laying the floor of the long parlor, the workmen discovered marks of the old benches. It is now owned by the estate of the late Benjamin Merrill, and occupied by Mr. James Kent. Like most of the New Hampshire schoolhouses of that period, it was doubtless painted red, and the "old scholars" and new boys may still find patches of this ruddy color near the old side door. How many stern, yet fond, recollections are associated with the little red schoolhouse of our fathers!

The second Academy building, erected in 1794, just before the death of the Founder, and under his personal supervision, was located twenty feet to the west of the present structure, and in such a manner that its rear wall rested on the front line of the main part of the present building.

It was a wooden building, 75 × 36 feet, surmounted by a handsome belfry, and according to a writer of that period was a model of the day. On the first floor, to the left of the front entrance, was the main schoolroom, seating about ninety pupils; while on the right was a smaller room, occupied by the English department. On the second floor was a spacious hall, used for those exhibitions for which the Phillips Exeter Academy was once so famous. Would that some new " revival of learning" might rouse Exeter to emulate those old-time contests! Then might the graduates of Exeter hope to win Lee prizes, and then might a second Edward Everett be taught to face an audience, and speak brave verses or braver prose.

William E. Sparks tells us: "Afterwards, when they ceased holding these exhibitions, this large upper hall was used only as a kind of lumber-room, but we boys sometimes got in there to add our names to those already on the woodwork of the hall; hundreds of names were cut and written all over the old building, many of men well known in after life. I have seen D. W. deeply cut in the bell tower, and it was always believed to have been put there by the great

Webster himself." In the southeastern corner of the building, on the second floor, was the school library,— a room in which many a lad has held a more profitable than pleasant interview with the good Dr. Abbot. This reminds us of the little room at Eton College, England, where a few years ago we were shown the rods and whipping-stool of that ancient seat of learning.

In 1822 the two wings were erected, which, besides affording additional accommodations, added much to the symmetry of the structure. Throughout his administration, Dr. Abbot presided in the main hall, and gave instruction in Latin. It was in this room, also, that morning and evening "prayers" were held, conducted by some one of the instructors in the morning, and always by the Principal at the close of school in the evening. For sixteen years, until 1838, Gideon L. Soule, as Professor of Greek, occupied the western wing of this building, while from 1808, throughout this same period, Ebenezer Adams, Hosea Hildreth, John P. Cleaveland, Charles C. P. Gale, Joseph H. Abbot, Francis Bowen, or William H. Shackford had charge of the Mathematical and Philosophical Department, — sometimes called the English Department, — in the eastern room of the main building.

From 1832 until the destruction of this building, in 1870, Dr. Soule, the Principal, presided in the main hall, while Joseph G. Hoyt and his successor, George A. Wentworth, had charge of the English Department in the eastern room. During the same years, Henry French, Nehemiah Cleaveland, Richard W. Swan, Paul A. Chadbourne, Theodore Tibbets, Henry S. Nourse, George C. Sawyer, and Bradbury L. Cilley succeeded one another in the possession of the western wing. The eastern wing was always occupied by the Golden Branch Society, and its library was in daily use by instructors and pupils.

About two o'clock on Sunday morning, December 18, 1870, the citizens and the students were roused by a cry of fire. Guided by the light of the flames, all hurried toward the Academy grounds, and there perceived that the old building, which had received Webster and Sparks and Everett and Hildreth, — yes, and hosts of others, — was in the grasp of the destroyer, fire. Water was scarce and far away, and although the students and citizens formed in line and passed along buckets of water, and although the fire department did its best, all their exertions were unavailing. By the persistent efforts of the students, some of the furniture and the valuable library of the Golden Branch Society were saved.

The scene of the fire must have made a lively picture. By the lurid flames, which only made the obscurity of the night more Cimmerian, one could see that the whole yard was in confusion. Through the windows of the eastern wing the boys were passing out the books of the Golden Branch library, while the doorways were blockaded by chairs, desks, and benches. The collapse of the belfry and the fall of the heated bell formed the climax of the painful scene.

Of all those who mourned the loss of the old building none were more deeply pained than the venerable Principal. It is said that, as he looked at the blazing and falling timbers, he wept like a child. Had his own dwelling been destroyed, we doubt if he would have sorrowed as much. The different halls about town were at once engaged, and the work of the Academy was but slightly interrupted.

The Academy was burned, as we have stated, on the morning of December 18, 1870. On the following Wednesday a circular, recounting both the past influences and the present distress of the institution, was sent to every Alumnus throughout the length and breadth of the land. On Saturday, the 24th, at a meeting of the Alumni held in Boston, the following resolutions were adopted: —

"*Resolved*, That it is desirable to raise the sum of one hundred thousand dollars, and by a contribution from the Alumni of Exeter Academy, and the other friends of the Academy, to good learning, and to the public welfare, for the uses of the Academy, and especially for the restoration of the building totally destroyed by fire.

"*Resolved*, That for the furtherance of the above object a committee of thirteen Alumni be appointed, to consist of the chairman of this meeting and twelve other gentlemen, to be appointed by the chair; also, that this committee have power to fill all vacancies."

The committee consisted of the following gentlemen: —

JOHN G. PALFREY.
FRANCIS B. HAYES.
SAMUEL SEWALL.
WILLIAM BOOTT.
REV. JOHN H. MORISON.
HENRY J. GARDNER.
REV. CHARLES LOWE.
EBENEZER BACON.
CHRISTOPHER C. LANGDELL.
JAMES C. DAVIS.
HENRY LUNT.
WILLIAM E. SPARKS.
WALTER A. BAKER.

These appeals were almost instantly answered, the widow of Jared Sparks sending the first contribution. From every side substantial aid was received. One of the Academy's most gifted and loving sons,[1] hastily penned and sent these unique lines to the Trustees: —

> " Alas! those dear old classic halls,
>   Where all the Muses sat,
> More loved than old Dardanian walls,
>   Amo, amas, amat.
> How have the flames that laid them low
>   New flames within us lit,
> And set our bosoms all aglow,
>   Uro, uris, urit !
>
>   .   .   .   .
>
> " From high and by way, far and wide,
>   Let all the builders come,
> And do good service, side by side,
>   Bonus, bona, bonum.
> With rapid strokes build strong and high
>   The everlasting stone,
> Τύπτω, τύπτω, τύπτοιμι,
>   Τύπτε, τύπτειν, τύπτων." [2]

[1] John B. L. Soule, D. D., Ph. D.
[2] These verses are given in full in the Appendix.

The money for the new building came from those who needed no exhortation. Old Exeter men never forget the school of their boyhood, and as she nurtured them, so will they ever care for her. Before the snows of winter had departed, the ground was cleared for a new building, which was completed so that the Class of 1872 had the satisfaction of reciting their last lessons in it.

The dedication, which took place June 19, 1872, was the scene of a glorious reunion of old friends, teachers, and schoolmates, who came thronging back to meet and greet each other, and to celebrate the completion of Dr. Soule's half-century of faithful service. The Soule Festival, as it was called, has already been more fully referred to in the historical chapters at the beginning of this volume.

We have been inclined in this country to build only for our own day and generation, and, instead of erecting enduring structures of stone or brick, we have darkened the sky with ghost-like wooden things, — court-houses, school-houses, — which, like the army of Indians who guard the tobacco-shops of our cities, soon become battered and unseemly.

> "Build to-day, then, strong and sure,
>   With a firm and ample base;
>   And ascending and secure
>   Shall to-morrow find its place."

" In the elder days of art," the buildings were erected which to-day receive the students of Eton, Harrow, and

Winchester. So, owing to the wisdom of the Trustees of the Phillips Exeter Academy, future generations — descendants of the present Exeter students — may go to school in the same building that received their great-great-great-grandfathers.

The architects of the new school building, Messrs. Peabody and Stearns, of Boston, were directed to reproduce the old structure as nearly as seemed to them advisable in stone or brick. The result was a building perfect in its proportions and graceful in its outlines, — a building which is said to be one of the most popular and pleasing structures of its kind in America. It is built of pressed brick with trimmings of gray sandstone, and consists of a main building seventy-two feet front by fifty-five feet deep, to which are added two wings having a front of thirty-two feet and a depth of seventy-two feet. The wings have roofs, somewhat of the Mansard style, but more sloping, and having their otherwise severe outlines broken here and there by dormer and gabled windows.

The main building is covered by a low but graceful hip roof, surmounted by a clock tower and belfry, on which swings a weather vane. The clock was the gift of Jesse Seligman, of New York City, while the bell was furnished by the Class of 1870.

The gilded weathercock, unlike many of the students, has had but one attraction for many years, and Exeter lads have watched it in the vain hope of some time seeing it change its direction. The clock, too, has played queer freaks, and afforded the tardy student many a slim excuse. Both vane and clock, we believe, are now performing their proper functions in a most creditable manner. Now, since the vane often indicates approaching storms, the new student will at least be weather-wise, while the clock will warn the tardy Junior to hasten his homeward steps; $νὺξ\ γὰρ\ ἔρχεται$, "for night comes on," says Xenophon. This warning of the old Greek general was printed above the clock of an English school we once knew, and the boys used to speak of it as $νύξ$, or more familarly as "snooks."

The interior of the school building is admirably arranged. Three hundred pupils may be easily accommodated, while another fifty would crowd the rooms to their utmost capacity.

All the school-rooms [1] are on the first floor, consequently the students are obliged to climb no stairs to go to their various recitations.

Each wing contains two convenient recitation-rooms (measuring 36 × 36 and 30 × 25 feet), while the main building contains two others (each measuring 36 × 28 feet), besides the corridors, the coat-rooms, and the great stairway leading to the second floor. This stairway is one of the most effective features of the interior. It

---

[1] Room No. 1 is occupied by Mr. Tufts, Instructor in English, &c.; Room 2, by Mr. Wentworth, Professor of Mathematics; Room 3, by Mr. Faulhaber, Instructor in French and German; Room 4, by Mr. Cilley, Professor of Ancient Languages; Room 5, by Mr. Kittredge, Instructor in Latin, &c.; Room 6, by the Principal of the School.

separates at a platform near the base, and by an easy ascent, to the right and left, one reaches the great hall or lecture-room (measuring 69 × 43 feet), overhung with the huge, dark beams of the open timbered roof. Here hangs Stuart's celebrated portrait of the founder, and portraits of benefactors, Alumni, and former instructors. Here one may gaze on the manly face of Webster, and on those of the historians Hildreth and Bancroft, and of many other Exeter graduates who have become famous, and old students may again look into the faces of much-loved masters now no more.

In this room the morning religious services are held, but some time we hope some wealthy alumnus will build a handsome stone chapel, and then this room will be only used for lectures and exhibitions. In this room, too, are held the class-day exercises, and here the Athletic Association holds its meetings, and elects the Captain who is to lead Exeter to victory. Here, too, "the school" holds its meetings, on which occasions the "head monitor" presides; at these times memorials and resolutions are adopted, and other school affairs arranged.

At the end of each school year the dreaded preliminary and final examinations for entrance to Harvard University take place; at these times the benches give place to long, narrow, well-remembered tables, and the vigilant Cambridge proctor lounges in the chair sacred to the honored head-master.

On this same floor, in the western wing, are the Reference Library and the Laboratory. The former contains the volumes collected since the burning of the old library in 1870, and such mementos and relics as the Academy possesses; the latter contains the apparatus used by classes in physics and chemistry.

In the eastern wing, nearer Abbot Hall, are the rooms of the two literary societies. The Golden Branch, founded in 1818, occupies the side room, while its younger but equally vigorous companion, the G. L. Soule Literary Society, holds its meetings in the front room. Both are furnished with good libraries, and hung with interesting pictures and mementos. In these rooms have occurred well-remembered contests and hard fought battles.

The building is heated throughout with steam heat, both by direct and indirect radiation from the apparatus located in the cellar. In the cellar is also an apology for a running track, soon to be abandoned, we hope, for a well-appointed gymnasium.

ABBOT HALL, situated just east of the Academy, is a four-story brick building (78×42 feet), with a slated gable roof. It was built in 1855 at a cost of about $17,000, and named to commemorate the services of the much-loved Dr. Abbot. This building contains twenty-six large, well-ventilated rooms, most of them containing an alcove ($7\frac{1}{2} \times 6\frac{1}{2}$ feet), which in the daytime may be shut off from the study by curtains.

These rooms are partly furnished by the Corporation,

GORHAM HALL.

and accommodate fully fifty students. On the ground floor are the kitchens and dining-room, all under the charge of a competent matron, who lives in the building.

GORHAM HALL is a four-story brick building, situated on the corner of Court and Front Streets. It is on the same site on which, in 1837, the daughters of Captain Samuel Gilman built a hotel, named the Swamscot House. In 1850 this building was destroyed by fire. In 1851, Major A. P. Blake built the present structure, which was also called the Swamscot House and used as a hotel. In 1872 it was purchased for a dormitory by the Trustees of the Academy, and renamed in honor of David W. Gorham, M. D., one of the Board at that time.

PORTRAITS AND BUSTS.

In the Chapel of the Academy there is a collection of portraits and busts, that have been presented to the institution largely through the agency of Hon. B. F. Prescott, a former member of the school. Most of these represent former teachers, Trustees, donors, or pupils. A list of these is here given.

BENJAMIN ABBOT. An original portrait painted by Chester Harding. Presented in 1838, by the Alumni.
GEORGE BANCROFT. An original portrait by Schaus of Berlin. Presented by Mr. Bancroft.
JOSIAH BARTLETT, one of the signers of the Declaration of Independence. A copy after Trumbull, by E. Billings, of

Boston. Presented by Josiah Calef Bartlett, of Cambridge, Mass.

PETER C. BROOKS. An original portrait by J. **Harvey Young**. Presented to the Academy by Mr. Brooks.

REV. CHARLES BURROUGHS. **Copy of an** original portrait by E. Billings, by the same **artist**. Presented to the Academy by Mrs. Burroughs.

BENJAMIN F. **BUTLER**. **A** medallion in marble, by Andrews of Lowell, **Mass**. Presented to the Academy by General Butler.

LEWIS CASS. An original portrait by Healey, in **a** standing posture, two-thirds length. Presented **to** the Academy by the children of General Cass.

PAUL **A**. CHADBOURNE. An original portrait by J. **G. Fletcher**. Presented to the Academy by President Chadbourne.

DANIEL DANA. An original portrait by Thomas A. Lawson, **and copy by same** artist. Presented to the **Academy** by **Miss Jane Dana, of** Derry, **N. H.**, **a** daughter.

JOHN A. DIX. **A marble bust,** presented to the Academy by himself. **The bust was chiselled** when General Dix was United States Minister **to** France.

NICHOLAS EMERY. **An** original portrait **by** H. C. Pratt ; copy by J. G. Fletcher, **of** Portland, Me. Presented to the Academy by Mrs. L. **G. S**. Boyd **and** Miss Charlotte G. Emery, of Portland, daughters of Judge Emery.

EDWARD EVERETT. An original portrait by J. Harvey Young. Copy made by same artist, and presented to the Academy by Peter C. Brooks., Esq., of Boston, Mass.

JOHN TAYLOR GILMAN. Plaster cast. Presented **by a member** of the family.

JOHN P. HALE. An original portrait **by Adna** Tenney. Presented to the Academy by the **Hon. and Mrs.** Moses T. Willard of Concord, **N. H**.

SAMUEL HALE. Presented to **the** Academy by his family. An original portrait by his daughter, Miss Martha Hale.

JOSEPH G. HOYT. An original portrait by Adna Tenney. Presented to the Academy by friends and pupils of Chancellor Hoyt.

RICHARD HILDRETH. A copy, by U. D. Tenney, of an original crayon. Presented by Dr. Charles H. Hildreth, of Gloucester, Mass., a brother.

JOHN KELLEY. An original portrait by N. B. Onthank. Presented to the Academy by the family of Judge Kelley.

THEODORE LYMAN. A marble bust, presented by Theodore Lyman and Mrs. Cora H. Shaw, of Boston, children of Theodore Lyman.

WOODBRIDGE ODLIN. An original portrait painted by U. D Tenney.

SAMUEL D. PARKER. An original portrait by Thomas Ball. Presented to the Academy by Mr. Parker.

REV. WILLIAM B. O. PEABODY. An original portrait by Chester Harding. Presented to the Academy by O. W. Peabody, Esq., of Boston, Mass., his son.

JOHN PHILLIPS, the Founder. Full length, in sitting posture ; the head an original by Gilbert Stuart ; copy by Adna Tenney. Presented to the Academy by Messrs. E. and E. G. Wallace, of Rochester, N. H.

HON. SAMUEL PHILLIPS, and LIEUT.-GOV. SAMUEL PHILLIPS. Presented to the Academy by the Phillips family of Andover, Mass. The former is a copy ; the latter is an original painting, and was designed for the Lee family of Virginia, but from some cause never reached them.

JOSHUA W. PIERCE. A copy by U. D. Tenney of an original portrait by the same artist. Presented by the family of Mr. Pierce.

LEVERETT SALTONSTALL. A copy, by Osgood of Salem, of an original portrait by Chester Harding. Presented to the Academy by Leverett Saltonstall, Esq., his son.

JOHN LANGDON SIBLEY. An original portrait painted by Fred. P. Vinton.

JEREMIAH SMITH. An original portrait by Alexander ; copy by Adna Tenney. Presented to the Academy by Mrs. Jeremiah Smith, and the Hon. Jeremiah Smith, his son.

GIDEON L. SOULE. An original portrait by Porter.

JARED SPARKS. A plaster cast. Presented to the Academy by Mrs. Sparks.

120   THE PHILLIPS EXETER ACADEMY.

Rev. Theodore Tebbets. An original portrait by Adna Tenney. Presented to the Academy by the relatives of Mr. Tebbets.

Amos Tuck. An original portrait by Ansel D. Clough. Presented to the Academy by his son, Edward Tuck, Esq., of New York City.

James Walker. A crayon portrait, presented by pupils of Dr. Walker.

Daniel Webster. An original portrait, three-fourths length, in a standing posture, by Joseph Ames. Presented to the Academy by the "Marshfield Club."

Henry Winkley. An original portrait painted by B. Uhle.

Rev. Augustus Woodbury. An original portrait by Miss Rosa F. Peckham, of Providence, and a present to the institution by Mr. Woodbury.

TONGUE OF OLD BELL.

[Purloined by the Class of 1870, before the burning of the old building.]

CHAPTER VII.

GOVERNMENT.

ACT OF INCORPORATION. — CONSTITUTION. — FACULTY. — MONITORS. — PUNISHMENTS.

BY the act of incorporation, the government of the institution is vested in a Board of Trustees, which forms a body politic by the name of "The Trustees of the Phillips Exeter Academy." This act declares that the school is established "for the purpose of promoting piety and virtue, and for the education of youth in the English, Latin, and Greek languages, in writing, arithmetic, music, and the art of speaking, practical geometry, logic, and geography, and such other of the liberal arts and sciences or languages as opportunity may hereafter permit."

By this act the Trustees are made the "true and sole visitors, trustees, and governors of the Academy," in perpetual succession forever. It moreover gives to them full power to elect such officers, and make such rules and laws, as they deem requisite for the good government of the Academy; and, after providing certain rules for the government of the Trustees themselves, it declares that, by a vote of two thirds of *all* the Trustees, the Academy may, "for good and substantial reasons," be moved to any other place within the State. Finally, it declares that all the property of the Academy shall be forever free from all taxes whatsoever.

The entire text of this liberal act of the good old "Granite State" will be found in the Appendix, together with that other celebrated document, written by the Founder himself, viz. : —

THE CONSTITUTION.

The Constitution first declares that the school is established more especially to teach young men "the great end and real business of living"; and, continuing, provides for the safety of the funds and the government of the school, making rules for the guidance of the Trustees, instructors, and students. The officers of the trust thus established are a President, a Clerk, and a Treasurer; and their duties are clearly and minutely defined. Since the Trustees are to be the custodians of a public fund, the Founder wisely provides that *the records of their meetings, and the accounts of all gifts and expenditures, shall be open " for the perusal of all men."* If a candidate for election is as near related as first-cousin to any member of the Board, such member is not to sit in determining the election. By such wise provisions did the Founder guard against any perversion of the trust. It states that the Principal must be a man of exemplary manners, good natural ability and literary acquirements, and that he must have a natural aptitude for the instruction and government of boys.

He must also indorse the religious sentiments expressed in the Constitution, and be a church-member.

The instructors are to be chosen by the Trustees, regardless of position, birth, place of education or residence, and no preference is to be given to any friend or relative,— another safeguard.

The Trustees are required to observe the conduct of the instructors, and to remove one or all, if unfit to continue in office ; to determine for what reasons a scholar shall be expelled, and the manner in which the sentence shall be administered ; to visit the school annually, and examine into the proficiency of the students.

The instructors are to make it a "principal duty to regulate the tempers, enlarge the minds, and *form the morals* of the youth committed to their care." They are also to pay especial attention to the health of the students, and urge them to be industrious. One of the most celebrated portions declares "that though goodness without knowledge, as it respects others, is weak and feeble, yet knowledge without goodness is dangerous ; and that both united form the noblest character, and lay the surest foundation of usefulness to mankind." The instructors are therefore directed to point out to the pupils under their charge the beauties of virtue and the evils of vice, and to impress them with the truths of the Bible.

Although the school is open to all sects and races, yet it is declared that the Trustees and instructors must be Protestants ; they must also approve the Constitution, and uphold it steadily, cordially, and vigorously. It declares that no student shall enjoy the privilege of the Academy who shall board in any family not licensed by the Trustees, and that none but well-governed Christian families are to be licensed.

The Principal of the Academy and his associates form what is known as

THE FACULTY.

This body is secondary to the Board of Trustees, and receives its power from it. The Faculty, although a terror to evil-doers, form a most beneficent body. They execute the rules, and are the guardians as well as teachers of the young men who come under their care. By provision of the Constitution, however, the rules and regulations which the instructors may make are subject to the examination of the Trustees, and may be amended or abolished by them. The business meetings of the Faculty occur once a week.

THE MONITORS

are selected by the Faculty from the students themselves. Each class has its monitor, whose duty is to keep order in the class-room during the absence of the instructor. There is a monitor, too, for each church, who marks and reports all absentees, and who, like the class monitors, may give "notes." The chapel monitor, during morning prayers, sits, with the monitor of the school, on a platform in the rear of the great hall in which the exercises are conducted; he marks all absentees, and reports them each week to the Principal. The school monitor receives the reports of the class monitors, and presents them to the Principal; he also, in the absence of a President of the School, presides at all School meetings.

The officers of Abbot Hall consist of a President, Vice-President, and Steward. The President and Vice-President act as monitors, and are expected to maintain order within the building: the former has first choice of rooms, and pays no rent; while the latter also has a choice of rooms. The Steward receives all moneys for board, and buys all provisions for the table; his accounts are examined by an auditor chosen from each class. For his services the price of his board is remitted. All these officers are approved by one of the Professors, who has the charge of both Abbot and Gorham Halls. At Gorham Hall the President and Vice-President are chosen by the boys living there, while a monitor for each floor is appointed in the same manner as are the officers of Abbot Hall.

PUNISHMENTS.

Corporal punishment no longer exists in the school. The three grades of admonition, suspension, and expulsion are in vogue as at Cambridge. If a boy is known to exert a bad influence among his schoolmates, he is simply "removed" by his parents, in accordance with the advice of the Principal. For minor offences the monitors and instructors give "notes." In that case, the boy is required to clean the boards in one of the class-rooms, or perhaps to sweep the floors during one week. He may, however, if he likes, pay some one to do it for him. A "capital letter" is supposed to be equal to three notes, and is considered a great disgrace. Sometimes "lines" and other tasks grieve the delinquent "Preps," and sometimes they are even ordered to "come up to my house at six to-morrow morning with this lesson fully prepared." We well remember one of those early recitations. It was a bright spring morning, and the august Professor of Latin was raking his little lawn. We waited at a convenient corner, — the gathering-place appointed for the clan, — and students could soon be seen assembling from all directions. Union is strength, and in a body we walked to the gate of that loved, yet fearful man. "What are you here for, young men?" "You told us to call and recite the lesson we failed in yesterday, sir." "Well, do you know it now?" "Yes, sir," in a chorus. "Well, then, hurry home and get your breakfast." We *did* hurry home, and, relieved at our unexpected escape, and full of love for our kind teacher, we determined to repay him with better lessons in the future.

The few necessary rules, which require punctual attendance, thoroughly prepared lessons, quiet during study hours, gentlemanly deportment, the shunning of vice and idleness, are so clearly understood to be necessary, and the public sentiment of the school is so strong in upholding them, that any young man who violates them finds himself in an uncomfortable position among the students themselves, and also that the Faculty are prompt to remove any real offenders.

In conclusion, we would say that the members of the Phillips Exeter Academy are, in the main, governed wisely and well. Though constant vigilance is maintained, no secret spies are employed, and the young man soon discovers that he is trusted. The result is manifest: teachers and pupils work together, both alike are interested in maintaining good order, and "rebellions" are unknown. The boys are thus taught to become independent and manly American gentlemen; and when they go forth from the protection of Exeter Academy, they are, let us hope, well fitted to become true citizens, full of high purposes, Christian truth, and ardent patriotism.

CHAPTER VIII.

BIOGRAPHICAL SKETCHES.

ALUMNI. — DANIEL WEBSTER. — EDWARD EVERETT. — LEWIS CASS. — JOHN P. HALE. — BENJAMIN F. PRESCOTT. — ROBERT T. LINCOLN.

> " Young art thou still, and young shalt ever be
>   In spirit as thou wast in years gone by ;
>   The present, past, and future blend in thee,
>   Rich as thou art in names which cannot die !
>   And youthful hearts already beating high
>   To emulate the glories won of yore,
>   That days to come may still the past outvie,
>   And thy bright roll be lengthened more and more
>   Of statesman, bard, and sage well versed in noblest lore."

IN this chapter and those immediately following we have attempted to form a group of Exeterians

> " Who 've battled in our Congress' stately walls,
>   Or labored long in Education's halls, —
>   Great Webster on my left, and Everett, Cass,"

and many others who have become more or less celebrated. In making this collection of biographical sketches we have but selected the names of a few of those who have become most distinguished in after life. A complete list of the divines, statesmen, jurists, men of letters, warriors, and others, who received their earliest intellectual training at Exeter, would far exceed the limits of this work.

DANIEL WEBSTER.

DANIEL WEBSTER, the son of Ebenezer Webster and Abigail Eastman (a lady both beautiful and of superior intellect), was born January 18, 1782, in Salisbury, N. H., in a log-house situated on the borders of the pathless wilderness. Until he reached the age of ten, his health was delicate. His tender mother, however, taught him the letters of the alphabet; she also taught him to read, and impressed on him, while still a child, the vital truths of the Bible. The first copy of that book he ever owned was given to him by his mother. His first schoolmaster was Mr. Tappan, who taught the district school three miles away. This good man soon perceived the remarkable abilities of the lad, and advised his father to give him the advantages of a college education. Daniel Webster never forgot his old teacher, and in later years, when he had become a great lawyer and senator, " Master Tappan " received many affectionate letters and gifts from his former pupil. For many months the father thought of the schoolmaster's advice, and although very poor he was not insensible to the advantages to be derived from education, as will be seen from the following extract from one of Webster's letters, written long years after. He says he was making hay with his father, and continues: —

" The Hon. Abiel Foster, M. C., who lived in Canterbury, six miles off, called at the house, and came into the field to see my father. . . . When he was gone, my father called me to him, and we sat down beneath the elm, on a haycock. He said, 'My son, that is a worthy man. He is a member of Congress. He goes to Philadelphia and gets six dollars a day, while I toil here. It is because he had an education, which I never had. If I had had **his** early education I should have been in his place in Philadelphia. **I came near it, as it was**; but I missed it, and now I **must work** here.' 'My dear father,' said I, 'you shall not work: brother and I will work for you and wear our hands out, and you shall rest,'—**and** I remember to **have** cried, and I cry now at the **recollection.** 'My child,' said he, 'it is of **no** importance **to me; I now** live but for my children; I could not give **your elder** brother the advantages of knowledge, but **I can do something** for you. Exert yourself! Improve **your** opportunities! Learn! Learn!—and **when I am gone** you will not need to go through the **hardships which I** have undergone, and which have made me **an** old **man** before my time.' The next May he took me to Exeter, to the Phillips Exeter Academy, and placed me under the tuition of its excellent Preceptor, Dr. Benjamin Abbot, **who** is still living."

And thus, at the age of fourteen, **Webster came to** the Phillips Exeter Academy, where for nine months he received the instruction and counsel of Dr. Benjamin Abbot.

His father found a home for him, **among** a number of other students, in the family of old **" 'Squire** Clifford," as he was always called, and on leaving it is said that among other requests he begged the good 'Squire to teach his son how to hold his knife and fork; "for," remarked **Mr.** Webster, "Daniel knows no more **about** it than a cow does about holding a spade." None saw this more clearly than Mr. Clifford, for, when not using his knife and fork, the boy was accustomed to hold them upright in his fists on either side of his plate. Daniel was a bashful boy of delicate feelings; and the 'Squire feared to wound his feelings by speaking to him directly on the subject. So he called aside one of the other students with whom he had been longer acquainted, and told him his dilemma. "Now," said he, "I want you this noon, at the table, to hold your knife and fork as Daniel does. I will speak to you about it, and see if the boy does not take a hint for himself." The lad consented to be the scapegoat for his fellow-student, and several times during the meal planted his fists on the table with his knife and fork straight up, as if he had received orders to present arms. The 'Squire drew his attention to his position, and courteously begged his pardon for speaking of the matter; then added a few kind words on the importance of having young men correct such little habits before going out into the world. The student was almost bursting with laughter, yet he soberly thanked the 'Squire, and promised to do better. Daniel from that time was most careful about his table manners.

Dr. Abbot also taught him lessons found in no book of that day, and the good master is said to have often sent Webster down to Kimming's Brook to wash his face and hands. This same brook still flows at the base of the hill just in the rear of the Academy, but it is now somewhat smaller, and its waters are far less clear than at that time. 'Squire Clifford's dwelling, where Webster boarded when at school in Exeter, is the "old Garrison house," still standing, near the white bridge. One may still see the room in which many a day he is said to have worked at the carpenter's bench.

Three days after Webster entered the Academy, he returned to his boarding-house in a most dejected mood, and said that the city boys were constantly laughing **at** him because he was at the foot of his class, and **came** from the "backwoods." Mr. Nicholas Emery, then an assistant tutor in the Academy, heard of his trouble, and, having especial charge of Webster's class, treated him with marked kindness. He urged him to think of nothing but his books, assuring him that, if he did this, all would come out right. Did Webster heed this advice? Listen! At the end of the next quarter, Mr. Emery marshalled the class in a line, and, taking Webster by the hand, led him to the head, telling the class that this was Webster's proper position. The class had suspected this for several days; nevertheless, the boys who had taunted him were surprised and chagrined. This triumph greatly encouraged Webster. He did not doubt that many of his classmates were equal, if not superior, to him in scholarship, but he resolved that, if study could do anything for him, he would continue to try his best. As the end of **the** second quarter approached, although he had worked hard, he grew anxious about the **result**.

When the day arrived, the class was called out as before, and Mr. Emery, standing before them, broke the silence by these words: " Daniel Webster, gather **up your** books and take down your cap!" The boy was stunned, fearing he was about to be expelled, and sorely troubled, not knowing the cause of his calamity. Mr. Emery soon dispelled the illusion, for, continuing, he said, " Now, sir, you will please report to the teacher of the next class; and you, young gentlemen, will take an affectionate leave of your classmate, for you **will** never see him again." That teacher became a man of distinction, and was ever a friend of his illustrious and fortunate pupil. In the class of this same Mr. Emery, Webster mastered the principles of the English grammar in less than four months, and upon his promotion began the study of Latin, and recited his first lessons in that language to Joseph S. Buckminster, the great Biblical scholar, **whose** early death **was so lamented.** Although Webster did well in his studies here, it is well known that he could not, by any appeal, **be in-**duced to declaim in the presence of his schoolmates. When the day arrived upon which his class was to speak, although the boy had learned his speech, and keenly felt the mortification of his position, yet, when his name was called, he seemed utterly incapable of rising from his seat. He says of this incident, " When the exercises were over, I went home and wept **bitter** tears of mortification."

When we consider the address, **the rare** diction, and

the matchless eloquence of his later years, — how he graced the halls of Dartmouth, the courts of justice, and the halls of national legislation, — we can but turn to that other picture, and wonder at the poor, trembling lad, shrinking beneath the gaze of his mates from his appointed task.

After leaving school, Webster was placed in charge of the Rev. Samuel Wood, a neighboring clergyman. This gentleman will always be gratefully remembered, since, free of any charge, he prepared young Webster for Dartmouth College, which he entered in 1797, one year after leaving Exeter.

Daniel read Virgil and Cicero, and was warmed by the latter to a love for oratory, which never afterwards failed him. At Dartmouth, he earned his way by teaching during the winter months. The expenses of his Junior year he paid by superintending the publication of the small weekly newspaper of the town. He also was paid for delivering the Fourth of July oration before the people of Hanover. So it seems that the "bitter tears of mortification" of but four years before were not shed in vain. At graduation he took no part, owing to a disputed election, but delivered before the foremost College society a stirring address on "The Influence of Opinion." Although not ranking first, Webster was acknowledged to be the leading man in his class. He excelled in the classics, in history, and in literature. He was fond, too, of athletic sports, and throughout his life enjoyed hunting and fishing. But the promise made to his father in the hay-field was never forgotten. He had resolved to succeed, and allowed nothing to interfere with the accomplishment of that purpose.

Many interesting anecdotes are related of him. One day, as he was entertaining one of the Gilmans, of Exeter, at dinner, Webster asked, "Is that old sign still hanging on your gristmill, Mr. Gilman?" — "What sign do you mean?" — "Why, the one that read, 'All sorts of grinding done here,'" replied Mr. Webster. He evidently remembered the "grinding" that he did at Exeter.

It is said that he planted the second elm in "Tan Lane" (now Academy Street), which one sees on his left upon entering from Front Street the west gate of the Academy yard. The first one was planted by his friend, Lewis Cass.

Throughout his life his connection with the Academy was most happy. As a Trustee he was efficient, thoughtful, and accurate.

An "old scholar,"[1] writing to us, says: —

"Some persons have questioned whether Daniel Webster ever looked so elegant as he is represented in one of the capital steel engravings in Curtis's Life of the great statesman. But the picture looks just as Webster did, when, in 1836, as an honored Trustee of the Academy, he assisted the venerable Dr. Abbot at our final examinations in Latin. The circumstances of that day have

---

[1] Edmund Chadwick, Esq.

caused me to remember exactly how he looked then, — very different from his plain, homespun appearance when he came from the backwoods to Exeter as a student, just forty years before. He had now been out of college thirty-five years, and had led a busy life as teacher, statesman, lawyer, hunter, and farmer. It was five years after his great debate with Hayne. **He** was fifty-four years of age, and at the very zenith of his powers as a lawyer, orator, and statesman. One would think it was high time he had forgotten all his Latin; but, luckily, **he** had not.

"I nearly trembled as Dr. Abbot said, 'Mr. **Webster**, Chadwick has read the whole of Virgil,' and **the great** constitutional lawyer selected **a** passage, **not in the Æneid**, but in the Georgics, to try my skill. **Turning to** the place, the venerable Doctor says, **'Scan!'** At the third or fourth line he shakes his big head, — 'Wrong! scan that line over again.' **I** tried the line again and again, with the same result, — 'Wrong, wrong!' What shall I do? The Doctor **never** helps a student at recitation. Will he tell me to construe, translate, or send me crestfallen **to my seat?** Awful moment! **To be so** disgraced, **in such a presence!** But, *mirabile dictu*, Mr. Webster lifts his keen, **black** eyes from his book, and says to Doctor Abbot, '**I think he is** right, sir.' Presto! Dr. Abbot's big head comes down; he and Mr. Webster compare books. All **is** courtesy. 'Go on! you are right, sir. It was only a difference in our books.' Never had the illustrious Webster a more grateful client than the humble pupil then before him. Thanks that he had remembered how to **'scan'**! All honor to the great teacher, Dr. Abbot, **and** to his greatest pupil, Daniel Webster!"

In 1834 Daniel Webster sent his son Edward to the Academy at Exeter, in order that he might be instructed by the same teacher who nearly forty years before had taught himself, then poor and almost friendless. How different his condition now! It was near the close of an unusually busy season, and fully occupied with the duties of state, Mr. Webster was obliged to send the boy in the care of an elder brother. The first letter Mr. Webster wrote to Edward is so interesting, and so full of good advice, that we cannot forbear quoting it here.

"WASHINGTON, June 23, 1834.

"MY DEAR SON:—

"Fletcher wrote me from Exeter the next day after your arrival, and informed me that you had been so fortunate as to be received at Colonel Chadwick's, and was commencing your studies. I am glad you are so well situated, and trust you will make progress in your studies.

"You are now at a most important period of your life, my dear son, soon growing up to be a young man and a boy no longer, and I feel a great anxiety for your success and happiness.

"I beseech you to be attentive to all your duties, and to fulfil every obligation with cheerfulness and punctuality. Above all, remember your moral and religious concerns. Be constant at church, and prayers, and every opportunity for worship. There can be no solid character and no true happiness which are not founded on a sense of religious duty. Avoid all evil company and every temptation, and consider that you have now left your father's house and gone forth to improve your own character, — to prepare your own mind for the part you are to lead in life. All that can be done for you by others will amount to nothing unless you do much for yourself. Cherish all the good counsel which your dear mother used to give you, and let those of us who are yet alive have the pleasure of seeing you come forward as one who gives promise of virtue, usefulness, and distinction. I fervently commend you to the blessing of our Heavenly Father.

. . . . .

"I wish you to make my best respects to Dr. Abbot, and remember me to Colonel and Mrs. Chadwick and their family. If I do not hear from you sooner, I shall expect to find a letter from you when I reach Boston.

"Your affectionate father,
"Daniel Webster.

"P. S. Since writing this I have received your letter, and am very glad to hear from you.

"Give my love to your friend Upham. I remember the great tree, and know exactly where your room is. Charles sends love."

In 1838, Mr. Webster presided at the "Abbot Festival," and "led the way in the hearty and eloquent expression of the sentiments entertained by the whole assemblage toward his and their old master." He also presented the elegant silver vase given to the venerable teacher by his former pupils, "as a token of their love and abiding reverence."

The following letter was written by him, a few months before his death, to the pupils of the Phillips

Exeter Academy. The original has been framed, and hangs in the rooms of the Golden Branch Society, at Exeter.

"WASHINGTON, June 7, 1852.

"To the pupils of Phillips Exeter Academy, an elder brother student presents these copies of an address lately delivered by him, in New York. My Brothers, let us do honor to the Founder of our Academy! Let us cherish, affectionately, the memory of the venerable and beloved Benjamin Abbot! And let us labor to repay to the cause of learning what a most excellent institution for learning has done for us!

"My Brothers, farewell!
"DANIEL WEBSTER."

From 1835 until the time of his death, in 1852, he was one of the Trustees of the school, and delighted in doing his share of the work. He died full of years and honors. His last words were, "I still live!"

Yes, Daniel Webster does live, and as long as young Americans throng the classic halls of Exeter his name shall be honored and revered as that of an "elder brother," and until all records of this nation be lost shall he live in the affections of a grateful people. His fame is immortal, — his reward, immortality.

EDWARD EVERETT.

EDWARD EVERETT was born in Dorchester, Massachusetts, April 11, 1794. In 1807 he spent a few months at the Phillips Exeter Academy, and under the tuition of Dr. Abbot and his own brother finished his preparation for Harvard College. From Harvard he was graduated with the highest honors at the age of seventeen. Two years later, he **became** the pastor of the Brattle Street Church, Boston, and **there his** eloquence soon attracted marked attention.

In 1814 Mr. Everett, having been appointed Eliot Professor of Greek at Cambridge, went abroad, in order to enjoy **the** advantages of foreign travel. At the University of Göttingen he spent two years, besides visiting many other seats of learning, and **enjoying the society of the most noted men of** the time. **He was abroad four** years.

Mr. Everett was one **of the first editors of the North** American Review, and held that position for two years. **He** afterwards developed **a** taste for political affairs, and was ten years a member of **Congress.** In 1834 he declined a re-election, and was chosen Governor of his native State, in which office he served four terms. **He** was appointed Minister to the Court of St. James by President Harrison, and four years later became President of Harvard University. The duties of this latter position, however, proved irksome, and at the end of three years he resigned.

In 1852 he was appointed Secretary of State by President Fillmore, to fill the vacancy caused by the death of Daniel Webster.

The next year he was elected a member of the United States Senate, but soon resigned the office on account of impaired health. He died on January 15, 1865.

Who may criticise the character of such a man? If Edward Everett possessed rare powers, the cultivation they received, and the use which he made of them, were rarer still. He was, without doubt, marked out for a scholar, but it was himself that did the carving. With him, to live was to conquer. His tastes and habits gradually changed as he grew older, and developed latent powers; and so it was the most natural thing in the world, that at different periods of his life he should have been preacher, essayist, professor, editor, statesman, and diplomatist.

Daniel Webster and Edward Everett have been happily referred to by one who well knew them both, as the Demosthenes and Cicero of the American forum. The orations of Everett differ greatly from those of Webster, and it would be interesting, if we had the space at our command, to trace this difference. The orations of Mr. Everett covered a great variety of subjects, but in each he seems equally at home. They were carefully prepared, and are most polished and exhaustive productions. Although they rarely startle, they always delight. His preparation did not cease with composition, but his voice was made to sympathize with his subject; his gestures were perfect, and his cadences musical; thus he held the entire attention of his audience.

Mr. Everett was not entirely fortunate in the latter part of his political career. It was just before the Rebellion, and the wheels of progress were smoking with the intense friction of the times. Like a kaleidoscope, the political complexion was ever changing, and events moved too fast for him. He was too conservative, too stoical, too refined. His smoothly turned sentences seemed tame, and, where downright forcible Saxon might have won, were ineffectual.

Edward Everett, however, was a glorious man, and right gloriously did he work out the life which God had given to him. Each minute he was submissive to the truth as he then knew it, in order that in the next he might enter into fuller knowledge.

Thus he lived, progressed, and lived again. Boston is proud of him; Massachusetts reveres him; the whole country claims him.

LEWIS CASS.

It is much to be regretted that little can be found relating to the connection of General Cass with the Phillips Exeter Academy; for, without doubt, there have been few of its Alumni who have risen as high among their fellow-men, and have acquired as great fame with either sword or pen.

Lewis Cass was born in Exeter, New Hampshire, October 9, 1782, and thus enjoyed by birthright, as it were, the great advantages of the Academy of that town. His parents were of the old Puritan stock of New England. His father, Jonathan Cass, was "a man of strong natural powers, and of great purity of purpose, — one of that band of patriots who were born for the time in which they lived." He served his country faithfully during the war of the Revolution, and was present at Lexington, Bunker Hill, and other important battles.

Lewis entered the Academy in 1792, at the age of ten years. Here he pursued his studies with great diligence and considerable success, standing well in his class, and applying himself diligently to the acquirement of knowledge throughout his course.

In regard to this period of the life of Lewis Cass, an alumnus [1] writes the following: —

"The incidents which Dr. Abbot related about the schoolboys who have since become illustrious were extremely interesting.

"'Lewis Cass,' he said, 'was a very wild boy. One day his father, Major Cass, came to me and asked me if I could take his son.

"'Certainly; but why do you ask?'

"'O, the youngster is headstrong, and hard to manage.'

"'What does he do?'

"'Plays truant, runs away from his work, steals off without my permission to go a-gunning, fishing, or swimming, and is full of all kinds of pranks.'

"'Well, send him to me, and I'll see what I can do with him.'

"The boy was placed under my charge. Several months later I met his father, and asked him how his son was getting along.

"'Well, sir,' said he, 'if Lewis was half as afraid of the

[1] Professor Sylvester Waterhouse.

Almighty **as he is of you, I should never have any more trouble with him.'**

"In relating this incident Dr. Abbot fairly shook with the laughter which the recollection of Major Cass's answer excited. It is scarcely necessary to add, that, controlled by the Preceptor's extraordinary *power* of discipline, the strong motive energies which led young Cass into all sorts of boyish mischief were directed to nobler objects. The results of the wise management, which quickened the ambition and roused into action the **faculties of** a powerful nature, are recorded in American history. It was, however, intimated that, at Exeter, **the future statesman** evinced more talent for practical affairs **than for the details of scholarship.**"

After he was graduated, in **1797,** the family removed to Wilmington, Delaware, where **Mr.** Cass took charge **of a** small academy.

We thus see that he had no classical education beyond that received at Exeter, and that this was of a high order is evident from the writings and speeches of his public life in after **years.**

Removing from Wilmington, Delaware, to Ohio, he began the study of the law, and was admitted **to** the bar in that State in 1802. In his profession Mr. Cass, **even at** the outset, was most eminent, and it was to this that he owed his rapid advancement in public life, so well known to all. He was at different times Colonel and Brigadier-General in the United States Army, and held during his life the offices of Governor of Michi**gan,** Secretary of War, Minister Plenipotentiary to

France, United States Senator, and, lastly, Secretary of State.

About 1833 Mr. Cass, returning to Exeter, visited the Academy; his reception is thus described:—

"The whole school was assembled to receive him, and he was conducted by Dr. Abbot to a seat on the platform by his side, the students standing as they entered. His imposing personal figure and a brief address made an agreeable impression upon the rising generation, one half of whom, probably, might expect to become great men also."

Mr. Cass was twice a candidate for the Presidency; but in this, the great object of the latter part of his life, he was unsuccessful, chiefly because of the ascendency at that time of the Whigs over his own party, the Democrats.

Mr. Cass died in June, 1866. He was always a strong advocate for the preservation of the Union, although he did not recognize the right of the general government to coerce individual States. He ranks without doubt among the first on the rolls of the Phillips Exeter Academy.

JOHN P. HALE.

JOHN PARKER HALE was born in Rochester, New Hampshire, in 1806.

He entered the Phillips Exeter Academy in 1820, at the age of fourteen, and from there went to Bowdoin College. Of this part of Mr. Hale's life a classmate

speaks as follows : " When I entered at Exeter, **a green
boy** from the farm, I sat near the recitation **bench, and**
used to be much interested in observing the recitations
of an advanced Greek class, composed of John Hodgdon, John P. Hale, Alpheus Crosby, and another whom
I have forgotten. One morning **Hale, who** was a droll,
good-natured wit, full of fun and mischief, in translating
the little Anacreontic, —

> 'It is a hard thing not to love;
> It is a hard thing, too, to love;
> But the hardest thing of all is
> To love and not be loved,' —

made a sly but flagrant assault upon the Preceptor's
dignity by rendering the last line, hesitating a little, —

> ' To love and — get the mitten.'

There still lingers in my ears the gruff reproof of Dr.
Abbot, as he **turned** full upon him with 'What! what!'
John, in his peculiar, unruffled way, blubbered some
word of apology, and the recitation **went on."**

Upon graduating **he studied law,** and in 1830 was
admitted to the bar.

Mr. Hale immediately began the practice **of his**
profession in Dover, New Hampshire, where **he at once**
met **with** marked success. **In** 1832 he was **chosen** to
represent that town in the State legislature, and some
years afterward was appointed United States Attorney
for his District; after filling that office with distinction
for several years, Mr. Hale was in 1843 elected a member of the United States House of Representatives

from New Hampshire. Thus began his public life, in which he was afterwards so eminently successful. Mr. Hale was a firm Democrat; his political views prevented his re-election to Congress, and in 1845 he again became a member of the legislature of New Hampshire; but his talents were of too high an order for so limited a sphere of action, and in 1846 he was elected United States Senator. This office he held, without intermission, for seventeen years, and few have filled it with more distinction. Entering public life at a time when great men were plenty, and attaching himself to a party which was on the eve of disbanding forever, Mr. Hale met with strong opponents and many obstacles to success; but his perseverance throughout was great, and during his last years in the Senate there were in that body few more influential than he. Upon retiring from the Senate, Mr. Hale was, in 1865, appointed Minister to Spain; after holding this position for some years, he returned from abroad, and retired permanently from public life.

Mr. Hale died in Dover, New Hampshire, in 1873, lamented by all, and honored as a man whose education was of the best, and who possessed marked abilities.

BENJAMIN F. PRESCOTT.

BENJAMIN FRANKLIN PRESCOTT, son of Nathan Gove Prescott and Betsey Hills Richards, was born in Epping, New Hampshire, February 26, 1833. He inherited good health and a vigorous constitution, and during his boyhood was accustomed to all sorts of rough farm work. He attended the school of the district in which he lived until his fourteenth year, when he entered the Pembroke Academy, where he remained, with one or two exceptions, until 1850, when, in his seventeenth year, he entered Phillips Exeter Academy. Here Mr. Prescott's course was in every way creditable to him; he held the office of head-monitor in Prof. J. G. Hoyt's recitation-room (then a position of considerable responsibility), and was elected a member of the Golden Branch, of which society he was made President in 1852, delivering an oration at the anniversary in 1853. After leaving the Academy, Mr. Prescott entered the Sophomore Class at Dartmouth College; he graduated there in 1856, and began the study of law. Upon his admission to the bar of New Hampshire, Mr. Prescott opened an office in Concord, and began the practice of his profession, from which, however, he retired in 1861 to accept a position as associate editor of the *Independent Democrat*, at that time a leading paper of the State. In 1865 Mr. Prescott closed his connection with that paper, and was soon afterwards appointed agent of the United States Treasury Department for New England, but was removed, after a short period, on account of his opposition to the policy of President Johnson. From 1872 to 1876, Mr. Prescott was Secretary of State of New Hampshire, and in 1877 was elected

Governor, and re-elected in 1878. He was a delegate from New Hampshire to the National Republican Convention at Chicago in 1880. It is to Mr. Prescott that the Academy owes the extensive collection of busts and portraits which contribute so much to the beauty of its chapel; for it was through his strenuous and successful efforts that they were collected and placed there, just after the building of the new Academy in 1872.

ROBERT T. LINCOLN.

ROBERT TODD LINCOLN, the oldest child of President Lincoln, was born at Springfield, Illinois, August 1, 1843. His early education was received at the academy of a Mr. Estabrook, which he left at the age of twelve years, and shortly after entered the Illinois State University, at Springfield. After remaining there some years, he came to the East, and was for one year a member of the Phillips Exeter Academy, from which he entered Harvard College in 1860, as a member of the class of 1864. Mr. Lincoln's year at Exeter was, as he himself says, "devoid of excitement, and full of hard work." He seems to have been chiefly under the instruction of Mr. Wentworth, of whom he speaks as follows: "He was, and still is, I suppose, a 'driver.' I shall always think him the most thorough instructor I ever saw."

While at Harvard, Mr. Lincoln ranked well as a student, and was universally popular among his classmates.

He was a member of the Institute of 1770, and likewise of the Hasty Pudding Club. After graduation he was for a short time at the Harvard Law School, which he left in 1865, to accept a commission as Captain and Assistant Adjutant-General on General Grant's staff. This commission he resigned in June of the same year, and resumed the study of law in Chicago, where, after his admission to the bar of Illinois in 1867, he began the practice of law.

In 1880 he was one of the Electors from the State of Illinois, and immediately upon the inauguration of President Garfield was appointed by him Secretary of War.

CHAPTER IX.

BIOGRAPHICAL SKETCHES.

ALUMNI. — JARED SPARKS. — GEORGE BANCROFT. — RICHARD HILDRETH. — BENJAMIN F. BUTLER. — JOHN G. PALFREY — NATHAN A. HAVEN. — LEVERETT SALTONSTALL. — A. S. PACKARD. — SYLVESTER WATERHOUSE. — BUSHROD WASHINGTON. — J. G. COGSWELL. — LYMAN, DUNBAR, WYMAN, ETC.

JARED SPARKS.

ONE day, in the year 1809, a young man, dusty and foot-sore, walked into the town of Exeter, and sought the house of Dr. Abbot.

Brushing his travel-stained garments as well as he could, he let fall the old brass knocker, and as he heard the sound re-echo through the great house, no doubt he trembled, for he was weary, — perhaps hungry; and although the Doctor had been apprised of his coming, the young man was doubtful as to how he would be received. In a moment he was ushered into the Doctor's presence, and to him told a story much as follows.

"Dr. Abbot, last week I was working at my trade; I was a journeyman carpenter, and doing well. Long ago I had dreams of going to college and becoming a help to my countrymen, but I was so poor that I was forced to give them up. I left my jack-plane and saw, because

I heard that here you could give me the **help I can obtain** nowhere else. **I hope, sir,** that you will give **me a** place on the 'foundation,' for I have walked from Connecticut to this town in order **to** your school."

We can imagine the emotions of **the good** Preceptor, and the kind words of encouragement with which he responded.

Thus Sparks, **at the** age of twenty, **was** enabled, by the kindness **of** his friends and the beneficence of Dr. Phillips's bequest, to obtain a liberal education.

Sparks's early life forms as interesting and **instructive a bit of** biography **as one** can **find.** His watchword, from early boyhood, **was** "progress," and no obstacle could long prevent his going forward. He became interested in astronomy, and, wishing to observe the **heavens more** carefully, he erected a rude observatory in **a** neighboring field, and manufactured his own telescope. He learned carpentry quite by himself, and earned his living by working at his trade in summer, and teaching school in winter.

One of the friends of young Sparks, impressed by his progress in the classics and higher mathematics, as well as by his good character and industry, introduced him to the brother of Dr. Benjamin **Abbot.** Mr. Abbot, handing Sparks a copy of Virgil, asked him to construe. So well pleased was Mr. Abbot with the young man, that **he wrote** to his brother at Exeter, and succeeded in having Sparks placed on the Phillips foundation. Then, sending for Sparks, he asked him if he wished to go to college, and told him what he had done. There was but one answer to give. The young man was overjoyed with his good fortune. Mr. Abbot told him that it was necessary for him to go to Exeter at once, at the same time asking him how he would go. " Have you any money, Sparks ? " "No, sir ; I shall walk to Exeter." " But how will you get your box there ? " asked his benefactor. Sparks hardly knew. Mr. Abbot then told him that he was about to go to Brunswick, and that, if he would leave it at a certain corner at six o'clock the next morning, he would tie it under his chaise and take it nearly to Exeter for him. He added, " You yourself would be quite welcome to ride there, were there a vacant place." Thus Jared Sparks, afterwards President of Harvard College, came to Exeter.

Many years after Sparks had left Exeter, and had become famous in the republic of letters, his old teacher, Dr. Abbot, called at the bookstore in Exeter, — then kept by Francis Grant, — and purchased a book Sparks had just published. Turning to an old friend, he said, " Jared Sparks was the best scholar I ever sent away from the Academy. When he was graduated I was proud of him, sir, — I was proud of him ! I gave him the best recommendation I could write. In the same class was a superficial little fellow, and I did not know whether it was best to give him a recommendation or not. I did, however. Not long after, one of the examiners met me, and said, ' Doctor, we were disappointed in your friend Sparks, but there was one *sweet little fellow* who made up for all the rest.' When I inquired of Sparks the cause, he said that he was much embarrassed that day, and couldn't do well." But, fortunately, the real test is not the work of a few hours, but the work of a lifetime; and Jared Sparks, by his after labors in history and education, richly repaid the help given him by the Phillips Exeter Academy.

We can give but an outline of his life and labors. Jared Sparks was born in Willington, Connecticut, May 10, 1789. He was graduated from Harvard College in 1815, and was a Tutor in Mathematics there from 1817 to 1819; at the same time he studied theology. In 1819 he became pastor of a church in Baltimore, and in 1821 was Chaplain of the United States House of Representatives. He was Professor of History in Harvard College from 1839 to 1849, and President of that institution from 1849 to 1853. The biographies and histories which he has written make a long list in our library catalogues, and many of them are still standard authorities. He died in Cambridge, March 14, 1866.

GEORGE BANCROFT.

GEORGE BANCROFT, the eminent historian and statesman, was born at Worcester, Massachusetts, October 3, 1800. He entered the Phillips Exeter Academy in 1811, and there remained two years; he then entered Harvard College, and was graduated in

1817. His college course was merely the foundation of his education, for upon graduation he sailed for Europe, where he spent five years in the study of various subjects at Göttingen, Berlin, Heidelberg, Paris, and other cities, forming the acquaintance of many men celebrated for literary and scientific attainments.

Upon his return, Mr. Bancroft became an Instructor in Greek at Harvard University, remaining, however, but one year. He was then connected, for a brief time, with the Round Hill School at Northampton.

Mr. Bancroft, although at this time much interested in politics, and an avowed advocate of Democratic principles, refused to enter public life, as he had, when a student at Harvard, formed the plan of writing a History of the United States, and in 1834 the first volume of this History appeared; this was soon succeeded by the second volume, and in 1840 the third volume was published.

Turning his attention to politics, Mr. Bancroft was, in 1838, appointed Collector of the Port of Boston by President Van Buren.

In 1844 he was Democratic candidate for Governor of Massachusetts, but was unsuccessful, and was, in the following year, appointed Secretary of the Navy by President Polk. In this office Mr. Bancroft accomplished great good, as he thoroughly reorganized the Navy Department, and rendered it effective for service. It was he also who conceived and put into execution the plan of founding, at Annapolis, Maryland, a national Naval Academy, similar to the military school at West Point.

In 1846 Mr. Bancroft was appointed Minister to England, and remained abroad until 1849, when he returned, and once more gave his attention to literary work. The fourth and fifth volumes of the History were published in 1852, the sixth in 1854, the seventh in 1858, the eighth in 1860, and the ninth in 1866.

In 1867 he was again called into the diplomatic service, this time as Minister to Prussia; in which office he rendered important service to his country in negotiating treaties with certain German states.

Although justly celebrated as a diplomate, the great work of Mr. Bancroft's life has been his History of the United States, which is universally acknowledged as a standard work.

Mr. Bancroft while at the Phillips Exeter Academy had been greatly assisted by the aid which he received from the Phillips Charity Fund. He therefore, in 1870, founded the Bancroft Scholarship, by the gift of two thousand dollars. At the same time he writes: "A schoolboy is forgotten in the places of his haunts; but for himself, he can never forget them. Exeter is dear to me for the veneration in which I hold Dr. Abbot, my incomparable preceptor, and for the helping hand extended to me by its endowments. I desire to repeat for others that come after me what was done for me."

Mr. Bancroft resides, at present, in Washington, D. C., and is noticeably strong and vigorous; he is still engaged in literary work.

RICHARD HILDRETH.

RICHARD HILDRETH was born, June 28, 1807, in Deerfield, Massachusetts. His father, the Rev. Hosea Hildreth, in 1811 accepted a professorship in the Academy at Exeter, where young Hildreth entered, in 1816, at the age of nine. After remaining seven years at Exeter, he entered Harvard in the Sophomore Class, and was graduated in 1826.

He afterward read law in Newburyport, whence he removed to Boston, and commenced practice. In 1832 he became editor of the Boston Atlas.

A trip South, which he took about this time, suggested the idea to him of writing a novel against slavery, which he did. "Archy Moore," which appeared on his return, was the first antislavery novel. But Mr. Hildreth's mind was one which dealt more with facts than with fiction, as his works testify. He translated Bentham's Theory of Legislation from the French, besides writing a History of Banks, "Despotism in America" (a treatise on the subject of slavery), a "Theory of Morals," and a "Theory of Politics."

His most important work, however, is his History of the United States, in six volumes, published between 1849 and 1852, and bringing the history down to 1820. This is a work which evinces great industry, independent judgment, and unswerving adherence to facts, as he saw them. His style is clear and pure, and his arrangement of details excellent.

Mr. Hildreth likewise published a work entitled "Japan as it Was and Is," a compilation of some value. He was also connected with the New York Tribune, and frequently wrote for other periodicals.

As Mr. Hildreth was in delicate health, he went to Florence, where he died in July, 1865.

BENJAMIN F. BUTLER.

BENJAMIN FRANKLIN BUTLER was born at Deerfield, New Hampshire, November 5, 1818. "His father, John Butler, died when Benjamin was an infant, only five months old, leaving him, with an older brother, Andrew Jackson, to the care of his mother.

"Reading and writing seem to come by nature in New England, for few of that region can recollect a time when they had not those accomplishments. The district school helped him to spelling, figures, a little geography, and the rudiments of grammar. He soon caught that passion for reading which seizes some New England boys, and sends them roaming and ravaging in their neighborhood for printed paper. The boy hunted for books, as some boys hunt for birds' nests and early apples; and, in the great scarcity of the article, read the few he had so often as to learn large portions of them by heart; devouring with special eagerness the story of the Revolution, and all tales of battle and adventure.

"The Bible was his mother's sufficient library, and

the boy pleased her by committing to memory long passages, — once the whole book of Matthew. His memory then, as always, was something wonderful. His mother, observing this gift, and considering the apparent weakness of his constitution, early conceived the desire of giving him a liberal education, cherishing also the fond hope, as New England mothers would in those days, that her boy would be drawn to enter the ministry."

In the year 1829, at the age of eleven, we find him, a poor boy, entering the Phillips Exeter Academy, to prepare himself for college. His humble entrance to the Academy doubtless obscured, to an extent, his academic life, yet he is still remembered by his fellow-students, and also by many of the old residents of the town.

Edmund Chadwick, one of his classmates, writes of him: "Benjamin came to Exeter a young, slender boy, with pale and freckled face. He was brought to Exeter by his uncle. Benjamin was, as nearly as I recollect him, a modest and studious boy, of quick parts, but not much known among his fellow-students, and his circumstances never could have suggested his subsequent career."

Mr. William P. Moulton, of Exeter, in whose father's family Benjamin boarded, says of him: "He was the same Ben Butler, a boy, that he is a man. I recollect that he was a strong Jackson Democrat, in consequence of which he was unpopular with the boys, against whom he would stand up and fight for his party. He was a diligent student, and a great fellow at football."

Mr. Butler himself says: "Of my academic life there is little to be said. Sweet are the memories,

> 'And dear the schoolboy spot
> We ne'er forget, though there we are forgot.'

I was sent to the Phillips Exeter Academy when a child of very tender years. While there I learned the rudiments of Latin under Dr. Abbot, who was one of the kindest men I ever knew, and Greek — perhaps all the Greek I ever knew — under Professor Soule. I was the smallest boy in the Academy, with the exception of one who was a dwarf. It was part of my ambition to become a member of the Golden Branch, but I was too young to be admitted."

He was graduated from the Academy in his fifteenth year. "As the time approached for his entering college, the question was anxiously discussed in the family, 'What college?' The boy was decided in favor of West Point, but the cautious mother hesitated. She feared he would forget his religion, and would disappoint her dreams of seeing him in the pulpit of a Baptist church. She consulted her minister upon the subject. He agreed with her, and recommended Waterville College (now Colby University) in Maine, recently founded by Baptists, with a special view of educating young men for the ministry. It promised also the advantage of a manual labor department, in which the youth, by working three hours a day, could earn part of his expenses." The mother gave heed to her minister's opinions, and the youth was consigned to Waterville.

"His purse was most slenderly furnished. His mother could afford him little help. A good New Hampshire uncle gave him some assistance now and then, and he worked his three hours a day in the manual labor department, at chair-making, earning wages ridiculously small. He was compelled to remain in debt for a considerable part of his college expenses.

"If he was prone to undervalue some parts of the College course, he made most liberal use of the College library. He was an omnivorous reader. All the natural sciences were interesting to him, particularly chemistry; and his fondness for such studies inclined him, for a long time, to choose the medical profession."[1]

A prominent Professor in Waterville College once said to the late Dr. Soule, Principal of the Academy, "The few students from your Academy, Rogers, Butler, and Chadwick, have had the influence to raise the scholarship of our college twenty-five per cent."

The short space allowed in this volume does not permit more than a brief and cursory notice of some of the principal events of his life. He studied law, and became eminent in his profession. Previous to 1860 he was elected to the House and Senate of the Massachusetts legislature. In 1860, when the Rebellion broke

[1] General Butler in New Orleans. By James Parton.

out, he **was** the first general to lead a regiment of soldiers from the State of Massachusetts **to** the defence **of the** Capitol at Washington. His war record, made memorable by the capture of **and his** administration at **New** Orleans, testifies **that** he was not only a brave officer, but **also a** man of rare executive ability.

Since **the war** he has been elected several times a Representative to Congress, and in 1882 was elected Governor of Massachusetts, which office he now holds.

Perhaps **it can be said of him,** more truly **than of any other public man, that** he is the architect of his **own fortunes. The whole course of his life** has been **onward** and upward. **In his vocabulary** there is no **such** word as fail. **A striking instance** of this is his election to the gubernatorial chair of Massachusetts, after suffering defeat six times. As a lawyer, **soldier,** and statesman, his life has **become a part of the essential** history of the country.

A marble medallion of Governor Butler may be found **among** the **portraits of** Alumni, teachers, and benefactors, on the **walls of the** Academy hall at Exeter.

JOHN GORHAM PALFREY.

John Gorham **Palfrey** was born in Boston, Massachusetts, May **2,** 1796. He entered the Phillips Exeter Academy in **1809, at the** age of thirteen, and, after remaining there two years, entered Harvard College, from which **he was graduated in 1815,** delivering at

Commencement the Latin Salutatory address. After graduation he took up the study of theology, and in June, 1818, was ordained pastor of the Congregational Church in Brattle Square, Boston. From 1831 to 1839 he filled the chair of Sacred Literature in Harvard University, and from 1835 to 1842 was an editor of the North American Review. About this time Mr. Palfrey delivered a course of lectures on Religion before the Lowell Institute of Boston.

Mr. Palfrey was at one time a member of the legislature of Massachusetts, and for several years her Secretary of State. He was also Postmaster of Boston for four years. In 1851 he was one of the editors of "The Commonwealth," the chief organ in New England of the party of the Free-Soilers, in which he was a leader.

His latter days were devoted to literary works. Among his productions was a History of New England, in three volumes, bringing the narrative down to 1688. His style is spoken of as "clear and exact; if it is considered as lacking in vivacity, it shows conscientious care, and is free from the verbiage that sometimes passes for rhetorical ornament."

NATHAN A. HAVEN, Jr.

NATHANIEL APPLETON HAVEN, son of the member of Congress of the same name, was born at Portsmouth, New Hampshire, January 14, 1790. His elementary education was received under the instruction of Deacon

Amos Tappan, at Portsmouth; and at the early age of ten he entered the Phillips Exeter Academy, where he remained three years. In 1803 he entered Harvard College, and graduated there with distinction in 1807. He then filled the position of Assistant Instructor at the Phillips Exeter Academy for one year.

After leaving Exeter, Mr. Haven began the study of law, and was for a period of three years in the office of the Hon. Jeremiah Mason. He was admitted to the bar in 1811, but after a few years was compelled to give up work, on account of his delicate constitution, which had been impaired by excessive study.

Mr. Haven spent the year 1815 in foreign travel, and upon his return resumed the practice of law. In his profession Mr. Haven gained considerable celebrity as a man of deep and solid learning, and was notably one who disdained to use the talents with which nature had endowed him to avert the course of justice. "His fame was not as the transient flash of the meteor, brilliant and momentary, but, from the beginning of his course, as the gradual rising of the morning, its light continued to brighten to the fulness of meridian day."

From 1821 to 1825 Mr. Haven was managing editor of the Portsmouth Journal, and was at the same time a frequent contributor to the North American Review and the Journal of Education.

In the years 1823 and 1824 he was a member of the legislature of the State of New Hampshire.

Mr. Haven died of scarlet-fever at Portsmouth, on the 3d of June, 1826.

LEVERETT SALTONSTALL.

Hon. LEVERETT SALTONSTALL was born at Haverhill, Massachusetts, on the 13th of June, 1783. His ancestors were among the earliest settlers of the State, and had always been noted as eminent and benevolent citizens.

At the age of thirteen, Mr. Saltonstall entered the Phillips Exeter Academy, then under the management of the learned Dr. Abbot, for whom he is well known to have entertained the greatest love and respect throughout life.

During the two years spent at Exeter, young Saltonstall was distinguished for his ability and application, and took high literary rank as a scholar. Among his classmates and associates were Daniel Webster, Joseph S. Buckminster, and Lewis Cass. He always spoke of Exeter and of the Academy in terms of the deepest affection and gratitude, and at his death left one hundred dollars to increase the library of the institution.

In 1798, Mr. Saltonstall entered Harvard College, from which he was graduated in 1802. After leaving college he began the study of law, and was admitted to the bar of Massachusetts in 1805. In his career as an advocate he was eminently successful, and is described as "powerful, persuasive, and brilliant."

From 1814 to 1818 Mr. Saltonstall was a leading member of the legislature of Massachusetts, and during part of this period President of the Senate. In 1838 he was chosen a member of Congress, and served in the House of Representatives as chairman of the Committee on Manufactures. His political career was a brilliant one, and he was guided throughout by rectitude and by the dictates of his conscience. His honesty in his public, as well as his private life, was uniformly considered as inflexible.

Mr. Saltonstall died on the 8th of May, 1845, at Salem, Massachusetts.

ALPHEUS SPRING PACKARD.

ALPHEUS SPRING PACKARD was born at Chelmsford, Massachusetts, in 1798. When but twelve years of age he entered the Phillips Exeter Academy, where he was a holder of one of the scholarships founded by John Phillips. He remained but a year and three months at Exeter, and in 1812 entered Bowdoin College, from which he was graduated in 1816.

While at college he became a friend of Gideon L. Soule, with whom, at different periods of his life, he corresponded. After leaving college Mr. Packard taught in the Gorham Academy, from which he went to Wiscasset, and thence to Bucksport. He was then for a short time Principal of the Hallowell Academy, and in 1819 was made a Tutor in Bowdoin College, which position he held until, in 1824, he became Professor of Latin and Greek. While a Professor in Bowdoin he at different times has had charge of the department of

Rhetoric and Oratory, the department of Natural and Revealed Religion, and of the library, of which he is now Librarian.

In 1839 Mr. Packard edited the Memorabilia of Xenophon, and in 1841 issued a second edition. Besides editing the works of Dr. Appleton, he contributed a history of the Bunker Hill Monument, and other articles, to the Maine Historical Society, of which he is a member. He is also a member of the New York and of the Royal (England) Historical Societies. He received, in 1869, the degree of Doctor of Divinity from Bowdoin College. He is an ordained minister, and sometimes supplies charges in his vicinity.

Mr. Packard was married, in 1829, to Miss Frances E., daughter of President Appleton. She died in 1839. In 1844 he was married to Mrs. C. W. McLellan, of Portland. He had five children by his first wife, and one by his second.

Mr. Packard is a teacher of ability, and for more than sixty years has been an earnest supporter of the cause of education : his unswerving fidelity in its cause, maintained throughout so long a period, has placed his name among the foremost educators of the day.

SYLVESTER WATERHOUSE.

SYLVESTER WATERHOUSE, son of Samuel H. Waterhouse and Dolla Kingman, was born in Barrington, New Hampshire, September 15, 1830.

The accidental loss of his right leg, at the age of ten, changed the whole course of his life. It had been his intention to become an architect, but now, considering himself unfitted for an active profession, that design was abandoned.

Mr. Waterhouse entered the Phillips Exeter Academy in 1847, and distinguished himself throughout his course. He was President of the Golden Branch, and was also the Orator of that society at the close of his academic career. After leaving the Academy, Mr. Waterhouse entered the Sophomore Class at Harvard College, and was graduated in 1853. He then began the study of law, and in 1855 completed his course at the Harvard Law School.

In 1856 he was tendered the Professorship of the Latin Language and Literature in Antioch College. After remaining there one year, he accepted a position in Washington University, St. Louis. He has been connected with that institution from the first full year of its existence to the present time, — now more than a quarter of a century. He occupies the chair of Greek.

As an instance of the grateful regard in which Professor Waterhouse is held by his former pupils, we quote the following from the last Catalogue of Washington University.

"Under date of February 22, 1868, the anniversary of the institution, the sum of twenty-five thousand dollars was presented to the University, as a part of its permanent endowment, by Messrs. John P. Collier, William B. Collier, M. Dwight Collier, and Thomas F. Collier. The disposition of the income of this sum is left to the Directors, subject only to the request 'that until the Board of Directors shall officially determine a different employment of it to be required for the well-being of the institution, it shall be applied to the University Professorship of Greek, in grateful recognition, by his former pupils, of the fidelity, learning, and ability with which the present incumbent of that chair has for years past discharged its duties.'"

In 1871 Mr. Waterhouse was appointed by the Governor of Missouri a member of the Bureau of Geology and Mines, and in 1872 was elected Secretary of the St. Louis Board of Trade. In 1872-73 Mr. Waterhouse made a tour around the world, travelling about forty thousand miles. In 1877 he was a member of the convention for the improvement of the Mississippi River, which was held at St. Paul, Minnesota; and in 1878 he was appointed by President Hayes a commissioner to the World's Fair held in Paris.

The writings of Mr. Waterhouse have been many and influential. It is certain that his pamphlet on the "Resources of Missouri" brought many thousands of immigrants to that State; his article on the "Natural Adaptation of St. Louis to Iron Manufactures" was one of the potent factors that led to the establishment of the large and numerous iron and steel works of that city; and his "Memorial to Congress for the Improvement of the Mississippi River" undoubtedly exerted a powerful **influence towards inducing Congress to grant larger appropriations for that** work than ever.

In addition to the writings just mentioned are **the following**: "Reflections **on the** Southern Rebellion"; "**The** Dangers **of a Disruption of** the Union"; a Eulogy on Chancellor **Hoyt; and** many other newspaper and magazine **contributions,** including **a** large number on **the cultivation** of jute in America, **a subject** in which **Mr. Waterhouse was,** after **his tour abroad,** much interested.

BUSHROD WASHINGTON.

BUSHROD WASHINGTON, of Westmoreland, Virginia, **was born in 1759, and was** the nephew **of** General George Washington, and **one of** his heirs. He entered **the** Phillips **Exeter** Academy **at the** age of ten, and we find among **his** classmates Augustine Washington, Daniel Webster, and Francis Lightfoot Lee.

After leaving Exeter he began the study of law, and, **having** attained considerable distinction in the profes- **sion, was in 1797 appointed a** Justice of the Supreme Court of the United States **by** John Adams; this office he retained until his death.

Mr. Washington was also the **first President of** the American Colonization Society. **He is** described as a man of irreproachable integrity, and of **great** simplicity of manner, an earnest and faithful worker, and a sincere Christian. He died **at** Philadelphia, Pennsylvania, November 26, 1829.

JOSEPH GREENE COGSWELL.

JOSEPH G. COGSWELL was born in Ipswich, Massachusetts, on the 27th of September, 1786. He entered the Phillips Exeter Academy in 1801. He afterwards began the practice of law in Belfast, Maine, but in 1816 went abroad. Returning, after four years, he was made Professor of Mineralogy and Geology in Harvard College. In 1823, in conjunction with George Bancroft he founded the Round Hill School at Northampton, Massachusetts. He assisted John Jacob Astor in the management of the Astor Library in New York, and was for some time Superintendent and Trustee of that institution. Mr. Cogswell died, November 26, 1871, at the age of eighty-five.

THEODORE LYMAN.

THEODORE LYMAN entered the Academy in 1804; he graduated from Harvard in 1810, and was afterwards Mayor of Boston. He died in 1849.

CHARLES F. DUNBAR.

CHARLES F. DUNBAR was born at Abington, Massachusetts, entered the Phillips Exeter Academy in 1844, and was graduated from Harvard in 1851. He studied law, and was admitted to the bar in 1854. He became an editor of the Boston Advertiser on the 1st of January, 1861. In 1870 he was made Professor of Political Economy at Harvard, which position he still holds.

JEFFRIES WYMAN.

JEFFRIES WYMAN was born in Chelmsford, Massachusetts, August 11, 1814. He entered the Phillips Exeter Academy in 1826, graduated at Harvard College in 1833, and received the degree of Doctor of Medicine in 1837. He became, in 1843, Professor of Anatomy and Physiology in Hampden-Sidney College at Richmond, Virginia, and in 1847 Professor of Anatomy in Harvard College. He died at Bethlehem, New Hampshire, September 4, 1874.

The catalogue of the Academy contains the names of many others who should be mentioned on these pages, did not lack of space forbid. Among them are John A. Dix, Abiel Abbot, Ezra Abbot, David W. Gorham, Jonathan Chapman, Peter C. Brooks, Rev. John H. Morison, Charles H. Bell, Joseph B. Walker, and George S. Hale.

1.

3.

4.

CHAPTER X.

BIOGRAPHICAL SKETCHES.

INSTRUCTORS, PAST AND PRESENT. — HOYT. — BUCK-
MINSTER. — CHADBOURNE. — WARE. — WALKER. —
CLEAVELAND. — EVERETT. — LORD. — THE TWIN
PEABODYS. — HILDRETH. — HURD. — HALE. — BOWEN.
— THACHER. — PENNELL. — WENTWORTH. — CILLEY.
— FAULHABER. — TUFTS. — KITTREDGE.

JOSEPH GIBSON HOYT.

JOSEPH GIBSON HOYT was born on his father's farm, in Dunbarton, New Hampshire, January 19, 1815. The story of his struggle for a liberal education is truly remarkable. Obliged to work on the farm until the sixteenth year of his age, he was able to attend the district school only three months out of the twelve. His father was indifferent to culture, and it was due to the energy of his noble and gifted mother, coupled with his own perseverance, that, after various struggles as student and teacher, in Hopkinton, N. H., Andover, Mass., and various other places, he entered Yale in 1836, and was graduated the sixth scholar in a class of one hundred. His after life was wholly devoted to teaching, not only in the schoolroom, but also in town meetings, on the lecture platform, in State conventions, and through the press; and while on his death-bed the best lessons of his life were taught to hundreds of his friends and pupils who came to pay him homage.

In 1841 Mr. Hoyt was appointed Professor of Mathematics and Natural Philosophy in the Phillips Exeter Academy. On the 13th of April, 1842, Mr. Hoyt married Margarette T. Chamberlain, of Exeter. The issue of this marriage was a family of six children, five of whom survived their father. In December, 1858, he accepted the appointment of Chancellor and Professor of the Greek Language and Literature in Washington University, St. Louis. Six months later, the degree of Doctor of Laws was conferred upon him by Dartmouth College. His new friends had hardly ceased discussing his inaugural address, — an address which his generous culture had filled with rich learning, practical suggestions, and comprehensive plans, — when dread consumption seized upon the author. He died in his new home, November 26, 1862. His grave may be found near that of the Founder of the Phillips Exeter Academy, in the new cemetery at Exeter.

Exeter was the scene of Mr. Hoyt's life-work, and to him the town owes a debt of gratitude. Many of the fine trees which add so much to the beauty of the town and to the comfort of its people were planted by the hands of the Exeter Professor. The town hall, the public library, and many of the model schoolhouses of the State, are due to the efforts of this scholarly citizen, seconded by the more progressive of his friends and townspeople. Had Professor Hoyt lived, and still remained a resident of Exeter, we feel quite sure that no such architectural abortion as the building of the Robinson Female Seminary would have been inflicted upon the town. For many years he was the Superintendent of Schools in Exeter, and his brilliant reports were quoted far and wide. They are models for school reports to this day. Into the schools of Exeter he introduced improved classification and better systems of teaching, and by his efforts the standard of scholarship throughout the State was raised.

His exertions in behalf of the Academy were marked by the same sagacity and perception. It was mainly through his endeavors that the school was divided into four classes, and that the old system of studying in the building was abolished. Professor Hoyt was a model teacher. The remark which he once made of Dr. Abbot is eminently true of himself,—no one better understood the nature of young men. Honest himself, he trusted the young men under his charge, and they knew it. Like a general at the head of an obedient and enthusiastic army, he led them to success: he arranged for no retreat; he suffered no Waterloo. In the class-room he was at his best. His happy illustrations, his rich scholarship, and his keen wit cleared away all obstructions, and made his recitation hours memorable.

Goethe says, "A teacher who can arouse a feeling for

one single good action, for one single **good** poem, accomplishes more than he who fills our memory with rows **on** rows of natural objects classified with name and form."[1] This, **too,** was what Professor Hoyt believed. He never forgot the higher duty he owed to those under his charge, and often went outside the subject of the hour to dwell on the nobility of some character of history, the grandeur of some fine poem, or, again, to inspire his "boys" with a love for the truths of the Bible. He was greatly beloved by his **pupils**: just before leaving for St. Louis, the school at Exeter sent **one**[2] **of** their number to Boston, to purchase an elegant silver pitcher. This was presented to him with a speech full of affection and reverence.[3]

Mr. Hoyt was a man of great literary ability, and wrote **on** a variety **of** subjects. Politics, education, **music,** agriculture, criticism, tile draining, potatoes, and insects, are some of the subjects that engaged his fruitful pen. **He was a frequent contributor** to the North American Review, and several minor publications. **His** essays have been collected, and published in one volume.

One of the prominent traits of Mr. Hoyt's character was his physical and moral courage. Many times during life his strong, **brave** heart carried him safely through scenes of the greatest danger. One day, when

---

[1] Elective Affinitives, **Bohn's ed., p. 172.**
[2] J. Nelson Trask.
[3] The presentation speech was made by A. Hollis.

a schoolboy at Dunbarton, he went with a party of boys to a neighboring pond to enjoy a bath. While they were engaged in the sport of diving, one of their number became entangled in some underbrush at the bottom of the pond. His friends stood pale and irresolute, but young Hoyt sprang to the rescue. He soon found his friend, and commenced to swim ashore with his helpless burden; but, weighed down as he was, was forced to swim under water, dragging his friend along the bed of the pond. Twice he was forced to come to the surface to breathe, and twice he returned. At length he had the satisfaction of getting his mate to land, and of knowing that his courage had saved a life.

It is said that, " when Mr. Hoyt was in college, he was grossly insulted by a student of large and athletic frame. The bully was disposed to take unfair advantage of his physical superiority; but he suddenly found himself
> 'Laid low,
> With his back to the field, and his feet to the foe,'

and learned by personal chastisement the danger of insulting a brave man." Mr. Hoyt, from that day, was the champion of his class.

Dr. Hoyt was an earnest Christian. He had read the New Testament several times in the original, and amended translations which he deemed incorrect. He himself wrote, "I never entertained an unbelieving doubt of the divine authority and transforming efficacy of the Christian religion"; and again, "God's existence and man's immortality are the twin pillars of our faith"; and, last of all, "I die a believer in the Christian religion."

How shall we estimate this man of varied gifts? He had a keen relish for debate, and his brilliant wit — never used to give needless pain — was a trenchant weapon against the enemies of honesty and justice. He was a man of rare poetic sensibilities, and a great lover of the **bard of** Avon. His own writings, throughout, are studded with gems of rare thought and brilliant expression.

I will close with a few words from Professor Sylvester Waterhouse, of the Washington University, who has kindly furnished me with the materials[1] upon which I have so freely drawn for this sketch. He says: —

"Long years ago, as a student of Phillips Exeter Academy, I became acquainted with Mr. Hoyt. I remember, as though it were yesterday, his first salutation. The words of that kind greeting linger like music in the memory of the heart. Stimulated by his friendly encouragements, I gained new hopes of victory in the battle of life, and fresh determination to redress the wrongs of fortune. The friendship which began between the humble pupil and the warm-hearted teacher has never known a moment's interruption. It would require an eloquent gratitude to recount all his kindnesses. His personal interest, his latchless hospitality, his quick sympathy and cheerful encouragement in moments when life looked

---

[1] "Eulogy on Chancellor Hoyt."

sunless, are titles to my grateful regard, which Lethe shall not make me forget."

Professor Hoyt is not forgotten; he still lives in the memory of his friends and in the works of his own hand and brain.

JOSEPH STEVENS BUCKMINSTER.

JOSEPH STEVENS BUCKMINSTER, the eldest son of Rev. Dr. Joseph Buckminster, was born May 26, 1784, at Portsmouth, N. H., where his father, who was for eleven years a Trustee of the Phillips Exeter Academy, had long been an eloquent and popular preacher. The younger Buckminster in his earliest youth evinced an ardent thirst for knowledge, beginning the study of the Latin Grammar, we are told, when only four years of age. A great lover of books, he seldom joined in boyish sports, and in disposition displayed such amiability as made him a favorite among his acquaintances and beloved by all who knew him.

In 1795, at the age of eleven, he entered the Phillips Exeter Academy, and remained in it more than a year, under the instruction of Dr. Abbot. It is interesting to note the books studied by him at this early age, among which we find the Iliad, Xenophon's Cyropædia, the Epistles of Horace, Sallust, and Cicero. He translated Cicero's De Amicitia, and a part of Sallust. During his college life he was most industrious, and one of his classmates writing of him, says, — "Commencing his college course standing in the first rank, he sustained that rank unwaveringly to the end." Upon his graduation from Harvard in 1800, he was appointed to the position of assistant instructor in the Academy at Exeter. It is in this capacity that we are, perhaps, most interested in him, as the teacher under whom Webster experienced his first difficulties in declaiming in public ; speaking of which he says: " The kind and excellent Buckminster sought to persuade me to perform the exercise of declamation like the other boys, but I could not do it. . . . Mr. Buckminster always pressed and entreated with the most winning kindness that I would only venture *once ;* but I could not command sufficient resolution."

Mr. Buckminster remained three years at Exeter. In 1804 he entered the ministry, and was first settled at the Brattle Street Church in Boston, which was one of the leading congregations of New England. Here he became celebrated as a preacher of the Unitarian faith, differing in belief from his father, who had been of the Congregational persuasion. In 1806–7, he visited Europe, and while there took a deep interest in the purchase of books for the Boston Athenæum. In 1808 he supervised the republication of Griesbach's New Testament (in Greek), and in 1811 received the appointment of Lecturer on Biblical Criticism in Harvard College.

He was a member of most of the important literary societies of the day, and a contributor to the leading periodicals. His works have been published, in two volumes.

At the close of the year 1811, Mr. Buckminster's health began to fail, and he died on June 10, 1812. His loss was deeply mourned, as ending the brief career of a most eloquent and successful preacher, a versatile writer, and a deep student of biblical and secular literature.

PAUL ANSEL CHADBOURNE.

PAUL ANSEL CHADBOURNE, a distinguished author, scientist, and teacher, was born in North Berwick, Maine, October 21, 1823. During his boyhood he worked on a farm in the summers, and in a carpenter-shop during the winters. He studied medicine, and was employed for some time in a drug store. In 1842 he entered the Phillips Exeter Academy, and although in narrow circumstances, yet by copying law and insurance papers he paid his current expenses. He entered Williams College in 1844, and graduated in 1848 with the highest honors. After leaving college Mr. Chadbourne taught school for a year at Freehold, N. J.; while there, he began the study of theology, which he continued at a theological institute in Windsor, Conn. After finishing his Theological studies, Mr. Chadbourne was chosen Principal of the High School at Great Falls, N. H., and soon afterward was made a Tutor in Williams College. From Williams he was called to be Principal of the East Windsor Hill Academy, Connecticut, and in 1851 was made Professor of Ancient Languages in the Phillips Exeter Academy, remaining there one year. In 1853, he was elected to the chair of Chemistry and Natural History in Williams College, and three years later was called to fill the same position at Bowdoin College; during the next seven years he did double duty, spending half the year at each college. He was also a Professor in the Berkshire Medical College for three years, and Chemical Lecturer in the Mount Holyoke Seminary for thirteen years.

Dr. Chadbourne was greatly interested in science. In 1855 he explored Newfoundland. In 1859 he visited Europe, and also went to Iceland in order to study volcanoes and geysers. In 1857 he led a scientific expedition to Florida, and in 1860 he explored Greenland.

When Dr. Chadbourne was a member of the Massachusetts Senate, in 1865–66, he was chosen first President of the Massachusetts Agricultural College; but on account of ill health he was compelled to resign this position after one year.

He went to the West, and was soon afterwards elected President of the University of Wisconsin. During the three years of his administration of this University, he reorganized and established it on a firm basis. He afterwards spent two years in the Rocky Mountains in order to regain his health, and was then, in 1872, chosen President of Williams College. He remained at Williams for nine years, and his efficient administration contributed much to its prosperity.

Mr. Chadbourne received the degrees of Doctor of

Medicine from the Berkshire Medical College, and of
Doctor of Divinity and of Laws from Amherst College;
he was elected a member of the Massachusetts Board
of Agriculture to succeed Professor Agassiz; and he
was also a member of the Massachusetts Historical
Society, the Royal Society of Northern Antiquaries of
Copenhagen, and many other organizations.

Dr. Chadbourne always took an active interest in
politics. He was a delegate at large from Massachusetts
to the National Republican Convention in 1876, Chairman of the Republican State Convention of Massachusetts in 1880, and Presidential Elector in the same year.

Dr. Chadbourne was a business man as well as a
teacher; he was often engaged in business enterprises,
working land and operating mills. He was half owner
of two cotton-mills at Williamstown, Mass, and was
also a director of several business corporations. In
March, 1882, Dr. Chadbourne was again made President of the Massachusetts Agricultural College, which
position he held at the time of his death, February
23, 1883.

He is well known as an author; he published
"Natural Theology," "Instinct," and the "Relations
of Natural History." He wrote several pamphlets, and
also a tribute to President Garfield. The latter was a
very able production. At the time of his death he was
engaged on a work called "The Public Service of the
State of New York,"—chiefly devoted to the history
and industries of that State.

From the number of positions which Dr. Chadbourne held, it will be seen that he was a man of great industry. He always exhibited a genuine zeal and love for work, whether in teaching, in business, or in work of exploration. Dr. Chadbourne, throughout his life, cherished a warm regard for the Academy at Exeter, and often returned there to attend its festivals.

HENRY WARE, JR.

HENRY WARE, JR., a distinguished Unitarian divine, was born at Hingham, Mass., April 21, 1794. He was a direct descendant of Robert Ware, one of the earliest of the settlers of New England.

He prepared for college at Duxbury, Mass., under the instruction of a private tutor, but was sent, in 1807, to the Phillips Academy at Andover. Here he remained for one year, and then entered Harvard College. Mr. Ware was graduated in 1812, and was throughout his college course an earnest worker, always maintaining an excellent rank.

Immediately after leaving college, Mr. Ware, then but nineteen years of age, was appointed an assistant instructor in the Phillips Exeter Academy, of which Dr. Abbot was at that time Principal.

Here he spent two years, of which period he always spoke with pleasure; the following extract from a letter of Dr. Abbot gives evidence of the esteem in which he was held there : —

"The sweetness of his disposition, his open frankness of manner and acknowledged scholarship, soon gained him the love and confidence of his pupils, and the respect and affection of his brother instructors. His two years' residence in this place left an impression on all who had the happiness to know him, and is still fondly cherished in the recollections of all who survive him."

After leaving Exeter, Mr. Ware, in 1814, returned to Cambridge, and began the study of theology; he then became pastor of the Second Unitarian Church in Boston. In 1814 he married Miss Elizabeth Watson Waterhouse, daughter of Dr. Benjamin Waterhouse, of Cambridge.

During his ministry Mr. Ware travelled much for his health, especially through the Middle and Southern States. While on his journeys, he was often engaged in religious and charitable work, and occasionally preached at places where he stopped. He remained at his charge in Boston till 1829, when he resigned to become Professor of Pulpit Eloquence and Pastoral Care at Cambridge, in 1829. Before entering upon this office, which he held till July, 1842, he visited Europe, where he remained about seventeen months.

Mr. Ware had the misfortune to lose his first wife in 1824; and in June, 1827, was married to Miss Mary Lovell Pickard, of Boston. Besides attending to the duties of his pastoral charge, Dr. Ware wrote several works on religious subjects; among these may be mentioned a work on the Offices and Character of

Jesus **Christ; one on the** Formation **of** the Christian Character; and a Life of the Saviour.

In 1842, Dr. Ware's health continuing to become worse, he resigned his professorship, and removed to Framingham, Mass., where he died, September 22, **1843.** His biography has been published in two volumes.

In person, Dr. **Ware was** short in stature, **and in** later years somewhat bent. His countenance was pale, and gave **the** appearance of poor health; **its expression** was somewhat serious, though **rarely, if ever, gloomy.** His sermons were **clear and** forcible, and **were delivered in an** impressive manner. Although he was not considered a hard student, yet **he was** careful in the preparation of his sermons, and they bear **evidence** of deep thought. His ministry was, on **the** whole, very acceptable. He labored hard in the **cause** of his Master, and when his work was over **it** could be well said to him, "Well done, thou **good and** faithful **servant!**"

JAMES WALKER, D. D.

JAMES WALKER was born at Burlington, Massachusetts, August 16, 1794. From early youth it was his intention to enter the ministry, and with this end in view he was educated at Harvard College, where **he** graduated with honors in 1814, at the age of twenty.

Just after graduation he was chosen assistant instructor in the Phillips Exeter Academy; this position he accepted, and filled for one year. Mr. Walker left Exeter in 1815, and was soon after ordained. In 1818 he was installed as pastor of the Harvard Church in Charlestown, Mass., where he remained for twenty-one years.

He was from 1831 to 1839 an editor of the Christian Examiner (a religious periodical then published in Boston), and in 1839 accepted the Alford Professorship of Natural Religion, Moral Philosophy, and Civil Polity in Harvard College. In 1853 Dr. Walker was chosen President of the University, and filled this position until 1860, when he was compelled to resign, on account of bodily infirmity.

As President of Harvard University, he inspired all who came under his care or tuition with love and respect, and was universally revered and venerated for his dignity and kindness. His death, which occurred on December 23, 1874, occasioned deep regret among the friends of the College, which he had so long and so faithfully served.

JOHN P. CLEAVELAND.

REV. JOHN P. CLEAVELAND, D. D., was the son of Parker Cleaveland, M. D., of Rowley, Mass, who at one time represented his district in the legislature of the State. Mr. Cleaveland himself was "earnest and intense in all he undertook; study was a delight to him." His early education was received at Dummer

Academy, Byfield, from which school he entered Bowdoin College.

After his graduation, Mr. Cleaveland pursued theological studies at the Andover Theological Seminary. In 1825, soon after leaving this institution, he was chosen Professor of Mathematics and Natural Philosophy in the Phillips Exeter Academy, a position which he held for one year. After leaving Exeter, Mr. Cleaveland held, at different times, pastorates in Salem, Mass.; Detroit, Mich.; Cincinnati, Ohio; Providence, R. I.; Northampton and Lowell, Mass.

At the outbreak of the Rebellion, although over threescore years of age, Mr. Cleaveland entered the service as Chaplain of the 30th Regiment of Massachusetts Volunteer Militia. His health never recovered from the exposures undergone during this part of his life, and he died in Newburyport, Mass., March 7, 1873.

ALEXANDER HILL EVERETT.

THE subject of this sketch was born in Boston, March 19, 1792, and was graduated from Harvard College at the age of fourteen, the youngest of his class, but the highest in scholastic rank. He immediately became an assistant instructor in the Phillips Exeter Academy, but at the end of a year removed to Boston, in order to study law in the office of John Quincy Adams. When that gentleman was appointed Minister to Russia, young Everett accompanied him as an *attaché* of the embassy. On his return to Boston, he divided his time between law and literature, and became a prominent political writer. Later, he was Secretary of the Legation to the Netherlands, afterwards *Chargé d'Affaires*, Minister to Spain, and Commissioner to Cuba and to China. He was five years a member of the State legislature; and from 1829 to 1834 was the editor of the North American Review, to which for many years he had been a prominent contributor. In 1841, he was elected President of Jefferson College, Louisiana, but was soon compelled, on account of impaired health, to return to the North. He was sent by President Polk on a special mission to China, and died at Canton, May 29, 1847.

Mr. Everett was a man of great and varied accomplishments. He was quite equal to his brother Edward in native abilities; but a longer and more fortunate career gave the latter a reputation which has quite overshadowed the fame of the less favored Alexander.

Mr. Everett always remembered kindly the Academy at Exeter, and at the Abbot Festival was among those who returned to pay homage to the great teacher under whom he had once served.

His published works include many subjects. They are written in a delightful style, indicative of great originality and strong convictions. We cannot but think, had his convictions been less strong, he would have ranked much higher among statesmen.

NATHAN LORD.

NATHAN LORD was **born** in Berwick, Maine, on November 28, 1793. Preparing for college in his native town, he was graduated **at** Bowdoin in 1809, at the **age** of sixteen; throughout **his** course he maintained an excellent rank in his class, and even thus early gave evidences of unusual forensic ability.

Immediately after leaving college, he accepted **the** position of assistant instructor in the Phillips **Exeter** Academy, where he remained three years.

Mr. Lord then began the **study of** theology, and **entered** the Theological Seminary **at** Andover, where **he was** graduated in 1815. **In May,** 1816, he was settled **over** the Congregational **Church** at Amherst, N. H., where he remained for **twelve** years.

During the last seven years of his pastorate here, Mr. Lord served as **a** Trustee of Dartmouth College, and upon leaving Amherst, **at** the **age of** thirty-five, was made President of that institution. **Under** his administration Dartmouth College prospered as never before. Thornton, Reed, and Wentworth Halls were erected, a new chapel **was** constructed, an observatory built, and the entire Scientific Department was founded, as well **as** several new Professorships in other departments **of the** University.

In 1863, Mr. Lord resigned his position because he was unable to reconcile his views on the slavery ques**tion** with those of the Corporation of the College. He then withdrew to private life, and died, September 9, 1870.

WILLIAM B. O. PEABODY.

WILLIAM BOURN OLIVER PEABODY, son of Oliver Peabody, was born at Exeter, N. H., on the 9th of July, 1799. In 1808, when nine years of age, he entered the academy at Atkinson, N. H., but, remaining a few months only, was admitted to the Phillips Exeter Academy in the same year.

In 1813 he entered the Sophomore Class at Harvard College, and here, as at Exeter, maintained a high standard of scholarship. After graduation he returned to Exeter, and became an assistant instructor in the Academy, remaining however but one year.

In 1817 Mr. Peabody went to Cambridge, where he pursued theological studies. Soon after being ordained, he was settled over a congregation in Springfield, Mass., and there remained until the time of his death, which occurred on May 28, 1847. In 1842 the degree of Doctor of Divinity was conferred on him. Dr. Peabody gained considerable fame both as poet and author, and was universally beloved by his congregation.

OLIVER W. B. PEABODY.

OLIVER WILLIAM BOURN PEABODY, twin brother of the preceding, was born on July 9, 1799, became a member of the Phillips Exeter Academy in 1808, was graduated from Harvard College in 1816, and was then for one year an assistant instructor at Exeter under Dr. Abbot. In 1822 he became an editor of the North American Review. He was at one time editor of the Rockingham Gazette and Exeter News-Letter. In 1842 he was Professor of English Literature in Jefferson College, Louisiana, but afterward removed to Boston, and was for some years a member of the legislature of Massachusetts. He died on July 5, 1848.

HOSEA HILDRETH.

HOSEA HILDRETH was born at Chelmsford, Mass., January 2, 1782. He was the son of Timothy and Hannah Hildreth, and descended from Richard Hildreth, who had emigrated from the North of England to Massachusetts in 1643. While Hosea was still a child, his parents removed to Vermont, but afterward returned to Worcester County, Massachusetts.

A short time afterward, young Hildreth fell from an apple tree, and broke a cord in his right arm; this accident, since it incapacitated him for out-of-door work, turned his attention to study and education. He was therefore placed under the instruction of the Rev. Mr. Holcomb, at that time the Congregational minister of Sterling, and by him was prepared for Harvard College, which he entered in 1801.

In 1805, just after graduation, Mr. Hildreth began the study of theology, but, marrying soon after, was compelled to teach as a means of supporting his family.

After spending some years in this way at Lynn, Deerfield, and Brighton, he accepted, in 1811, the Professorship of Mathematics and Natural Philosophy at the Phillips Exeter Academy. This position he held for fourteen years, during which time he endeared himself to all who knew him, and gained the respect of all those who had the good fortune to be under his instruction.

During part of the period of Mr. Hildreth's residence at Exeter he filled the pulpit of the Congregational Church of that town, of which Isaac Hurd afterward became pastor. In 1825, Mr. Hildreth left Exeter; he afterwards, at different times, held several pastorates in various parts of Massachusetts. He was also an early and efficient worker in the movement in favor of temperance. Finally, in 1835, he left the parish which he then filled, in Westborough, Mass., and retired from active life to Sterling, where he died in July of the same year.

Mr. Hildreth was the author of several works, of which the following are the principal: A Discourse to the Students of the Phillips Exeter Academy; Book for New Hampshire Children; A Discourse on Ministerial Fidelity; Duties and Rights of a Congregational Minister; The Kingdom of Jesus Christ not of this World.

ISAAC HURD.

REV. ISAAC HURD was born in Charlestown, Mass., in 1786. He was graduated at Harvard College in 1806, and, after studying divinity, was ordained at Lynn, Mass., September 15, 1813. Mr. Hurd was then a Unitarian; but having changed his faith some years later, he became a Congregational minister, and was installed at Exeter, N. H.

From 1817 to 1839, while in charge of the Second Parish, Mr. Hurd was Theological Instructor in the Phillips Exeter Academy. The duties of this position were far from laborious, as the instructor only came to the Academy once during the week to give a few lessons in elementary theology. Mr. Hurd inherited considerable property, and, having ceased to perform his duties as Theological Instructor, this office was abolished in 1839.

Mr. Hurd was a man of small stature, mild and gentle in manner; his sermons, while excellent in every respect, were still remarkably moderate and liberal in style. He died in Exeter, October 4, 1856, and is spoken of as "a diligent student, a good scholar, amiable, exemplary, and faithful."

NATHAN HALE.

NONE of those who were assistant instructors under Dr. Abbot became more distinguished in after life than Nathan Hale. He was born in Westhampton,

Mass., August 6, 1784, and was the son of Rev. Enoch Hale, and nephew of the Nathan Hale of Revolutionary fame. Mr. Hale was graduated from Williams College in 1804, and, after studying law for a few months in Troy, New York, was appointed an Instructor in Mathematics in the Phillips Exeter Academy, which position he filled until, in 1810, he removed to Boston to practise law. Four years later, he became one of the editors of the Boston Weekly Messenger, the first weekly periodical in America devoted to literature and politics. In 1814 he purchased the Boston Daily Advertiser, the first, and for many years the only, daily paper published in New England. It was first Federal, and afterwards Whig, and exerted a great influence on the politics of the day.

Mr. Hale was a man of progress, and was connected with nearly all the great movements which gave to Boston the high rank she holds among cities. At his death, February 9, 1863, his son, Charles Hale, succeeded him in the management of the paper which he had so faithfully conducted for forty years. Another son, Rev. Edward Everett Hale, is well known as the author of many interesting tales of American life.

FRANCIS BOWEN.

FRANCIS BOWEN was born in Charlestown, Mass., September 8, 1811. He was one of a large family, and was from early youth compelled to depend for support almost entirely upon himself.

His early education was received at the Mayhew Grammar School of Boston; and after some years spent there he became a clerk in a publishing house in the same city. In 1829 Mr. Bowen entered the Phillips Exeter Academy, and at the end of a few months completed his preparation for Harvard College, which he entered as a Sophomore in 1830. Upon graduation he became Professor of Mathematics and Natural Philosophy at the Phillips Exeter Academy, remaining there until 1835, when he returned to Harvard College, and, after serving one year as Tutor in Greek, was appointed Instructor in Mental Philosophy and Political Economy.

In August, 1839, Mr. Bowen resigned his position in the College, in order to enjoy the advantages of a year of travel and study in Europe.

Upon his return, he took up his residence in Cambridge, and devoted himself to literary work. In 1842 he published an edition of Virgil, and a volume entitled, "Critical Essays on Speculative Philosophy." The next year Mr. Bowen became proprietor of the North American Review, which he edited for upwards of ten years. He also edited and published for six years, "The American Almanac and Repository of Useful Knowledge." In 1848 and 1849 he delivered, before the Lowell Institute, two courses of lectures on Metaphysics and Ethics, which have since been published.

In 1850 he was appointed McLean Professor of History, which office, however, he held only for a brief period. Some years later he became Alford Professor of Natural Religion, Moral Philosophy, and Civil Polity, which position he now holds.

Mr. Bowen has been the author of many celebrated metaphysical and ethical works, as well as of treatises on Logic and Political Economy. Among these are the following: "The Principles of Political Economy applied to the Conditions and Institutions of the American People"; "A Treatise on Logic, or the Laws of Pure Thought"; "American Political Economy"; "Modern Philosophy"; and "Gleanings from a Literary Life."

Mr. Bowen has throughout life shown himself devoted to the interests of the Phillips Exeter Academy. He served as a Trustee from 1853 to 1876, and is the author of the historical sketch of the Academy which appeared in the General Catalogue issued in 1869.

PETER O. THACHER.

PETER OXENBRIDGE THACHER, son of the Rev. Peter Thacher, D. D., pastor of the Brattle Square Church, Boston, was born at Malden, Mass., in 1776. In 1792 he entered Harvard College, at the age of sixteen. From here he was graduated with distinction in 1796, and immediately accepted the position of assistant instructor in the Phillips Exeter Academy. According to the custom, he remained there but one year; and, having afterward taken up the study of law, was in 1823 chosen Judge of the Municipal Court in Boston, which position he filled for twenty years, with much credit to himself and to the city. He was a member of the American Academy of Arts and Sciences, and is said to have been a well-read lawyer, an accomplished scholar, a good citizen, and a Christian gentleman.

Mr. Thacher died, February 22, 1843, "much respected for his integrity and humanity."

ROBERT FRANKLIN PENNELL.

ROBERT FRANKLIN PENNELL was born in Freeport, Maine, on July 13, 1850. He was the son of Robert and Caroline (Soule) Pennell, the latter a daughter of Deacon Moses Soule and a sister of Gideon Lane Soule, so well known as Principal of the Academy at Exeter.

In August, 1864, Mr. Pennell, then a boy of fourteen years of age, came to Exeter, and, entering Dr. Soule's family, became a student in the Academy. Under the careful instruction of his uncle, he became conspicuous for his accurate scholarship: indeed, his native ability and his powers of application gave him easy pre-eminence. During his first year at the Academy a change occurred in the fortunes of his family, and from that time he was obliged to work his own way.

In 1868 Mr. Pennell entered the Sophomore Class at Harvard College. There his scholarship was early recognized, and throughout his course he held a high rank. The expenses of his course at Cambridge he paid by giving private instruction, not only to members of the lower classes, but to his own classmates. Under such pressure his health became impaired, and for a brief period he was obliged to leave his studies and seek needed rest.

Upon his graduation, in 1871, Mr. Pennell at once became an instructor in the Academy at Exeter. Later he was elected Professor of Latin in the same institution. This position he resigned in December, 1882, in order to obtain a long period of needed rest. The eleven years spent by Mr. Pennell at the Phillips Exeter Academy were characterized by earnest, faithful work of a very high order. He was respected among his colleagues, and among his "boys" was greatly loved and admired. As a teacher it was his aim, not only to ascertain what the pupil himself knew, but to impart something in return. Consequently his recitation-room was never dull; to enter it became a pleasure, and at the close of his hour the student felt that he had indeed been rolling along the "road to knowledge" at a rapid rate.

Mr. Pennell has assisted in editing a number of educational works, and is himself the author of several text-books of value. These include a History of Greece, a History of Rome, and a study of the Latin Subjunctive.[1]

[1] Published by John Allyn, Boston.

GEORGE ALBERT WENTWORTH.

GEORGE ALBERT WENTWORTH was born in Wakefield, Carroll County, N. H., July 31, 1835. He acquired the rudiments of learning in a district school in that town, and attended the Wakefield Academy for about one year. In 1852 Mr. Wentworth entered the Phillips Exeter Academy. Leaving here in 1854, he entered the Sophomore Class in Harvard College, graduating in 1858. Mr. Wentworth was immediately elected Instructor in Ancient Languages in the Phillips Exeter Academy, and the next year was chosen Professor of Mathematics. Professor Wentworth is the author of many mathematical works, as follows: a Primary, a Grammar School, and a Higher Arithmetic; an Elementary Algebra; a Plane and Solid Geometry; a Book of Geometrical Exercises; a Plane and Spherical Trigonometry; a work on Surveying and Navigation; and a Five-Place Table of Logarithms.[1]

BRADBURY LONGFELLOW CILLEY.

BRADBURY LONGFELLOW CILLEY, son of Joseph Longfellow and Lavinia Bagley (Kelley) Cilley, was born in Nottingham, N. H., September 6, 1838. In 1842 the family removed to Exeter, and Mr. Cilley attended the schools of the town until the fall of 1851, when he entered the Phillips Exeter Academy. Mr. Cilley re-

---

[1] Published by Ginn and Heath, Boston.

mained a member of the Academy until 1855, when he entered the Sophomore Class in Harvard College, graduating in 1858. After graduating, Mr. Cilley moved to Albany, N. Y., and there taught in the Albany Academy until 1859, when he became Professor of Ancient Languages in the Phillips Exeter Academy.

OSCAR FAULHABER.

OSCAR FAULHABER was born at Isny, kingdom of Würtemberg, South Germany, in 1832, and received his education for the most part at Stuttgart and Tübingen, where he received the degree of Doctor of Philosophy in 1855. Mr. Faulhaber then went to France, and, after three years spent there, proceeded to England and later to the United States, where he has been for the most part occupied in teaching, both in the East and the West.

In 1874 Mr. Faulhaber was chosen Instructor in French and German in the Phillips Exeter Academy.

JAMES ARTHUR TUFTS.

JAMES ARTHUR TUFTS was born in Alstead, Cheshire County, N. H., April 26, 1855, and there spent his early boyhood, until, in his eleventh year, he joined the military school in Brattleborough, Vt. At the end of three years he returned to Alstead, and was for two years a clerk in his father's store. In April, 1872, he entered the Phillips Exeter Academy, graduating in 1874; he took a high rank in his class, and was, during a part of his Senior year, President of the Golden Branch. Mr. Tufts entered Harvard College with distinction in 1874, and while in College was President of the Everett Athenæum and a member of the Signet. Immediately after graduation, in 1878, he was appointed Instructor in English in the Phillips Exeter Academy, a position which he still holds.

GEORGE LYMAN KITTREDGE.

GEORGE LYMAN KITTREDGE, the son of Deborah Lewis and Edward Lyman Kittredge, was born in Boston, February 28, 1860.

In 1875, after studying for some time with a private tutor, he entered the Roxbury Latin School, where, under the learned Mr. Collar, he was fitted so as to enter Harvard University in 1878. His college course was marked by faithful work, and his rank upon graduation was very honorable.

At Commencement, Mr. Kittredge was assigned an Oration, and in addition to receiving an "honorable mention" in Greek, Latin, English, and English Composition, he was one of the two members of the Class of 1882 who received highest honors in the classics.

In January, 1883, while at Cambridge studying for the degree of Doctor of Philosophy, Mr. Kittredge was appointed an instructor in the Phillips Exeter Academy.

CHAPTER XI.

BIOGRAPHICAL SKETCHES.

BENEFACTORS AND TRUSTEES. — JEREMIAH KINGMAN. — JOHN L. SIBLEY. — WOODBRIDGE ODLIN. — JEREMIAH SMITH. — AMOS TUCK. — CHARLES BURROUGHS. — ANDREW P. PEABODY.

JEREMIAH KINGMAN.

THE Kingmans are of ancient English stock. Their lineage has been traced back through several centuries of honored ancestors. The founder of the New Hampshire branch of the family settled in Rye. William Kingman, the grandfather of Jeremiah, moved to Barrington, N. H. His son, John, was the father of the subject of this sketch. For three successive generations, the family occupied the same farm.

Jeremiah Kingman was born in Barrington, September 23, 1793, and died on his birthplace, December 7, 1872.

His education, received almost entirely in the common schools of his native town, was limited. In his boyhood, the public instruction given in the rural districts of New Hampshire was very superficial. Only the elements of the ordinary English studies were taught. The teaching, which continued but a small portion of the year, was too brief and imperfect to develop correct habits of study, or satisfy a native fondness for the pleasures of literature. Two terms spent in the academy at Gilmanton, N. H., then under the skilful direction of Mr. Samuel Fletcher, completed the lad's scanty education. The better methods and richer discipline of his academic training strengthened a natural taste for letters into a life-long craving for the acquisition of knowledge.

In early manhood, Mr. Kingman himself taught school for several winters. It is stated that his practical and suggestive illustrations invested dry facts with an interest that impressed them upon the minds of his pupils.

Mr. Kingman was married, March 23, 1828. His wife was Elizabeth, the daughter of Paul Hayes, of Barrington. No children resulted from this union.

In 1836, Mr. Kingman was elected Superintendent of the public schools of Barrington. He held this office for twelve years, and discharged its duties with rare success. He always spoke without notes, but his informal addresses on the trite subject of education were replete with suggestive thought. Under his supervision, the schools were improved by the employment of better teachers, and the proficiency of the pupils was tested by personal examinations. The dread of his searching questions was often a motive to greater studiousness: his wise reflections have quickened many a youth to a truer appreciation of the value of knowledge. His interest in education lasted through life, and his visits to the schoolroom did not cease till physical infirmities prevented their continuance. The aid of his loans enabled several young men to complete their collegiate courses. His devotion to letters survived death; since, in the final disposition of his property, an endowment of $11,000 was given to Dartmouth College, and one of $56,000[1] to the Phillips Exeter Academy.

In 1831–32, Mr. Kingman was a representative in the State legislature, where his sound judgment and familiarity with business were actively exerted for the promotion of wise legislation.

His military experience began while he was still a boy. In 1812, a threatened invasion of the State by the British summoned young and old to the field. Mr. Kingman was drafted, and went to Portsmouth to aid in the repulse of the foe. But the rumor of an attack proved baseless, and his patriotic valor was not tested by the ordeal of battle: the young soldier, however, was for many years the captain of a company of cavalry.

Familiar with the principles of mensuration, he was often employed to survey the lands of his neighbors, and determine the exact position of the boundary lines.

Through all the period of his mature and active life, he was a Justice of the Peace. In this capacity, he transacted a great deal of business. Many of the local deeds and wills of his day were drafted by his hand. In the transfer and settlement of estates, the adjust-

---

[1] Out of this sum, however, the Trustees of the Academy were obliged to pay several claims, so that the net amount received was $42,421.43.

ment of probate claims, and the administration of town affairs, his judgment was often consulted. In the management of both public and private interests, the counsel of no man in town was more frequently sought. Though as lavish of advice as he was frugal of money, his suggestions were always valuable.

His love of society was intense, and his highest happiness was found in the companionship of congenial friends. In their presence, his versatile powers of entertainment never flagged. The mystery of ingenious puzzles, the charms of song, and an endless flow of sprightly talk, never failed to interest visitors. His presence heightened the pleasure of every company.

He was very fond of music, and for many years he played the bass-viol in the church choir. The neighbors often gathered in his parlor, and there, accompanied with the sweet tones of the organ, sang anthems. These meetings, blending secular airs and lively conversation with sacred song, were occasions of rare enjoyment.

In the prime of manhood, Mr. Kingman was attacked with sciatica. This malady, which medical skill failed to cure, increased in severity with the advance of age. Unable, in consequence of this infirmity, to work on his farm, he devoted his leisure to reading. He enriched his mind with the wealth of literature and poetry. He read, not only every volume in his own cases, but also every book in the town library, and many works in those of Dover and Rochester. He had a collection of all the best English poets, and knew by heart many of their finest **passages.** Fascinated with the romantic **witcheries** of the Scotch magician, he was not content with a single perusal of the Waverley Novels. His medical reading was probably quite as extensive as that of many a rural physician.

In metaphysics, he studied with critical care **the systems** of Locke, Stewart, Kant, and Cousin. **His theological** learning would not have been discreditable to a professional student of divinity. The different creeds and religions of mankind were frequent themes of **conversation. Paley's** Evidences of Christianity was one of **his** favorite books. His interest in the young science **of** geology was evinced by the perusal of every accessible work on the subject, **and** his acquaintance with history was wide and exact. His special heroes were Samuel Johnson, Frederic the Great, and the first Napoleon. **He read** all of Alison's voluminous History of Europe, and many other works that describe the campaigns of the brilliant Corsican. It is probable that Mr. Kingman was as familiar with the career of the great Bonaparte **as any** man in the **United States.**

His rarest gift was his common sense. An unusual power of philosophic analysis enabled him to discern at **once the vulnerable points** of an argument. A singularly **keen** insight gave him clearness of views, while a strong memory retained in its grasp the facts which had been committed to its keeping. The results of original reflection upon the recorded experiences of mankind, as well as upon his own observations of human life, were held in readiness for **instant use.** Hence, in social discussion or public debate, he was a dangerous opponent. He had the faculty of reasoning on his feet, and could talk by the hour in a strain that never failed to interest **and** instruct his audience. **He** was never eloquent, but always clear, direct, and sensible. His conversation, though seldom brightened by flashes of wit, was often enlivened by sallies of humor. Without apparent effort or consciousness of superiority, he rose to easy eminence **in social** discussion. His mind, richly stored **with the treasures of reading and** reflection, needed **no** special **preparation. He could,** on any occasion, make a speech without premeditation, **and the sound sense** and clear expression of these **off-hand** remarks, **most** men, even **with** the advantage **of** study, would find it difficult to equal. He always avoided low topics: personal slander, local gossip, and public scandal were never permitted to pollute with their harpy touch the clean food of **his** social repasts. With native refinement and elevation of mind, he always sought pure and ennobling subjects of conversation.

Once, during the session of a convocation, some half a dozen of the leading clergymen were entertained by Mr. Kingman. The evenings were naturally **spent in the** discussion **of** theological topics. With untrained native strength, Mr. Kingman proved himself more than **a match** for his professional antagonists. Some of the best speeches made in the convocation were unconscious reproductions of the thoughts which Mr. Kingman had expressed in these evening debates. On one of these occasions, the visitors amused themselves with a novel test of the breadth and accuracy of their reading. Happening to find in a late paper a poem composed of lines taken from the works of different poets, they diverted themselves with efforts to trace the authorship of the several verses. The host knew the source of more lines than all of his guests put together.

Mr. Kingman was constitutionally timid. He once took a trip to the White Mountains. The coach was whirled down the steep hills by four horses driven at full speed. The swift motion, which filled all the other passengers with delightful exhilaration, blanched his cheeks with terror. At points of unusual wildness, the coach was stopped to give the tourists time to admire the grandeur of the scene. Afterwards, in relating his experience, he said that "the driver tempted Providence, and halted his horses in the very worst places on purpose to give an accident a chance to happen"!

On another occasion, he went to Halifax. On the return voyage, the steamer encountered a very violent storm. In the unequal combat with the elements, the brave vessel was nearly overwhelmed. Mr. Kingman was greatly terrified. The intensity of his fear seemed to shake the confidence of his religious hope. When asked what he thought of in the midst of the tempest which threatened to engulf him, he said, "I thought of home and heaven, and came to the conclusion that I should never see either."

Mr. Kingman was a Unitarian. He was reared in the Congregational faith, but the arguments of Channing and Sparks converted him to their views. He was the first, and for years the only, Unitarian in the town of Barrington. In those days of austere creeds, the stand which he took evinced moral intrepidity and fidelity to his convictions.

Mr. Kingman was kind and gentle-hearted. The sight of suffering easily moved him to tears. He was a man of good presence. Indeed, all the members of this branch of the family were fine-looking. His brother John and his four children were distinguished for physical beauty, conversational ability, and musically rich voices. In boyhood, the cheeks of Jeremiah Kingman were red as a rose. The amiability and keen intelligence of his expression were very winning. A large, well-shaped head, a fair complexion, bright, thoughtful blue eyes, a slightly Roman nose, a broad, firm chin, and a massive frame, are the traits that will convey an impression of his personal appearance. The salient qualities which his features expressed were good nature, thoughtfulness, and judgment.

But no character is perfect. Although temperate in all his habits, Mr. Kingman had one grave fault, which, growing with the lapse of years, weakened his hold upon popular respect, impaired his public spirit, and lessened the possible usefulness of his life. Over the details of his weakness it is well, with backward step, to throw the mantle of forgetfulness. But loyalty to truth, which requires a faithful delineation of character, and seeks to avoid the unwholesome influence which springs from a suppression of unwelcome facts, will not permit a concealment of the sole defect which marred the symmetry of an otherwise faultless nature. With this single exception, the character of Mr. Kingman was one of rare purity, elevation, and nobility.

JOHN LANGDON SIBLEY.

AMONG the benefactors and distinguished Alumni of the Phillips Exeter Academy no one is to be noticed with more respect and affection than John Langdon Sibley. He was born, December 29, 1804, in Union, Maine, where his father, Jonathan Sibley, was a physician and a small farmer.

At the Phillips Exeter Academy, which he entered in the summer of 1819, he was supported by aid from the Phillips Charity Fund, by small sums of money occasionally received from home, and by his own exertions.

Entering Harvard College in 1821, Mr. Sibley was appointed "President's Freshman." His connection with the library of the College began while still an undergraduate, as he spent considerable time in writing for the library, and in otherwise assisting the Librarian. By these means, and by various other occupations, Mr. Sibley passed through college free of debt, maintaining throughout an excellent standard of scholarship. After graduating, in 1825, he entered the Divinity School, and became then, for the first time, officially connected with the library, holding the position of Assistant Librarian, which had at that time a salary of $150 per annum.

In 1829, after leaving the Divinity School, Mr. Sibley was ordained as pastor of a church in Stow, and there remained until 1833. Returning then to Cambridge, he devoted himself almost exclusively to literary work, editing, for some years, "The American Magazine of Useful and Entertaining Knowledge."

In 1841 Mr. Sibley was again appointed Assistant Librarian, and in 1856, upon the death of Dr. Harris, who was then Librarian, he was appointed to that office, which he held until 1877, when he retired on account of bodily infirmity.

Of the many and valued services rendered by Mr. Sibley to Harvard University it is needless to speak at length; but there is one charity of this truly great and good man less widely known. Remembering with the deepest gratitude the assistance which he himself had, when a schoolboy at Exeter, received from the Phillips Charity Fund, Mr. Sibley began, in 1860, a series of gifts to the Phillips Exeter Academy, the amount of which is now estimated at $34,000, to be employed for the support of meritorious and needy students; at his own request, Mr. Sibley was not known to the public as the donor of this fund until the Soule Festival, in 1872, when he was prevailed upon by his friends to divulge the secret.

In 1879, at the request of the Trustees of the Academy, Mr. Sibley's portrait was added to those of the benefactors and illustrious Alumni which hang in the chapel of the school.

Mr. Sibley, upon his withdrawal from active service in the library of Harvard University, was made Librarian Emeritus. He resides at present in Cambridge, Massachusetts.

WOODBRIDGE ODLIN.

WOODBRIDGE ODLIN, who was descended from John Odlin, one of the first settlers of Boston, was the son of William and Elizabeth (Leavitt) Odlin, and was born in Exeter, N. H., May 29, 1805. After receiving his education, principally at the Phillips Exeter Academy, which he entered in 1817, at the age of twelve years, Mr. Odlin began his business career as a painter and carriage-maker in Exeter. He afterwards engaged in the wool trade, in which he was uniformly successful. In politics Mr. Odlin was a strong Abolitionist. He represented his town in the State legislature for several terms, and, after retiring, was for some time President of the Exeter Savings Bank. He was justly celebrated for his charities, which were many, and at his death, in 1879, "every good and worthy cause lost a kind patron; the community, a citizen of rare integrity; the church, a faithful worker; his family, a considerate and loving husband and father." Some time before his death, Mr. Odlin gave to the Academy the sum of twenty thousand dollars, to establish an English course, designed for students who do not desire to pursue classical studies. This course includes three years, and may, at the discretion of the Faculty, include Latin. It is also stipulated by the same gift, that ten students from Exeter may be admitted to this course free, provided that number of competent students belonging to the town apply, who lack the means to pay the usual tuition fees. In this munificent gift Mr. Odlin has left a monument to his memory "which will remain when monuments of stone shall have crumbled to dust."

JEREMIAH SMITH.

JEREMIAH SMITH was born in Peterborough, New Hampshire, November 29, 1759. He exhibited a fondness for books early in life, and is said to have taught himself to write, using pieces of birch bark, and ink made from vegetables. He received his preparation for college under the instruction of the Rev. Mr. Emerson, of Hollis, New Hampshire, and entered Harvard in 1777. Just at this time came the news of Burgoyne's invasion, and, notwithstanding his youth and excellent prospects of an education, young Smith enlisted. When he presented himself for enlistment, he acknowledged that he came without the consent of his father; thereupon, the captain, who was a personal acquaintance, informed Mr. Smith of his son's action, and persuaded him to allow the boy to enlist. The father reluctantly consented, but begged that, in case of a serious engagement, his son might be sent to a place of safety. Just before the battle of Bennington, in accordance with this request, the boy was despatched, on some errand, to a place of security, and great was the surprise of his captain when, in the thickest of the fight, he found young Smith at his side. " How came you here ? " he asked. " O, sir, I thought it my duty to follow my captain," was the reply.

Mr. Smith afterwards returned to Harvard, and two years later entered Rutgers (then Queen's) College, from which he was graduated in 1780. After teaching in various places, he became an instructor in the Phillips Academy at Andover ; here Dr. Benjamin Abbot, afterwards Principal of the Phillips Exeter Academy, was among his pupils. Fifty years later, at the Abbot Festival, Judge Smith, looking around upon the assembled Alumni, told them that they were Dr. Abbot's pupils, but that, great as was their honor, his own was greater, for he had been his teacher.

Judge Smith filled many offices of distinction faithfully and successfully ; he was District Attorney, Justice of the United States Circuit Court, Chief Justice of New Hampshire, and Governor of the same State. He also represented his district in Congress during four terms. From 1828 to 1842, Mr. Smith was Trustee and Treasurer of the Phillips Exeter Academy. Thus he became intimate with young men, to whom he was always a firm friend. His interest in the young, and in their education, only ended with his life.

In 1838, Judge Smith delivered the Centennial Address in Exeter, at the close of the second century of the existence of the town. In September, 1842, he ended his long and useful life.

AMOS TUCK.

HON. AMOS TUCK was born in Parsonsfield, Maine, August 2, 1810.

In 1838 he was graduated from Dartmouth College, and immediately afterwards became Preceptor of Hampton Academy, in Hampton, New Hampshire, which place had for years been the home of his family. After remaining two years in Hampton, Mr. Tuck removed to Exeter, where he began the study and practice of law.

In 1842 he represented Exeter in the legislature of the State, and afterwards was a member of the United States House of Representatives.

On the accession of Mr. Lincoln to the Presidency, Mr. Tuck, who had always been one of his firmest supporters, was appointed by him Naval Officer at the Boston custom-house.

Mr. Tuck's interest in education was always marked. He was a Trustee of Dartmouth College, also one of the first Trustees of the Robinson Female Seminary in Exeter, of which institution he was for a short time President. From 1853 until his death, which occurred on December 11, 1879, Mr. Tuck was one of the most active and interested of the Trustees of the Phillips Exeter Academy.

CHARLES BURROUGHS.

CHARLES BURROUGHS, the fourth son of George and Mary (Fullerton) Burroughs, was born in Boston, Massachusetts, December 27, 1787. He resided in his early youth chiefly at Boston, but was for some time at Billerica, under the instruction of Dr. Pemberton, at that time a noted teacher. In 1802, Mr. Burroughs entered Harvard College, where he was universally popular with his classmates, being spoken of as a person of winning manners and most amiable disposition. Throughout his college course he maintained a good rank, and at graduation had the honor of delivering the Latin Valedictory. After leaving college, Mr. Burroughs for some time studied theology; he received deacon's orders at Philadelphia in 1809, and in 1812 was ordained. He was from 1835 to 1867 a Trustee of the Phillips Exeter Academy, and was during the greater part of that period President of the Board.

Dr. Burroughs was at all times an ardent friend of the school, taking the deepest interest in all that concerned its welfare, and was especially noted for the promptness and carefulness with which his duties were always performed. During the latter part of his life he held many positions of trust and eminence; he was President of the Howard Benevolent Society, of the Portsmouth Athenæum, and also of the Board of Trustees of the New Hampshire Insane Asylum. In 1833 he received the degree of Doctor of Divinity from Columbia College.

At his death, which occurred in March, 1868, he was not unmindful of the institution to which he had been so devoted throughout life, but by a gift of $1,000 increased the beneficiary funds of the Academy, founding the scholarship which bears his name.

ANDREW PRESTON PEABODY.

ANDREW PRESTON PEABODY was born in Beverly, Massachusetts, March 19, 1811, and at the age of twelve years passed the entrance examinations to Harvard, but did not commence his course until the following year, when he entered the Junior Class. He was graduated in 1826, and immediately became a private tutor of the Huidekoper family in Meadville, Pennsylvania. In 1829 he entered the Harvard Divinity School, where he spent three years, during which time he was also a proctor and an instructor in Hebrew in the College; in 1832 he was a Tutor in Mathematics in the College.

In 1833 he was ordained pastor of the South Parish Church, Portsmouth, New Hampshire, which position he filled for twenty-seven years, until, in 1860, he accepted the appointment of Preacher to the University, and Plummer Professor of Christian Morals. Both his duties in the University and those of his church have been performed with the utmost fidelity.

His literary work has been so considerable that it is impracticable to give here even the titles of his various essays, reviews, addresses, and discourses. For several years, Dr. Peabody was a leading writer for the American Monthly and the New England Magazines, besides being a large contributor to the Christian Examiner, and for nearly a quarter of a century connected with the North American Review, which he edited from 1853 to 1861. It is said of him, that "he handles a ready and vigorous pen, is clear and animated in style, and well skilled in the arts of a reviewer."

In 1872, at the dedication of the new Academy building, Dr. Peabody was the orator of the occasion: his scholarly address has since been published.

Dr. Peabody is a member of the American Academy of Arts and Sciences, the Massachusetts Historical Society, the American Oriental Society, and the American Antiquarian Society.

He received the degree of Doctor of Divinity from Harvard in 1852, and that of Doctor of Laws from Rochester in 1863. He was acting President of the University during 1862, and again during the academic year 1868–69. For forty consecutive years he has been one of the Trustees of the Phillips Exeter Academy, and for sixteen has been President of the Board.

CHAPTER XII.

REMINISCENCES AND ANECDOTES.

EXETER SCHOOL LIFE IN 1808. — RECOLLECTIONS OF 1811. — THE ACADEMY IN 1822. — LIFE IN EXETER IN 1855. — AUNT RINGE. — ANECDOTES.

"Forsan et hæc olim meminisse juvabit."
ÆNEID, I. 203.

THE following recollections of Exeter school days have been kindly contributed by gentlemen who years ago were students at the Academy. We feel sure that old and new scholars will alike be deeply interested in this chapter of memorabilia.

EXETER SCHOOL LIFE IN 1808.

I WAS just twelve years of age when I entered the Phillips Exeter Academy, in 1808, having travelled alone in the stage-coach from my home in Concord, New Hampshire, to Exeter, by way of Haverhill, Massachusetts, then the only public mode of conveyance to my destination. My father's acquaintance with Governor Gilman and the Hon. Oliver Peabody led to my early and easy introduction to them, — by whom I was treated with great kindness, and through Judge Peabody found board secured for me in the pleasant family of Captain

Luther Dana, a retired shipmaster. Here I continued for more than a year, and then took board with Mrs. Giddings, nearer to the Academy. **Dr.** Abbot was then its esteemed Principal, and the accomplished N. A. Haven, Jr., the assistant in the large, or Classical room. In the other, or "Philosophy room," as then called, Prof. Eben Adams, soon after transferred to Dartmouth College, was the teacher in the various English branches. Of this department Prof. Hosea Hildreth was soon after the head, and Reuben Washburn, who became the father of Governor P. T. Washburn, of Vermont, succeeded to Mr. Haven after the summer term.

My intimacy with the students was not very great, most of them being older than myself. Of those who afterwards became prominent, Jared Sparks was the foremost; he came as a "charity scholar" from Connecticut (from Killingly, I think), and was reported to have come on foot, through his extreme poverty and the lack of cheap travelling facilities at that time. Charles Briggs, who afterwards became a clergyman and preached in Roxbury, Mass., was his near associate in age, in studies, and in pecuniary circumstances. Contrasted in this last respect were the Tayloes (William H. and Ben Ogle) from Richmond, Va., and their cousin Ben Ogle from Maryland; Thomas H. Perkins, the Debloises (T. A. and John), Apthorp, Baxter, and Bazin, from Boston; Thorndike, from Beverly; the Allens (Zachariah and Crawford), from Providence; the Sheafes, Sherburnes, and Havens, from Portsmouth; Willis from Portland, Me., Duncan from Haverhill, Mass., Hale of Barrington, Steele of Durham, Barker of Rochester, the Peabodys and the Gilmans of Exeter, and others of that grade in wealth or society. There were also Bidau and Bonhomme from France, and Tyler and one or two others from the West Indies. Prof. John G. Palfrey should not be overlooked as in scholarly connection with President Sparks, though not in such straitened circumstances, or at so advanced an age; nor should we forget the Hon. John A. Dix.

We had not adopted the college "hazing," but there was a custom in my Exeter day, "more honored in the breach than the observance," of subjecting the newcomers to climbing a high post in the Academy building, until they could touch the top ceiling; and another custom, on the first fall of snow, to subject one to being thrown down and "washed," or his face and hands scrubbed by the snow, not unfrequently by a mixture of grit as well as snow. In regard to "post climbing," I remember a student, Alfred Smith, of Durham, — almost a man in age and stature, — having a new coat nearly torn from his back and into tatters on his refusing submission.

Football was the principal game at which we played for exercise or amusement, — sometimes at bat and ball, — and there was some occasional by-play, out of the accustomed ring. I recollect some sport being made, at one time, by a little adventure in Leavitt's tavern stable.

One of the scholars had been taken into the stable, at the charge of a sixpence, to see "a horse whose head was where his tail ought to be." Coming out with a full realization of the "take in," and willing that others should be caught in the same trap, he was disposed to be silent as to the fraud, and fell in with the precautionary measure of the showman, to allow the entrance of but one person at a time, that the horse might not be frightened at a greater number. In this way many of the school were "taken in," each one, on coming out, being ashamed to confess that, for his money, he had seen only a common animal backed up into his stall.

On a "general muster" occasion at Kingston, where we were allowed to go for the day, some of us were accompanied by a schoolmate whose name was Brown, the son of a poorly paid clergyman at Deer Island, Maine. Brown, though not generally credited with average capacity or shrewdness, on this occasion displayed considerable ingenuity in order to accomplish a desired object. There was the side show of a bear, or some other animal, which demanded the old-fashioned ninepence for admission. Several of us went into the show; but Brown, in his poverty, stood outside, endeavoring to beat down the showman in his price. Failing in the mode adopted, and unwilling to lose the sight, he finally tempted the good nature or appreciative humor of the man, by asking whether he might not go in at half-price, in case he would shut up one eye.

Many of the early students will remember a man of

venerable appearance, who occasionally **was seen in the** street, and who, for some indebtedness, was **said to be** restricted to the jail limits, — the jail yard, or bounds, being rather extensive. This gentleman, who had seen better days, and **who had borne** civil office and military rank, was **known as** General Nathaniel Peabody. He was a man sufficiently gracious in manner, but regarded as rather lax and graceless in religious " walk and conversation." The following incident, occurring a little after my time, was related to **me by an Exeter** student **as** witnessed by him. A theological student, occupying himself, one vacation, in obtaining subscribers **for a work to** be published in Andover, by Mark Newman, entitled " The Christian's **Great** Interest," being in Exeter, and seeing the General's venerable form and somewhat clerical attire, accosted him respectfully, with quite confident appearance of success. On telling his object and the title of the book, he was soon met by an unexpected rebuff, in the General's abrupt declaration, " that he did n't want any such work, — that he had no need of it, — that he had learned what that interest was, from Parson C—— years before, — it was twelve, eighteen, and twenty-four per cent."

In the recess of Congress, we often saw in the street a stately gentleman, **of courtly** address, whose perfect straightness of **form was said to** have been caused, or continued, by his uniform practice of sleeping as nearly horizontally as possible, **with no** bolster, and but a **slight** pillow under **his head. This** gentleman was the

Hon. Nicholas Gilman, then a Senator in Congress from the State of New Hampshire. Being a bachelor, he made his Exeter home with the family of his brother, the Hon. Nathaniel Gilman. An anecdote is told of him, in connection with a well-known "darky" at the seat of government, who, in common with many of the colored race, was accustomed to wait upon gentlemen at Christmas time, and solicit something in return for their greeting of "A merry Christmas." This individual, well knowing and well known to the Senator, made the customary call, with the usual appeal for the sixpence or shilling. The Senator made strange of him, and demanded to know who he was. "Why, ole Harry," was the answer: "don't you know ole Harry?" — "Go away," was the reply: "they call the Devil old Harry." — "Yes, Massa Gilman," was the rejoinder, "some time ole *Harry,* some time ole *Nick.*" The Senator was so amused by the apt hit upon his own Christian name, that he gave Harry a dollar.

For lack of time and space, I am obliged to omit many well-remembered incidents of my Exeter days. I cannot close, however, without mentioning "Lawyer" Tobias Cutler (as he was called), and "Knockaree" Marsh, characters whom all students of my day must remember. The "cakes and ale" of the latter are well-remembered refreshments, but I do not suppose they are things only of the past, notwithstanding the fact that the present generation claims to be more "virtuous."

GEORGE KENT.

RECOLLECTIONS OF 1811.

WHEN I was but twelve years of age I was taken by my father, Rev. Hezekiah Packard, from my home in Wiscasset, District of Maine, to Exeter, where I had been admitted to the "Phillips Foundation." It was in June, 1811. My father left me at Captain Haliburton's, the boarding-place of the students who were entered on the Phillips Foundation. It was to be my first experience in living away from home; and I watched the square-top chaise which had brought me to Exeter until it disappeared from sight down the street by Leavitt's tavern, on its way home, some hundred and twenty miles distant. Then with a sad heart I went into the house, feeling like a forsaken one among strangers.

I was introduced to Silas Holman, of Boston, as his room-mate. Holman, Jared Sparks, Jonas Underwood, John Gorham Palfrey, and Charles Briggs were fellow-foundationers. I remember well their kind consideration to me, a stranger lad, and their friendly invitation to join them in a walk that evening. Such kindness tended to keep away home-sickness, for the first day or two at least. I remember how, in one of these walks, Sparks narrated his study of stars while at his home in Connecticut, and how he had constructed a rude observatory in an open field from which to observe the heavenly bodies.

The gentle, motherly care of the excellent Mrs. Haliburton soon made the place seem home-like to me. I recall, gratefully, the orderliness of this household of student boarders. Sparks, Underwood, and Holman were men in age and bearing, and had been in the Academy a year or two, so they were looked up to and respected by the younger members. The foundation scholars were doubtless carefully and officially observed by Principal Abbot, but I knew nothing of that. We seemed, in the best sense, to be a law to ourselves. During the year and three months that I was a pupil in the school, I recall no instance of interference, either from landlord and wife, or from the authorities of the Academy.

In the fall and winter months the foundationers studied together in the dining-room at Mr. Haliburton's, at a long table which stood on the right of the entrance, regulating ourselves by what was called "a bill." While "the bill was on," as the phrase was, any breach of silence was noted by our monitor, and, as a penalty for such an offence, the offender had to build the morning and evening fire. If one of us wished to "communicate" while we thus sat studying, a majority of raised thumbs "took off the bill," for the time; later, we resumed our work.

During the evening an occasional recess of a few minutes was taken, which was passed by breaking into some sort of fun. In summer, those who preferred to do so, studied in their chambers. The school lessons of the day, with rare exception, were prepared in the schoolroom, under the eye of our teachers. Occasionally, an older student was allowed to study at his boarding-house.

I recall the existence of a kind of literary club in that group, and I remember of having read at one of its gatherings a sketch of Linnæus, which I prepared from reading the account of him, I think, in Coxe's Travels in Sweden, Norway, etc. I think I am the sole survivor of that group, and cherish the memories of those halcyon days.

When I first took my seat in the Academy, in the front row of seats, Nathan Lord (Bowdoin 1809), afterwards President of Dartmouth, was the Assistant, and Hosea Hildreth (Harvard 1805) was Professor of Mathematics and Natural Philosophy. Lord was universally popular in the school. The second term of my pupilage, and the new year of the Academy, opened with H. W. Fuller as assistant, just graduated from Harvard, who for some personal peculiarities was less a favorite. Once during that year, I saw Principal Abbot assume the frown of Jupiter himself, as he looked toward us. The assistant's desk had been shamefully defiled during the night. In the morning, we assembled as usual, a few minutes before the Principal entered. The desks of the scholars ascended from the broad aisle on the east and west sides of the room. Those of the Principal and assistant were each enclosed by a low railing, which was entered by a gate, and were placed on each side of the fireplace, opposite the hall entrance. The slow, measured step of the Principal was heard in the outer hall. When he entered, we arose and stood, as was our custom, while he passed, dressed, according to the fashion of that day, in knee-breeches and high boots. With his usual royal bearing he entered his desk. The assistant already sat in his place grim and disgusted. A brief communication from him, and Mr. Abbot descended to the area in front. A look revealed the outrage; and, standing before the fireplace with a stern glance over the school, he pointed toward the assistant's desk, and exclaimed, "Who has committed that violence?" Resuming his seat, he asked, "Who had charge of the Academy last night?"

I arose from my seat. It was the duty of the "foundationers," each in his turn, to close the building at night, and to open it and ring the bell in the morning. I happened to be on duty that week. "Take the key and go up to the library," said Dr. Abbot. The library was in the second story. The Principal followed me, and examined me concerning my service. A day or two after, the attention of the school was called by the Principal. The culprit had been discovered. The vote of the Faculty, "that he should be expelled, and his name be stricken from the roll of membership," was announced in due form, and as he read the sentence he drew his pen across the name of the offender. The scene was a memorable one; and the impression which it left on us all was not soon forgotten.

The spacious hall in the second story was used for

exercise in declamation, also for the annual examinations, and the exhibition, near the end of August. Well do I remember the first exhibition which I attended, when J. G. Palfrey gave the Latin Salutatory, and Jared Sparks was a performer. The circumstances of the day have caused me also to remember distinctly the second one which I attended. It was, however, one of those exhibitions which were held each week, and consequently less formal than the first, but it is worth recalling. Holman and George Bancroft each had a part in a dramatic piece, and the latter, though a lad of only twelve years, personated, with admirable effect, an old man, in a full bottom wig, knee-breeches, and gray hose, to the great diversion of the spectators. I have a perfectly distinct picture in my memory of the scene, and of how the Principal shook his sides with laughter at the spectacle.

The instructors and the students generally attended public worship with the Second Society, in the unpainted church edifice on the street a few rods above, or south of, the Academy grounds. The services were conducted for a time, in the absence of a permanent pastor, by Mr. Nathaniel Whitman (Harvard 1809), formerly an instructor in the Academy, who read the sermons of some approved author. The students occupied the galleries; and I recall the more noticeable members of that congregation, such as Governor Gilman, and others of that honored name; also Judges Smith and Peabody, Hon. Samuel Tenney, Captain or rather Colonel Rogers, and the family of each. These we looked down upon from our height of observation. In the winter months, service was held in the Academy Hall, as this was more comfortable (this was before the Yankee stove had come into use). The preacher occupied the platform at the upper end, and the students their benches on the sides, while arrangements were made for families in the area, or upper part of the hall.

Besides those already mentioned as "foundationers" in my day, there were also Abel F. Hildreth (Harvard 1818), Lyndon A. Smith (Dartmouth 1817), Reuben B. Lowell, from Thomaston, Me., and Elias Hull, from Seabrook. Among my schoolmates who were not on the foundation I specially recall George G. Ingersoll (Harvard 1815), Benjamin Ogle Tayloe (Harvard 1815), and his brother Edward, nicknamed "Giant," from his diminutive stature. There were also William and Edwin Channing, Jonathan P. Cushing (Dartmouth 1817), afterwards President of Hampden-Sidney, Virginia, the twin Peabodys (Harvard 1816), John A. Richardson (Dartmouth 1816), and Richard Bartlett (Dartmouth 1815), whom we called "our politician," as we thought him to be a disciple of that somewhat noted political character, General Peabody, who was then an inmate of the debtor's prison across the river.

It may be of interest to some to know that in my school days the Græca Minora was required for admission to Harvard College. At Bowdoin and other colleges, the Greek Testament was required. Owing to this, both were studied at the Academy, and although my examination in that language was confined to the Greek Testament, yet I did not regard it a loss of time that the Minora was added to my scanty stock of Greek.

Besides walks in the village and its environs, the out-door amusements were football in autumn, skating on "Little River" in its season, and bat-ball in the spring. The military company of the school afforded ample recreation during the summer term. Of this company Charles Briggs was the first captain; Silas Holman was second captain, under whom I served. We drilled every day in the Academy yard. As soon as we became sufficiently organized and practised, we, in our way, paid our first military honor to our teachers. After our dismission from the afternoon session of school on that day, we hurried to seize our equipments, which were stored in the entrance hall. Passing into the yard, we formed in open column in front of the Academy in order to salute with "present arms" the Preceptor, Professor, and Assistant, as they left the building. We had a genuine "field day," when, with drum and fife, we marched through the streets of the village, and drew up in front of the residences of the Trustees of the Academy and magnates of the town, and were refreshed by the courteous hospitalities of those thus complimented. The Cadets, as they would

VIEW ON WATER STREET.

be styled in these days, paraded again at the close of the annual exhibition.

The evening before the Fourth of July it was the custom of the students to light a tar-barrel in a portion of the Academy grounds. A severe drought in my year rendered it somewhat hazardous. By direction of the Faculty this year the sport was transferred to "Jady Hill," across the river, and there we welcomed the coming day.

We bathed in the lower Swamscot, just outside the village. As I pass on the railroad, even now, I always look for that spot, and think I recognize where was situated the pier from which we were wont to make the plunge, and swim to the two-story dwelling on the high river-bank just below, a dwelling then unpainted, but now showing modern improvement and taste. There I learned to swim.

A favorite stroll was on the road leading southerly from the village, on the left of the Haverhill road, where stood the solitary abode of a gray-haired negro, with a rude drawing over the entrance. The drawing portrayed a man shooting a bear. The same road led to a pasture, — our nutting ground. On a wood path on the left was the abode of a Dinah, who used to entice the students with her root beer and cakes. Exeter was specially favored by that race, as one might have seen on the "bobolition" celebration of the abolition of slavery in England and her colonies by the efforts of Wilberforce and Clarkson. My recollection is of a motley procession of them, on that day, with music, banners, guns, and pikes, parading the streets, and saluting the residences of prominent citizens, courteously, though not with entire gravity, received or observed by all.

When the courts were in session, we occasionally, as boyish curiosity prompted, strolled in to see what was going on. I there first saw Jeremiah Mason and Daniel Webster, Portsmouth lawyers, just entering on a famous career, and the towering stature of the one, and the tall, somewhat spare form of the other, together with his dark brow and eye and his raven-black hair, made an impression upon me never to be forgotten. George Sullivan and Ex-Governor Judge Smith were also to be noted. The spring elections were held in that court-room, and I have before my mind's eye the imposing figure of Governor Gilman, rising from his seat of honor, assigned him by the town officers, to cast his vote in the election. He himself was one of the gubernatorial candidates. In that day of simple, dignified honesty, I thought to myself that the Governor, of course, would not vote for himself.

It gives me great pleasure to review in this way the memory of the admirable discipline and manners of the school of seventy years ago, if that could be called *discipline*, where was never heard a loud tone of censure or command, — no motion seen to quell disorder, except now and then a light tap at the desk of the Principal. There were rebukes, and sometimes severer methods, but such were always administered in the library, and always with effect; for in presence of the school the erring one was directed to go to the library, while the Principal followed with impressive bearing, and we knew that it was a grave occasion. Mr. Abbot, who soon became Dr. Abbot, was feared, respected, and loved alike by student and townsman; and the decorum and manly bearing which characterized the school while he was at its head must have deeply impressed itself upon the lives of those who were so fortunate as to be his pupils.

A. S. PACKARD.

THE ACADEMY IN 1822.

ENTERING at Exeter in 1822, I remained about four years. My teacher in Latin was Dr. Abbot; in Greek, Gideon L. Soule; and in Mathematics, John P. Cleaveland. Of all my classmates I remember James C. Richmond, of Providence, the best. He was a brilliant and rapid scholar. I remember, too, James Sullivan, of Exeter, a rough young boy, who showed the diamond as fast as it was cut. I tried to hold a decent rank in the languages, was a member of the Golden Branch, and on leaving was assigned the Latin Salutatory; having occupied the Monitor's chair during my last year.

The Monitor was appointed from among the oldest and most advanced students. It was an honorable office, and the holder sat in a conspicuous seat. When the office was vacant, a successor was commissioned by the Preceptor, who simply announced, "Jones, you will take the book." The Monitor kept a register, and for any misconduct he placed a mark against the delinquent's name. From this book there was no appeal. The school was as orderly under the Monitor as under the Principal. Indeed, if, as rarely happened, an occasion for some slight correction occurred, in the presence of the Principal the Monitor's book was the medium of correction; the Doctor denouncing, "Monitor, note Smith."

The assembled school, over which my eye so often swept, seems still fresh before me; but during these sixty years nearly all the individual faces have faded from me. I clearly recall John H. Morison, a large, awkward country boy, whose benevolent countenance glowed with intellect, and who was very popular. In our time, the students sat in the Academy under the care of their teachers during the day. They assembled in the Preceptor's room, in the morning, for religious exercises. The boys read from the Bible a chapter or part of one, two verses each in rotation as they were seated, each rising to read. The boy sitting next the one who ended the lesson carefully noted the place, and began there the next morning. After a prayer by the teacher whose turn it was to conduct the service, teachers and pupils repaired to their respective rooms, and recitations commenced. In this large room the

Monitor always presided in the absence of a teacher. When the Doctor entered, all arose and stood till he took his place at his desk; and the same respect was rendered whenever he passed out and left the Monitor in charge. When the hour for closing the day arrived, at the tap of the bell all assembled, as in the morning, to hear the Preceptor read the Bible and pray. Then he called, "Monitor, whose duty is it to sweep?" The Monitor, with his eye on the two names against which stood the most marks, answered, "Smith and Jones." "Smith and Jones sweep," ordered the Doctor; and the doom was irrevocable. Then the school was dismissed, the boys filed out in order, and bowed as they passed the Preceptor's desk. The duty to sweep was no sinecure. The pair appointed had to remain and sweep the room thoroughly, and, if fire was necessary, to bring from the basement sufficient wood for the next day's supply, and to have a good fire early and to tend it during the day. Two were always appointed; and if the Monitor's book did not furnish culprits, then he drew the requisite names from the alphabetical list. In this drawing, any student in the room was liable to be chosen. In the morning when the Doctor took his place at his desk, which was closed, like an old-fashioned pulpit, he glanced around it, and if the space within the railing had not been well swept, he called, "Monitor, who swept last?" "Smith and Jones, sir." "Smith and Jones, sweep to-morrow!" To-morrow the desk was not neglected.

The "Tardy Monitor" kept account of absence and tardiness. His book was laid on the Preceptor's desk at the end of each week. A single tardy mark against a name the Preceptor cancelled without question; but more marks or an absence subjected the delinquent to close scrutiny, and perhaps to further trouble. The rule for attending prayers on Sunday morning was rigid. No fire was lighted, yet neither weather nor distance excused one from attending that service. The first bell on Sunday morning, in the winter time, was rung at sunrise. Fifteen minutes were allowed to the end of the second bell, and it was interesting, on a morning when the blue snow was sweeping across the paths, and the thermometer stood at zero, to see the boys tightening their cloaks about them, and hastening from all points to the glad covert of the cold Academy.

Among my earliest memories of the town, I recollect the old meeting-house that stood on the west side of the main street, a little way south from the entrance to Tan Lane. I attended meeting in it one Sunday. The sermon was by Rev. Thomas C. Upham, afterwards Professor in Bowdoin College. His theme was the unrighteous condemnation of Christ, judged even by the laws of his accusers. I think this was the last time the house was used for worship, it being taken down directly after. It was a wooden structure, with a very tall, slim spire springing from the ground, and connected with the main building only on one side.

The carpenters proceeded first to detach this spire, "emoti procumbunt cardine postes," and, with a shock that startled the villagers, it fell diagonally across the road. "Dedit ampla ruinam." The gathering boys wondered at the size of the weathercock, and curiously noted the shot with which some unhallowed gunner had peppered it long ago.

As with the schoolroom, so with the playground. The whole picture is full of life, but the particulars have faded. I have hardly forgotten Jeremiah Kimball, a large, elderly, sober lad, not much given to play. One day, the football fell far away from the crowd, and lay tempting before him. He drew back, and spent his full force; but the ball did not move, because — he had aimed too low, and kicked the solid root of a tree! Jerry is still dancing on one foot, and squeezing the toes of the other in his hand, — and with what a grimace!

Next, the contending players came to close quarters in a jam against the front fence, with the ball in the midst. In the hubbub one of us caught up David Wells, of Deerfield, and threw him over the fence, into the street. He was tall, and his long legs were some impediment in crossing the fence; but when he was well over, what with shouting on one side, and howling disgust on the other, the fence separated very distinct styles of vociferation. Thirty years after this, a lady in a far-off city laughingly reminded me of the scene; she, a girl, having witnessed it from her window across the common.

MOSES SOULE.

LIFE IN EXETER IN 1855.

I SHALL never forget John Emery's house, on Water Street, and the long, narrow room which I occupied, with its windows looking toward the woods, and down the river; nor shall I forget the old man and his kind wife. I had never been away from home before, and the life at Exeter was new and strange. The room opposite mine was occupied by C. C. Salter, of Portsmouth, a new boy, who afterwards became a successful Unitarian clergyman, but who was early **called** away from his labors on earth. The other boys were from New York, Texas, Northern New Hampshire, Massachusetts, and Louisiana, all of them older than **myself.**

The first interview with Dr. Soule, when he gave me a brief examination to determine in what class I should be entered, took place in his pleasant study, which looked out on to a large garden. It was an experience to be remembered, though now somewhat dimmed by the remembrance of my first day of Exeter school life. The large schoolroom, in which so many had studied, who afterwards won for themselves national honor, was filled **with** boys from all parts of the country. How well I recall my surprise at the rising of all the scholars when the Doctor **entered** to open the school **with the** well-remembered prayer, — a prayer which we could soon repeat as well as the Doctor himself. How well I recall my first recitation to Mr. Hoyt, afterwards

Chancellor of Washington University. These first impressions will never be effaced.

I arrived in Exeter at the opening of the summer term, and enjoyed to the full the walks in the woods in search of May flowers, the visits to the pottery, where we were never weary of watching the skilful fingers of the potter, the rides occasionally enjoyed, to Hampton and Rye, and the exciting games of football. Not so pleasant was the "sweeping out," in punishment for some transgression of order; or the anxious watching of the Doctor's fingers, as he took one name after another from the box, — in terror lest mine should come, when my lesson was not well learned; or the various kinds of hazing to which I, with other newcomers, was subjected.

I shall ever remember the Christmas season, when we "confiscated," as we called it when afterwards in the army, one from John Emery's flock of geese, and how we stewed it, for we had no other means of cooking, and wondered at its unusual toughness. This was all explained when the old man remarked at breakfast, the next morning, in tones of sorrow, that he could not find the gander which he had owned for over ten years. And I shall never forget the expeditions after apples in the orchards surrounding the town, — apples which I shall always believe to have been the best in the world; also the fights between the "townies" and the "cads," as the Academy boys were then called. I specially remember the ringing of the Academy bell, one Fourth of July, when no watchman was on hand, because, as the Doctor remarked, when addressing the school after the holiday, he had trusted in the honor of the students. After this address, how small and mean we all felt, and how we resolved never again to do a dishonorable act!

Fresh in my mind is the first entrance into the mysterious room in the east wing of the old Academy, appropriated to the Golden Branch, and my pride when I wore the Golden Branch badge with "F. S. T." thereon inscribed. Plainly before my mind come the forms of my friends, some dead, others gone, I know not where, and yet others, who to-day are conferring honor on the Academy which did so much to prepare them for the duties of life. But this is no place to speak of them; what is needed is a reminiscence of life in Exeter.

The old wooden club-house was in existence when I was there, the brick one was not yet completed, and many of the boys boarded about the town. On the whole, we were a quiet set of boys, and but few gave any trouble. Dr. Soule, Mr. Hoyt, and Mr. Sawyer were the teachers, and they did good work.

A few of the boys rowed on the river, all played football and other games, though there were no clubs, and many of us spent the half-holidays in going on tramps through the woods, with an occasional night of stolen pleasure, when we camped out, little dreaming that most of us would camp out under far different circumstances when we had donned the blue and shouldered the musket.

At the close of the summer term, the custom had been before my time, and it was continued afterwards, to hold a celebration in the large hall over the Academy; there a poem and an oration were delivered. A hot contest for the offices, prolonged for several days, engendered such an uncomfortable feeling that in 1856 no celebration was held.

I have often intended revisiting Exeter, but am glad that I have never seen it since I left for Harvard, in the summer of 1856; for now the picture has never been dimmed, and it is as fresh in my mind as it was when I walked its streets, rambled through its woods, examined the books in Lovering's bookstore, and sat in the old Unitarian Church to listen to Rev. Mr. Cole. At this church several of us fell into sad disgrace, when a minister from abroad detected us in reading magazines instead of listening to his eloquence. As I sit in my study more than a thousand miles from the old town, the unaccustomed snow all about the streets of this city, which was only just starting when I was at Exeter, I forget the years which have passed, annihilate the distance, and am once more starting from my room to hurry through the snow, that I may be in time for "chapel." Again the old, familiar forms come trooping into the great room of the Academy, and, seeing an old graduate on the platform, we give him the time-honored salute, which even the grave Doctor permits. I wake from this dream, wondering whether I shall ever revisit Exeter, and whether the students would welcome me as we greeted the "old scholars" in that time, so long ago.

WILLIAM E. COPELAND.

AUNT RINGE.

IN the days of Doctor Abbot, a woman who always went by the name of Aunt Ringe took students to board. In those days but few boys had fires in their own rooms, and so it was customary for them to study in the living room of the family with whom they boarded. In the house of Aunt Ringe, however, the boys each evening had the dining-room quite to themselves, and on this account it was a favorite boarding-place. A custom of the house was the ringing of a nine-o'clock bell; this was the signal for the boys to fold their books, and like the Arabs, to "silently steal away." They seldom grumbled, or begged to be allowed to sit up later, but, one night after the bell had been rung, they all remained and studied with a zeal which, during the day, would be more commendable than common. Aunt Ringe observed that the young men were not disposed to retire, and so began, after the manner of women, to ask questions. "Boys, did n't you hear that bell?" "O, let us stay a little while longer," said the boys, suddenly disposed to be studious. "Did n't you hear that bell?" was the only response.

"Just a few moments more." "Didn't you hear that bell?"

Not even students could stand such a volley of questions, and, worsted in the debate, they retired from the dining-room. Once up stairs, however, they all began to march back and forth, from room to room, in a manner which would have been a model even for the Exeter police force. They took great care not to close the doors *carefully*, and the good lady of the house listened patiently until midnight to the ceaseless tramp of the young Trojans. Then, taking her stand at the foot of the stairs, she called one of the boys down, and, taking him affectionately by the collar, plunged him forthwith out of the front door into the snow. We assure you that he was not long lonesome out in the dark night, for before the bewildered youth could pick himself up and collect his scattered senses, he had company.

Thus, calling all the young patrolmen one by one, she escorted them to the door, and saw them across the threshold. Among the number is said to have been the son of Dr. Gideon Soule. Once out in the stormy night, for the snow was falling fast, these young mischief-makers either walked about in a dazed way till dawn, or else found shelter and solace with some schoolmate.

The next day Aunt Ringe told Dr. Abbot that a few of the boys could return, but some of them never could board with her again. The result was, that she had no boarders the next year, but only for that year, for afterwards her house was ever full. The boys well knew the real kindness of her heart, and, after all, admired her resolution and old-fashioned New England pluck. In fact, she became quite a heroine.

ANECDOTES.

A FORMER student writes: —

"Messrs. Cilley and Wentworth were in my time much as you see them now, — good teachers, who did their work on the cast-iron principle of 'Do the work and fill the pattern, or go when the term ends.'

"Professor Wentworth was, I think, the best-educated teacher we had. He was the only one in my time who ever said anything in the class-room, outside of the lesson. I remember once or twice when we got the laugh on him, and the boys applauded to the echo. I was up in Greek history one day, describing the battle of Marathon, and inadvertently said 'fit' for 'fought.' In a moment he was on me, with 'Well, ———, do you find that word in your vocabulary?' 'Yes, sir,' I said, "third person singular indicative present, from *fio*." The boys fairly yelled, and amid the din he 'flunked' me and called up the next victim.

"Mr. Wentworth was a red-hot Republican during the war times. Decrying one day the general ignorance of young Americans about things much talked about, he declared that not three boys in the class could tell the meaning of the word *liberty*. An ambitious Democrat, knowing that Fort Warren was then filled with political prisoners, held up his hand. The Professor nodded an assent, and was told that it meant filling jails and bastiles with free citizens, — to the amusement of the applauding class."

Of Dr. Soule, one writes: — "The old Doctor was constitutionally opposed to drinking. One day, a classmate of mine, whom I will call Smith, got gloriously drunk. The Doctor called him up, and made him detail the course of the spree, which included a visit to the three or four groggeries of the village, and the absorption of four or five glasses of ale, three glasses of wine, and a horn or two of whiskey. In holy horror, as Smith ended the enumeration, the Doctor held up his hands, saying, 'Why, Smith, if I at my age had drank that much, I should have been carried home on a stretcher.' 'Possibly,' said the imperturbable Smith, 'some heads are constitutionally weak to spiritual influences.' The Doctor smote off Smith's academic head that instant, and he went home on the evening train."

CHAPTER XIII.

SOCIETIES.

THE CHRISTIAN FRATERNITY. — THE GOLDEN BRANCH. — THE G. L. SOULE LITERARY SOCIETY. — THE BOAT CLUB. — THE ATHLETIC ASSOCIATION.

THE societies of the Phillips Exeter Academy are, at present, six in number; namely, the Christian Fraternity, the Golden Branch, the G. L. Soule Literary Society, the Boat Club, the Athletic Association, and the Π K Δ. Of these the first is a religious society, which holds its meetings every Sunday evening for the discussion of some portion of the Scriptures; the two next are literary, and aim at giving their members practice in parliamentary law and in debate; while the Boat Club and Athletic Association are merely organizations for the support of the various athletic interests of the students. The Π K Δ is secret in its aims and in its meetings, and comes under the head of what are generally known as Greek-letter fraternities.

We have endeavored, in the following pages, to give a brief but accurate account of each of these societies, from its foundation to the present time, showing what have been its objects, and with what success it has met. Of the Π K Δ, as will be readily understood, but little can be said.

SOCIETIES.

In addition to the organizations mentioned above, other societies have from time to time been formed in the school; of these but slight mention is made, as they no longer exist.

THE CHRISTIAN FRATERNITY.

"Remember now thy Creator in the days of thy youth."
ECCLES. xii. 1.
"For righteousness exalteth a nation." — PROV. xiv. 34.

ONE Sabbath evening, many years ago,[1] nine young men,[2] all students of the Phillips Exeter Academy, met together for the first time, to hold a prayer-meeting. After a few preliminary remarks on the proper mode of instituting such a meeting, it was proposed "that we all kneel, and ask God in prayer for Divine guidance and direction."[3] So reads the old record.

On the Wednesday following this meeting, these young men again met, and, on the principle that "Union is strength," determined to found a permanent organization. At this meeting a committee was appointed to draft a constitution. April 23, 1856, the report of this committee having been received, the constitution was adopted, and the Christian Fraternity

---

[1] April 13, 1856.
[2] The names of the nine founders of this society are as follows: George W. Atherton, H. M. Sanborn, S. C. Richardson, A. S. Symmes, T. S. Dodge, Daniel B. Fitts, Albert L. Norris, George W. Barber, and Gilman C. Hickok.
[3] Records of the Christian Fraternity, Vol. I.

of the Phillips Exeter Academy became a duly organized society. Although the meetings of this young and feeble society were for many years but thinly attended, they were nevertheless delightful occasions, and did much good, as the records plainly indicate. These old records are themselves wonderful writings. Thoroughly fresh and wholesome, they revive one like a sudden breeze from a mountain height. Among the signers of the constitution we find, written in round, schoolboy characters, the autographs of many men who have since become distinguished for great and good works, and honest, brave lives.

The officers of the society are but three, — President, Vice-President, and Secretary. Application for membership may be made by any student of the Academy, who "believes his sins are forgiven for Christ's sake," but his election must be unanimous. The meetings, formerly held semiweekly, at private houses, are now held each Sunday, in room No. 3 of the Academy; they are open to all, and are largely attended by the students. The anniversary of the founding of the society is celebrated in the school chapel on the last Sunday in the spring term; on these occasions the President makes a brief address, essays are read by the members, and hymns are sung.

From the introductory address of the President[1] delivered at the twenty-sixth anniversary of the society, one will perhaps obtain as good an idea of the growth

[1] Frank H. Cunningham.

and work of the society as in any other way. It is as follows : —

"Members and friends of the Christian Fraternity, — We come together for the last time this year, and we come to celebrate the twenty-sixth anniversary of our beloved society. During these twenty-six years the society has enrolled three hundred and fifty-three members, an average of thirteen, increasing from nine to twenty-eight, the present number. The average attendance of its meetings has increased, from eight in 1856, and seventeen in 1870, to over fifty during the present year. Since 1856 it has held over thirteen hundred regular meetings, beside many informal prayer-meetings, in private houses, in the jail, and at the bedsides of the sick. Throughout all these years the Lord has been with us, to aid and to bless; but I feel sure that, had we lived nearer the Lord throughout all these years, much more good could have been done, many more saved, and our own lives made richer and more valuable. What shall we do with the power we possess? Shall we wilfully waste it, — shall we hide it, in fear and trembling, like the slothful servant, — or shall we go courageously forward, leading prayerful Christian lives, raising the helpless, encouraging the weak, helping the needy, — in short, doing actual work? Visiting the old Phillips manse in North Andover, two weeks ago, the great-granddaughters of our Founder's brother sent you a message. Shaking her forefinger, one of these good ladies said, with great earnestness, 'Tell the boys to cling to the faith! Tell them to cling to the faith! For just as sure as they desert it, I believe the ghosts of the founders will rise and haunt them.'

"**Let** us cling to the faith. **Acts** make habits; habits, **characters;** and characters, destinies; and rest assured **that, if we** but hold fast, if **we** are humble, **yet** brave, and **if** we work and pray, our destinies will not fail to crown **our hopes with** success."

THE GOLDEN BRANCH SOCIETY OF THE PHILLIPS EXETER ACADEMY.

"𝔉𝔯𝔦𝔢𝔫𝔡𝔰𝔥𝔦𝔭'𝔰 **𝔖𝔞𝔠𝔯𝔢𝔡 𝔗𝔦𝔢.**"

"Latet arbore opaca
Aureus et foliis et lento vimine ramus,
Junoni infernæ dictus sacer." — ÆN. VI. 136.

THE Trojan war was **ended. Troy was** in ashes and the kingdom of Priam **was no more,** when Æneas and his little band **of** followers **sought** the base of Antandros to **build** the fleet which was to carry them **over** the deep to a better land, and away from the smoking ruins of their once beautiful city. After much preparation they set sail, and for many long and weary months **we** find them tossed about **on** the sea. But one bright morning **the** fleet **sails into the** harbor **of** Cumæ. The sails are furled, and Æneas goes in **haste** to consult the Sibyl, so famous for her oracles, **and into her** ear he pours the request that he may visit the world **of** Pluto and **see his beloved father Anchises.** No king **on his** throne **was ever more happy** than he, as, in obedience to the Sibyl**'s words, he goes** in search of the "Golden Branch" **of the golden** tree, which is to give **him** an entrance into **the** lower world, and the opportunity once more to see Anchises. Having found it, he easily persuades the gray-haired Charon to ferry him over the dark river, and, protected by the mighty influence of the "Golden Branch" which he carries in his hand, he gazes upon an unknown world.

With passing years the Golden Branch has lost none of its power. The Golden Branch of Æneas conducted him into the world of *spirits* in safety, and the Golden Branch of the Phillips Exeter Academy for sixty-five years has been ushering its members into the world of *men*, where, like the Trojan hero, they gaze in astonishment upon things before unseen. The Golden Branch is to-day trying to train young men to speak in the pulpit, at the bar, and in the senate, and is succeeding admirably, as can be shown by the large number of statesmen, lawyers, and clergymen who are proud to confess that they began their careers with fear and trembling, with downcast faces and hands in their pockets, before a Golden Branch audience. From the very time when Anchises bade farewell to his son, and in words most eloquent told him of the kingdom that he was to found, and of the glory of Rome and of the Cæsars, the Golden Branch has always been an inspiration to eloquence.

Before this society came into existence there was for a time an organization called the Rhetorical Society of the Phillips Exeter Academy. Its constitution resembled that of the Golden Branch, and among its members we find the names of A. F. Hildreth, Jonathan Phillips (a relative of the Founder of the Academy), George Bancroft, the historian, Gideon L. Soule, and Charles Soule, who afterwards became the Founder and first President of the Golden **Branch**. They held meetings **every two** weeks, and **each one** present was obliged to be prepared with a declamation, either original or otherwise. In 1820 this society ceased to exist. Two years before this the Golden Branch had been founded. On the evening of July 16, 1818, the ten original members [1] **of** this society assembled **in** the Academy, where **Professor** Hildreth performed the initiating ceremonies with the assistance **of Mr. O. W. B. Peabody, who read the** constitution and laws which **were then adopted.** At the next meeting Charles Soule was chosen President, **and** the following question was discussed : "To which should we submit with less reluctance, the privation of sight or hearing?" No doubt that question was discussed and settled for all time by the wise words and votes of the members, as many other weighty matters have been discussed and decided upon by their successors in the same society. The constitution, by-laws, **and** form of initiation, as presented to the society by Professor Hildreth **and** accepted, differed only in a few **points** from those we now use. It was then a secret society, and each candidate for admission must solemnly swear, before God **and** the assembled witnesses, that if,

---

[1] John G. Merrill, David R. Straw, George **W.** Gordon, Jonathan Ward, Jr., John Kelley, W. A. Whitwell, Elijah Colburn, Thomas W. Dorr, John P. Robinson, and Charles Soule.

after becoming acquainted with the objects of the association, he should decline to become a member, he should never reveal what he had already heard and seen. This " iron-clad " oath was too much for some of the more timid boys, and many of them, having been initiated thus far, did not desire any further knowledge of the mysteries of the Golden Branch, and were cast among the gentiles without. The society adopted the motto " F. S. T." (which interpreted means " Friendship's Sacred Tie "), and even kept the translation of these mysterious letters from those who were not " brothers."

The presidents and the critics are continually exhorting their brothers to stand firmly together, as if they were the common enemies of all outsiders. The constitution provided that meetings should be held once in two weeks, and so every other Saturday afternoon they met in the exhibition hall if it were summer, but if winter in the main hall or Latin room, where the Trustees furnished them with fuel. There for about four hours they held secret session. This of course aroused the curiosity of the other students, and we shall see later how it was the cause of trouble and ill-feeling.

The first inaugural address of the President of the Golden Branch was delivered by President Robinson, in 1824, and ever since that time it has been customary for that officer to address the society when he enters upon the duties of his office. A part of President

Robinson's address **is** interesting, as it shows how little **the** town-boys and students loved **each other**. But a **few** years before his time, he says, "the boys **used** to go out armed to a **man** with cudgels, clubs, and **even** pistols, and meet the foe armed in a like manner (**with** the addition of a fife and drum), with almost as much spirit and animosity **as two armies** meet to decide some long-debated contest, . . . when the instructors, the Trustees, and **even** the town officers were called **out to** still the commotion." He adds, **that the good old matrons used to** wonder what made the **boys so** much **more peaceable in his** time, and thought it because they were smaller; but President Robinson shows us that it **was** the effect of the Golden Branch. The boys knew well **that** to enter this society they must be of good character, **as** well as good scholars. They therefore restrained their desires for a riot and a fight more on account of the Golden Branch than on account of their smallness of stature. However, sometimes after becoming members they seem to have forgotten their desire to be virtuous, and **the** records tell **us** that several were caught in the act **of** whittling chairs, and fined for the offence. We now come to the stormy times **of** 1840 and thereabout.

The Golden Branch was at the **time, and** had always been, a secret society. The members, bound together by an iron-creed and "Friendship's Sacred Tie," were happy in one another's love; but outside this little company the boys were "nursing their wrath to keep it warm."

Whenever the shingle bearing the mystic letters
"F. S. T." (the sign for a Golden Branch meeting)
was hung out, it was always greeted with cries of
"Fools Stick Together," and "Father Soule's Todd-
hoppers." Many were kept out of the society by some
single enemy, as at that time it required a unanimous
vote for admission. When the rejected candidates and
several members of the Golden Branch undertook to
found a new society under the name of the Phillips
Debating Club, they were informed by the Preceptor
that one society only could be allowed in the school,
and some of the leaders of the new society were
expelled. The Preceptor thought that two rival societies could not dwell together in peace; but we have
lived to see the day when side by side, in perfect
harmony, the Golden Branch and the G. L. Soule
Literary Society exist and do their work. The late
President Chadbourne of the Massachusetts Agricultural College, who was a member in 1845, writes
that politics at that time ran high, and there was
as much excitement about the election of officers as
we see now in the wider field of politics. There could
be seen traits of character which later life has only
made clearer. Sometimes the debates were loud and
long.

One evening they assembled to discuss "immigration." The Secretary thus describes the meeting · "An
ever memorable scene took place then, in relation
to the reconsideration of a vote passed at a previous

meeting **to hold the** election **of** officers after the anniversary. **My** humble abilities quail before the task of recording it. Some one **has** spoken of a certain brawl in the House of Commons as resembling the great earthquake of Calabria. I do not know what to compare this to, unless I **say it** was equivalent to the debate **in** Commons and **the** earthquake combined. Speaking **of** foreign immigrants naturally suggested ideas of Irish wakes and shillelah fights, and, although **no** heads **were broken, yet** a goodly **number had** their **tongues forced into their** mouths." Soon after **this the** first **critic was** appointed **to criticise at each** meeting the proceedings **of** the **previous one.** Each critic was obliged to write **whatever he** wished to say, and some **of** the suggestions made and some of the breaches of etiquette criticised **are** quite amusing. One says that "the member from Pittsfield had his feet on the President's desk during **most of** the meeting," and speaks of the member **from** Washington as "being clamorous to obtain **possession of a bottle that** was passing around."

 Prof. George A. Wentworth, when critic, tells how one of the members placed his feet on the President's table, in closer proximity to the Vice-President's olfac**tory organ than** was agreeable; **and** also says that "the **gentleman from Boston, when** it came his turn to speak, **jumped up, rose** on tiptoe, thrust his hands into his pants' pockets (rather a difficult operation, his coat being buttoned), drew out a plug of tobacco about eight inches long, bit off about half an inch, adjusted his quid, and commenced to speak." No wonder that soon after the critic's report was dropped from the programme, after a few months' trial, and not resumed for sixteen years. We have often heard those older than we say that the boys now are not as they used to be, and we begin to see the force of the remark. But of course the critic brings before our eyes only the faults, and a thorough search anywhere will bring plenty to light. The society now has critics, but they report orally, and the records are not preserved, so that future generations can exclaim, like the Pharisee, "Lord, I thank thee that I am not as other men!"

The Golden Branch has a cabinet of curiosities, which have been presented by friends. It has also a fine library, of about 2,500 volumes; this contains books of reference upon almost every debatable subject, besides all the works of the standard authors, and the later novels. In 1824, the library contained 293 volumes, and in 1834 it had increased to over 1,000 volumes. At first it was increased by the gifts of friends, and some money was donated by the Trustees; but of late years the society has expended its own money for books, until we now have a library unsurpassed by that of any society in a school of this character. During the past year the books have been re-covered, re-numbered, and a new catalogue has been printed. In 1842 originated the custom of having a lecture at the end of each year. These have proved of great interest to the school, amusing **as well** as instructing. The following gentlemen addressed the society previous to 1858: —

ABRAM JAQUITH	1842
CHARLES J. GILMAN	1843
JAMES F. BROWN	1844
AUGUSTUS WOODBURY	1845
HORATIO STEBBINS	1846
PATRICK H. TOWNSEND	**1847**
CHARLES J. GILMAN	1848
Anniversary not celebrated	1849
SYLVESTER WATERHOUSE	1850
JOHN PERRY ALLISON	1851
WILLARD FLAGG BLISS	1852
BENJAMIN F. PRESCOTT	1853
JOSHUA W. BEEDE	1854
GEORGE W. C. NOBLE	1855
Anniversary not celebrated	1856
GEORGE S. YORK	1857

Since 1858, until within a few years, the anniversaries **have** not been celebrated; but recently the society **has** had the pleasure of listening **to** some of the best speakers in the country, among them President Chadbourne, Ralph Waldo Emerson, and Charles Theodore Russell, of Boston. Last June, Edward Atkinson, **Esq.** delivered an interesting and practical address, upon "**The** Advantages **of being** an American Boy." If possible, **the lecturer of this** centennial year should **tell us some of the** advantages of being a Golden Branch boy. Surely such men as Ex-Governor B. F. Prescott, of New Hampshire, and a host of others, ought to be able to do something creditable for the society which gave them their early training in declamation. Three of the present instructors, Professors Wentworth, Cilley, and Tufts, besides Professor Pennell, who has lately resigned, have been members of the Golden Branch.

If one needs proof of the kind of men the society has trained, he needs but to look over the names on its roll, to be satisfied that few such organizations have accomplished as much.

There are a large number of gentlemen who have accepted honorary membership, and such men as Webster, Emerson, Sumner, and Whittier have not thought it beneath their dignity to accept the proffered honor. There are about seventy-five honorary members on the roll. The Golden Branch began its career with ten members. Its average membership has been about twenty. During the fifty-seven years ending with 1875, the whole number of members was as follows: —

Whole number of Initiated Members	1063
Number deceased	186
Number surviving	877
Whole number of Honorary Members	59
Number deceased	38
Number surviving	21

Since that time, two hundred and sixteen students have been initiated, making a total membership of twelve hundred and seventy-nine. At present there are forty members in the society, which is as many as the room will accommodate. A former member, returning and looking in upon a meeting after an absence of thirty or forty years, would scarcely recognize the society as the same that he himself once charmed with his eloquence. Time has wrought many changes in the Golden Branch during these years. It is no longer a secret society, but many are invited to hear the literary exercises of its meetings. The programme consists of a debate, participated in by four regular disputants appointed for the purpose, and by any from the house who wish to speak. Then follow readings and declamations. The aim of the society is to give as much practice in parliamentary law and extemporaneous speaking as time will permit. In a school like this, where there is no teacher of elocution, a debating club is invaluable. The society now has a pleasant room in the Academy building for its meetings. It is true, the floor is uncarpeted, and the walls adorned with pictures a trifle too ancient, but it is hoped that, by the efforts now being made, and the assistance of the friends of the society, it may offer to future members a room simply and tastefully, if not æsthetically adorned. Across the hall are held the meetings of the Soule Society, and here in peace they dwell together.

The Golden Branch never was in a more prosperous condition than it is to-day. Each man tries to do his part, wherein lies success. Napoleon, when exhorting his soldiers to deeds of valor, looked up at the mighty Pyramids, and exclaimed, "My men, forty centuries are looking down upon you!" Some young member of the Golden Branch rises to speak for the first time: he trembles and falters, but, inspired by the thought that the members of the past sixty-five years are looking down upon HIM, he takes courage, and, forgetting that his fellow-students sit before him, wins his first debate. With the records of this noble society before us, who will say that the coming years shall not see him at the bar, or in the halls of legislation, or in the pulpits of our churches, repeating this success of his youthful days?

THE GIDEON LANE SOULE LITERARY SOCIETY OF THE PHILLIPS EXETER ACADEMY.

"*Fortiter, Fideliter, Feliciter.*"

ALTHOUGH the Golden Branch offered to the students of the Academy rare opportunities for practice in debate and literary work, yet, as its membership was naturally confined to a few, it did not entirely satisfy the wants of all the students. This, rather than any spirit of rivalry, was the cause which led to the formation of a new society.

In the fall term of 1881 it was proposed by the students rooming in Gorham Hall to organize a society for literary work, confined exclusively to themselves, but they were induced by others interested in the movement to throw it open to all in the Academy.

A petition for organization was at once circulated by G. P. F. Hobson, '82, and J. M. Merriam, '82, who were foremost in the project, and received about forty signatures. The Faculty immediately granted this request, and a preliminary meeting of the petitioners and others was held, November 5, 1881. F. H. Cunningham, '82, H. W. Hinde, '83, and Thomas Hunt, '82, were appointed a committee to draft the constitution.

The officers for the first term were J. M. Merriam, '82, President; G. P. F. Hobson, '82, Vice-President; A. A. Gleason, '82, Secretary; and W. F. Gleason, '82, Sergeant at Arms. The constitution was prepared with great care by the committee, and has proved a safe groundwork for the proceedings of the society. In memory of him who by his energetic management and teaching did so much to place the Academy in its present high position, this society was named the Gideon Lane Soule Literary Society.

The first few meetings were held in recitation-room No. 1 of the Academy building. The exercises consisted of an original composition, a debate, on which four disputants were appointed, a declamation, a reading, and extemporaneous remarks on subjects selected by the President. This last feature, suggested by Dr.

Perkins, is to be especially commended, as it tended to develop confidence, and power of ready response. In addition to these regular exercises, an inaugural address was delivered by each President as he took possession of the gavel. The society adopted as its motto the words, "Fortiter, fideliter, feliciter," and it is to be hoped that every member will strive to keep this motto before him, to do his work bravely, faithfully, and thus, in the end, to achieve success.

The officers for the second term were E. J. Swift, '82, President; Thomas Hunt, '82, Vice-President; H. T. Shepard, '84, Secretary; E. J. Wells, '82, Sergeant at Arms.

As the society grew in numbers, and as it became evident that it was to become a permanent institution in the school, need was felt for a special society room, and, by petition, the privilege was obtained of using the front room on the upper floor of the eastern wing. In order to furnish this room, a public entertainment was given in the Town Hall on the 25th of February, 1882, by the members of the society, assisted by a quartette from the Harvard Glee Club. The debate of the evening, on the subject, "Resolved, That Ireland should remain under British control," was presented by J. M. Merriam, '82, and G. P. F. Hobson, '82, in the affirmative, and by L. M. Garrison, '84, and E. J. Swift, '82, in the negative. Paul K. Ames, '83, delivered an oration on "Character and Influence," and John L. Ames a declamation. This entertainment was eminently successful. **It was also said to be** highly creditable.

Soon after, the Soule library, consisting of about **one** thousand volumes, **was** placed in the charge of the society.

The following officers for the third term were elected: G. P. F. Hobson, **'82,** President; Paul **K.** Ames, '83, Vice-President; G. B. Taylor, **'85,** Secretary; and W. H. Payne, '85, Sergeant at Arms.

The members of the society from **the Class of '82** presented, as **their** parting gift, an engraving **of** "Henry Clay delivering his farewell address before the United **States** Senate." At the express **wish of Mrs.** Soule, a crayon portrait of her husband **was** presented to the society by the members of the Soule family.

The second year of **the** society found it still full **of** zeal and earnestness. The officers for the first term were H. T. Shepard, '84, President; J. L. Ames, '83, Vice-President; Alan Cunningham, '85, Secretary; G. P. Buck, '85, Librarian.

During this term many members **were** initiated, and **all** the meetings were well supported.

The following officers were chosen for the winter term: C. S. Elgutter, '83, President; W. J. Chase, '84, Vice-President; W. N. Chase, '84, Secretary; L. A. L. Gale, '83, **Librarian.**

On March 9, **the** Harvard Glee Club gave a concert **in the** Town Hall, for the benefit of the society. This concert **was** well attended, and **met** with the success due to the efforts of the members of the society, and to the excellence of the concert. The proceeds were used to increase the library.

The officers of the spring term were G. B. Taylor, '85, President; C. H. Pennypacker, '84, Vice-President; G. W. Wheeler, '85, Secretary; O. C. Joline, '85, Librarian.

The exercises were varied on several occasions, and other interesting programmes substituted. A mock trial was held in the winter term of the second year, and eloquent pleas were made by embryo lawyers in support of their clients. Many profound questions of State and national importance have been clearly argued by this society, and conclusious have been reached with fewer words and with much less loss of time than in our national houses of Congress.

Thus for two years this society has flourished, and if its prosperity during that time can be made a criterion of the future, then there is in store for it a long and prosperous existence.

THE BOAT CLUB.

As will be seen hereafter, in the chapter on "Sports and Games," boating was first recognized as one of the sports of the Academy in 1864. Although it soon became quite popular as an amusement, still no movement was made until 1872 to form an association for the purpose of encouraging rowing, or of establishing it permanently as a branch of the school athletics. In the fall of that year, after one or two preliminary meetings of those interested, a committee was appointed to draft a constitution suitable for a Boat Club. On October 5, this committee reported, and the constitution which they then submitted was adopted. The following officers were then elected to serve for the ensuing year : President, W. N. Swift, '73 ; V. P. and Commodore, D. V. P. Loring, '73 ; Secretary and Treasurer, H. J. Harwood, '73; Directors, R. B. Blodgett, '73, R. P. Hastings, '73, J. H. Murray, '74. At the next meeting, T. Heminway, '73, was added to the Board of Directors.

The plan on which this society was first organized was as impracticable as it was novel. It embraced the formation of a stock company, the shares of which were to be assessable for all current expenses, and were to be forfeited for non-payment of dues and assessments. The scheme was at first successful; the stock was readily disposed of, and the treasury soon filled. But subsequent events proved the inconvenience of this organization, and a club was formed on October 17, 1874, on a more practical basis.

The first boat-house used by the students was the cellar of the old church, near the ice-houses ; the crews at this time rowed on Fresh River. In the latter part of 1872, after the Club was formed, the boat-house now in use was built, at a cost of three hundred and fifteen dollars.

Although burdened by debt and heavy expenses, and often threatened by the jealous zeal of the devotees of other branches of athletics, the Boat Club has had, in the main, a prosperous course, and has found many enthusiastic supporters.

In the earliest days of the Club, the custom was introduced of holding a regatta at some time during the spring of each year, consisting at first of races between four-oared or six-oared crews, selected from the school at large, and, later on, between six-oared class crews.

To defray the current expenses of the Club, an entrance fee of two dollars is required of each member, and an annual fee of the same amount. The regular meetings and the elections of officers are held on the second Wednesday of the first and last terms of the school year. Special meetings may be called at any time.

The beautiful and tasteful ensign of the Club was adopted in 1872; it consists of a light-blue swallow-tail flag, on which appear in silver-gray (the school color) the letters B. C., P. E. A.

A detailed account of all races and regattas of the Boat Club will be found in the chapter on "Sports and Games."

THE ATHLETIC ASSOCIATION.

THE Athletic Association was founded in 1875, in order to more thoroughly protect, support, and unite the various athletic interests of the school. At the first meeting, which was held on the 6th of September, the following officers were elected : President, Hastings, '76 ; Vice-President, Winsor, '76 ; Secretary, Babcock, '78 ; Directors, Huidekoper, '76, House, '78, and Bartlett, '78 ; Executive Committee, Bond, '76, Burleigh, '77, and Thomas, '77.

Although, as we have seen, the preliminary steps towards forming the association were taken as early as 1875, still it did not become a permanent organization until 1878. In the fall of this year, Messrs. Burke, '81, Perry, '80, and Hooker, '80, were appointed a committee to draft a suitable constitution. They reported in the following December, and the constitution which they then submitted was adopted. By the provisions of this constitution, as it now stands, the association has full and entire supervision over the base ball and football interests of the school; indeed, no one can become a member of either team unless he be a member of the association.

The captain of the nine and the captain of the eleven are elected at the last regular meeting of each year, to serve for the next year. Those who compose the two teams are selected by a committee of three, consisting of the captain, and two others chosen at large from the members of the Association. Before becoming final, however, the acts of these committees, as well as all measures of every committee, must be referred to the Board of Directors. The Directors have the power of sanction or veto, and from their decision there is no appeal.

To meet the expenses of the association, an entrance fee of one dollar, and a fee of fifty cents per term, are paid by all members. Regular meetings of the Association are held on or before the second Saturday, and also on the last Saturday, of the first and third terms of each school year. Special meetings may be convened at any time, at the request of ten members. Due notice of all meetings must be posted by the Secretary on the bulletin-board.

CHAPTER XIV.

THE EXONIAN.

ITS ORIGIN. — THE CENSORSHIP OF THE PRESS. — MATERIAL PROGRESS. — EDITORS. — MISCELLANEOUS.

ITS ORIGIN.

IN the last days of the winter term of 1878, Mariett, '78, Balch, '79, and Needles, '80, conceived the idea of establishing an Academy paper. The honor of making the first suggestion lies between Mariett and Balch. They were rooming together in Abbot Hall, and while conversing the suggestion was made, which soon ripened into a settled purpose. Needles was invited to join. At first he hesitated, but after some discussion his doubts vanished, and he became as enthusiastic as the others. This, then, was the situation: three young men, without experience in newspaper work, but having energy, some common sense, and such a training as gives to boys of nineteen a fairly good literary taste, had resolved, if possible, to edit and publish a school paper. Those who understand the many details of editorial work, even in small publications, will appreciate how doubtful were the prospects of success; but the boys took the risks and gayly launched their little craft upon the ocean of journalism, hopeful, but not too confident of success. Care and hard work brought prosperity, and in spite of mistakes and mishaps the "Exonian" became firmly established.

THE CENSORSHIP OF THE PRESS.

THE first requisite was the permission of the Faculty. This was only obtained after much discussion and some coaxing. Some members of the Faculty were incredulous as to success, some thought that the editorial work would interfere with studies, while all doubted whether it was desirable for the students to publish a school paper. Finally, however, their opposition yielded to the entreaties and promises of the editors, and they have had little occasion to regret giving their assent, as the work has been for the most part creditably done, and the paper, becoming a power in the school, has used its influence fairly, maintained a dignified yet modest style, and always aimed to uphold the eminent reputation of the Academy. The editors have usually stood high in their classes, and their school work has never suffered by reason of their connection with the Exonian. Members of the Faculty during the last few years have approved the paper and shown warm interest in its welfare, often furnishing items and suggesting topics for its columns.

The Exonian, however, has not always pleased the Faculty. At the outset, some of the editorials were too free in criticizing the government of the Academy, and the editors were "invited to confer" with Dr. Perkins. They repaired to the Doctor's residence, and an extended talk ensued. Their errors were pointed out, and they were warned that a repetition thereof would be followed by the suppression of the paper. About the same time, another professor informed one of the editors that the government of the Academy was an absolute monarchy, and one of its functions was a "censorship of the press," which would hold the Exonian to a strict accountability. This hint, together with Dr. Perkins's warning, was sufficient. The actions of the Faculty were criticised no more that term.

During the next year one of the editors made a narrow escape. He wrote a "slashing" article about what had been said by a professor in a recent recitation, which was duly set up, and the whole edition containing it printed. But before distribution, it somehow came to the knowledge of the professor, who at once notified the writer of the serious consequences which would follow the appearance of such a criticism. The editor at once ordered a new edition printed, with the objectionable article omitted. The first edition was destroyed, the life of the paper saved, and the expulsion of the offender averted. With these exceptions, the Faculty's interference has seldom been necessary.

MATERIAL PROGRESS.

THE financial history of the Exonian is, almost without a break, a record of prosperity. At the beginning the business details were puzzling to the boys. The size and shape of the paper, subscription price, advertising rates, etc., were arranged with the advice of the editor of the News-Letter. A goodly number of advertisements and a subscription list of fair proportions were secured. With scarcely an exception the Trustees, Faculty, and students subscribed, as did also a considerable number of Alumni and townspeople. An agreement was made with the News-Letter office to print an edition of four hundred weekly, for eighteen dollars. The first term the paper just about paid its way. In the second year financial difficulties were met, and the paper had its severest struggle for existence, but the editors by energetic efforts finally succeeded. The edition was reduced to three hundred, and the price of printing to fourteen dollars a week; the subscription rate was raised to seventy-five cents a term, or two dollars a year. When the accounts were closed for that year (1878–79) there was a deficiency which was balanced by assessing each editor a dollar and a half. In 1879–80, with the same prices and expenses, the paper prospered and paid five dollars to each editor of a year's incumbency, and three dollars each to those who had been members of the board for a shorter time.

At the beginning of 1880–81 the careful estimates

made for the coming year seemed to indicate that the paper would run in debt. After some negotiations, the News-Letter reduced its charge to twelve dollars a week. At the end of the year the financial result was better than had been expected, for in June, 1881, after all the bills were settled and an expensive supper paid for, a surplus of one hundred and eleven dollars remained. The year 1881–82 brought still greater prosperity, and the present year (1882–83) promises as well.

THE EDITORS.

E. H. MARIETT, '78, of Armand, Quebec; E. B. Balch, '79, of Plymouth, N. H.; and W. N. Needles, Jr., '80, of West Chester, Pa., were the first editors, and continued in office until the summer of 1878; after which Mariett entered Harvard, Balch became connected with the New Hampshire Press Association, and Needles went to the Harvard Law School for a year. In May, A. A. Wyman, '79, of West Acton, Mass., and W. C. Baylies, '80, of Taunton, Mass.; and in June, F. B. Fay, '80, of East Calais, Vt., and G. N. P. Mead, '81, of Everett, Mass., were chosen by the old board as their successors. These four conducted the paper during the fall term of 1878. They then elected M. H. Cushing, '79, of South Hingham, Mass., L. E. Sexton, '80, of Cleveland, Ohio, and C. A. Strong, '81, of Rochester, N. Y. In June, 1879, Wyman, Cushing, and Fay, having passed the examination, entered Harvard, and

C. E. Hamlin, '80, of Bangor, H. L. Dawes, Jr., '81, of Pittsfield, Mass., and G. R. Parsons, '82, of Providence, R. I., were chosen. Parsons immediately resigned, and Dawes resigned at the end of the first week of the new term, so that their connection with the paper was short. The only other changes during the year 1879–80 were the election of F. A. Aldrich, '81, of Flint, Mich., in October, and H. Osgood, '82, of Rochester, N. Y., in February. In 1880, Baylies, Sexton, and Hamlin entered Harvard. In June, W. M. Hall, Jr., '82, of Bedford, Pa., and R. P. Winters, '83, of Boston, were added. Strong and Aldrich did not return after vacation, the former entering Rochester University and the latter going into business.

In 1880–81 numerous changes took place on the editorial board. Mead and Winters were the only editors who continued in office throughout the year. In September, J. F. Holland, '81, of Milford, Mass., and J. A. Ordway, Jr., '82, of Boston; in October, J. A. Hill, '81, of Temple, N. H., and H. H. Wentworth, '82, of Niagara Falls, N. Y.; in November, E. I. K. Noyes, '82, of Antrim, N. H.; and in December, W. W. Colburn, '81, of Boston, were elected. Holland, Osgood, and Wentworth resigned in November. Hill retired in February, and Ordway left the Academy in March. In April and May, John Codman, '81, of Boston, C. F. Clement, '83, of Rutland, Vt., and W. C. Smith, of Chatham, Mass., were added. In May, Hall resigned. In June, Colburn, Mead, Smith, Noyes, and Codman finished their course and left, the first named to enter the Harvard Medical School, and the others to enter Harvard College. This left only Winters and Clement on the board. In September, 1881, C. C. Felton, '82, of Thurlow, Pa., W. W. Baldwin, '82, of Baltimore, W. K. Barton, '82, of Washington, and G. E. Bales, '83, of Wilton, N. H., joined them. Felton retired in November, and Baldwin and Clement in March, 1882. W. C. Boyden, '82, of Sheffield, Ill., and F. H. Stanyan, '83, of Milford, N. H., were added in April. At the end of the year, Barton and Boyden went to Harvard, and Winters went into business. Bales and Stanyan remained, and the vacancies were filled by the election of T. R. Varick, '83, of Manchester, N. H., C. S. Elgutter, '83, of Omaha, Neb., and W. H. Rand, Jr., '85, of Chicago, Ill. The management has so continued without change to the present writing (February, 1883).

Since leaving the Academy, Balch has been connected with the New Hampshire Press Association. Cushing is on the Harvard Advocate; Sexton and Felton are on the Harvard Lampoon; and Barton, on the Harvard Herald. Baylies was business editor of the Advocate for a time. Aldrich has been local editor and general manager of the Flint (Mich.) Globe. The majority of the former editors are still at college, mostly at Harvard. Of the others, Mariett is at the Episcopal Theological School at Harvard; Balch is connected with the Camp School for Boys at Plymouth, N. H.; Needles is practising law in Philadelphia; Strong is at school in

NO 12 ABBOT HALL

STUDENT'S ROOM ON PINE STREET.

Germany; Aldrich is a banker at Flint, Mich.; Osgood is in business at Chicago; Winters is in railroad business in Texas; and Colburn is at the Harvard Medical School.

MISCELLANEOUS.

THE Class of 1884 has not as yet been represented on the board, although frequent invitations have been extended to the members of that class to compete for a position.

The typographical appearance of the Exonian has always been a source of pride to its friends, and reflects great credit upon the printer. It may be added, that the liberality of the proprietor of the News-Letter, and his uniform kindness and that of those in his employ, have been of great assistance to the successive editors, and will always be held by them in grateful remembrance.

The Exonian is not the first attempt at journalism of the Phillips Exeter Academy students. In 1871, John B. Olmstead, B. C. Starr, and W. W. Sleeper, under the caption of "Exetonia," edited three columns of a small weekly published at Patten and Sherman's Mills, in Maine. Although conducted with fair ability, this enterprise was not of long continuance.

The Exonian is a "close corporation." It is the property of the editors, who are responsible for the expenses, and enjoy the profits. When the paper was established, some complaint was made because the founders did not make it a school concern, and provide for the election of the editors by the students. But its success has vindicated the propriety of making it a private enterprise, since it avoids the "red-tape" of an official undertaking.

CHAPTER XV.

SPORTS AND GAMES.

> "They man the oars, now poised upon the tide
> They rest, the signal shot they eager bide.
> 'T is off! they move, they fly along the waves' blue crest,—
> Each crew, in turn, by lovers fond caressed,
> Now this, now that, by skilful toil prevails.
> How bend they to their oars! nor one who quails
> Beneath the sturdy strokes; how waters part
> Before the boats' sharp bows! high beats each heart.
> And now the foremost flies beyond the goal,
> The flag-boat's bow is passed, and honor's roll
> Is proudly won. The air is rent with cheers."[1]

AT the beginning of the present century, the variety of athletic sports at Exeter was extremely limited. The only games seem to have been old-fashioned "bat and ball," which, in the spring, was played on the grounds around the Academy building, and football. The former differed widely from the modern game of base ball, which was introduced later. The old game had fewer rules, and was played with a soft leather ball. In the autumn, football was the standard game, and was played by the entire school. The boys who sat on the north side of the aisle in the chapel, or Latin Room, as it was called, were the oppo-

[1] "Exeter School Days, and Other Poems," by Seymour I. Hudgens.

nents of those who sat on the south side. The old game was played quite differently from the modern "Rugby" game. It consisted mainly of kicking, as no one was allowed to take the ball from the ground.

There does not seem to have been much change in the sports until about 1864. That year was noted for the introduction of boating. Five members of the class of '65 purchased a four-oared boat at Haverhill, and formed a crew, which was composed of Messrs. Whitewell, Rawle, Richards, Gold, and Sparks, who owned the boat and took turns as coxswain. Richards afterwards left school, and Bridge, '66, took his place. This boat was called the "Winona," and was kept under the old church, known as the "Christian Church," which stood near the banks of Fresh River, on which they rowed. Another boat of the same kind appeared the next year, owned by the members of the class of 1866, but no races were rowed between them.

In the spring of 1865, cricket was introduced, but soon gave place to base ball, which was played a little that season. The first base ball club was organized in the spring of 1865, and used to play on the field near the station. Base ball soon became popular, and for several years the classes played against one another on the "Plains." Football, however, still held the first place, although they had no organized club, and played the old-fashioned game.

The first record we can find of any game between the Phillips Exeter Academy nine and any outside nine was in 1875, when they played the Eagle Club of Exeter. In this game the Academy nine was Duncklee, '76 (p.), Byington, '77 (2 b.), Winsor, '76 (c. f.), Wright, '76 (1 b.), Watson, '75 (3 b.), Wheeler, '75 (l. f.), Bond, '76 (r. f.), Folsom, '77 (s. s.), Faulkner, '76 (c.). The result was a victory for the Academy nine, by a score of 28 to 12. The game was played on the new athletic grounds, which the Trustees, at a cost of $3,500, had purchased, four years before. The Campus was later enlarged, and now contains about nine acres.

The different classes in the school still played against each other, but the school nine does not seem to have played regularly with outside clubs, until May 22, 1878, when the first game between Andover and Exeter took place. In this game the Exeter nine was composed of A. Cohen (s. s.), Shattuck (p.), Byington (c.), Brown (2 b.), Olmstead (1 b.), Crawford (3 b.), E. Cohen (l. f.), Bean (c. f.), White (r. f.). The result was a victory for Exeter, by a score of 12 to 1. This was the first of a series of games between Exeter and Andover. In the return game, played at Andover, June 1, 1878, Andover was victorious, by a score of 10 to 8.

In the fall of 1878 the first attempt was made to organize a school eleven, which was to compete with Andover, and other schools. The first game was played with Andover, November 2, 1878, and resulted in a victory for Andover, by a score of 1 goal and 5 touchdowns to 0. The Exeter eleven were: Rushers, Baxter, '79, Baker, '79, Hayford, '79, Codman, '79,

Crawford, '80, Codman, '81; Half-tends, Byron, '80, Carter, '80, Shattuck, '79; Tends, Hooker, '80, Curtis, '81, and Kirk, '82, Haines, '82, substitutes. This game was played by the Rugby rules, which had been lately introduced in this country.

On the 14th of June, 1878, the first regatta was rowed, in which they used two boats. The four crews, chosen irrespective of class, took turns in rowing against each other. Captain Wylie's crew won the regatta in 2 minutes 50 seconds. The course was about one third of a mile. In 1880 class races were instituted, and '83 won both in that year and in the year following.

Within the last three years, tennis and lacrosse have been introduced. Both are deservedly popular. In a tennis tournament held in June, 1882, E. E. Graham, '82, won the single, and W. B. Goodwin, '82, and E. E. Graham, '82, the double.

An athletic tournament is held each year, under the auspices of the Athletic Association, and in the fall of each year one or more runs are made to Newmarket, by hares chosen for the occasion, pursued by as many hounds as may be mustered.

In this brief sketch we have endeavored to give an outline of the way in which the various games were introduced, and the success with which they met. For those who wish a more detailed account, we append tables of records.

FOOTBALL.

Opponents.	Where Played.	Date.	Opponent's Score.	Exeter's Score.
Andover	Andover	Nov. 2, 1878	1 g. 5 t. d.	0
Adams Academy	Exeter	Oct. 11, 1879	0	0
Harvard Freshmen	Exeter	Oct. 18, 1879	0	1 g. 3 t. d.
Andover	Exeter	Nov. 1, 1879	0	1 g. 4 t. d.
Harvard Freshmen	Exeter	Oct. 27, 1880	0	1 g. 2 t. d.
Adams Academy	Quincy	Nov. 11, 1880	1 t. d.	1 g.
Andover	Andover	Nov. 17, 1880	2 t. d.	2 t. d.
Institute of Technology	Exeter	Oct. 29, 1881	2 g.	0
Andover	Exeter	Nov. 12, 1881	1 g.	0
Harvard Freshmen	Exeter	Oct. 21, 1882	3 t. d.	0
Andover	Andover	Nov. 21, 1882	3 t. d.	0

BASE BALL.

Opponents.	Where Played.	Date.	Opp. Score.	Exeter's Score.
Andover	Exeter	May 22, 1878	1	12
Andover	Andover	June 1, 1878	10	8
Harvard Freshmen [1]	Exeter	June 5, 1878	0	9
Andover	Exeter	June 7, 1879	10	2
Harvard Freshmen	Exeter	May 15, 1880	3	17
Adams Academy	Quincy	May 22, 1880	6	7
Lawrence Academy	Exeter	May 29, 1880	4	6
Andover [2]	Andover	June 5, 1880	9	0
Harvard Freshmen	Cambridge	May 28, 1881	14	2
Andover	Exeter	June 8, 1881	13	5
Lawrence Academy	Exeter	May 27, 1882	5	6
Beacons	Exeter	May 30, 1882	11	6
Ætnas (of N. Andover)	Exeter	May 31, 1882	6	11
Andover	Andover	June 7, 1882	5	7

[1] This game was **given to Exeter** by the umpire, Harvard not appearing at the appointed time.

[2] The above game was stopped in the seventh inning by Exeter's refusing to play after a disputed ruling of the umpire; the score then actually standing 1 to 1, but awarded as above by the umpire.

BOAT RACES.

Date.	Race.	Winner.	Time.
June 11, 1873 ..	Single Scull ..	Weidman, '74	5 m. 25 sec.
June 19, 1874 ..	Single Scull ..	Price, '75	Time not known.
June 19, 1874 ..	Double Scull ..	Brooks, '76 Brooks, '77	Time not known.
June 17, 1875 [1]	Single Scull ..	Teschemacher, '76 ..	5 m. 17¼ sec.
June 17, 1875 ..	Double Scull ..	Teschemacher, '76 Wright, '75	5 m. 35½ sec.
June 17, 1875 ..	Four-oared ...	Capt. Learnard, '76..	6 m. 48½ sec.
June 17, 1875 ..	Six-oared ...	Capt. J. A. Wright '75	4 m. 48½ sec.
June 17, 1876 ..	Six-oared ...	Capt. Bartlett, '78 ..	4 m. 51 sec.
June 17, 1876 ..	Double Scull ..	Duncklee, '76 Allen, '76	6 m.
June 17, 1876 ..	Four-oared ...	Capt. Skinner, '76...	6 m. 6 sec.
June 17, 1876 ..	Single Scull ..	Merrill, '78	4 m. 53 sec.
June 14, 1878 [2]	Six-oared ...	Capt. Wylie, '79 ...	2 m. 50 sec.
June 14, 1878 ..	Six-oared ...	Capt. Salter, '80....	3 m. 21 sec.
June 14, 1879 [2]	Six-oared ...	Capt. Hooker, '80 ..	2 m. 9 sec.
June 9, 1880 [3]	Six-oared ...	'83, Capt. Brooks ...	6 m. 13½ sec.
June 5, 1881 ..	Six-oared ...	'83, Capt. Stoughton .	5 m. 44 sec.

[1] Course from stake opposite boat-house to Fernald's Wharf and return.
[2] Course about ½ mile.
[3] Course from Rocky Point to boat-house, one mile.

CHAPTER XVI.

STATISTICAL AND MISCELLANEOUS.

LIST OF OFFICERS. — LAWS. — REGULATIONS FOR BOARDING-HOUSES. — COURSES OF STUDY. — SCHOLARSHIPS. — EXPENSES.

THE following is a complete list of the officers and teachers of the Academy since its foundation.

The Founder.

HON. JOHN PHILLIPS, LL.D.

Trustees.

Hon. John Phillips, LL.D.	1781–1795.
Hon. Samuel Phillips, LL.D.	1781–1802.
Thomas Odiorne	1781–1794.
Hon. John Pickering, LL.D.	1781–1802.
Rev. David McClure	1781–1787.
Rev. Benjamin Thurston	1781–1801.
Daniel Tilton	1781–1783.
William Woodbridge, A.M., *ex officio*	1783–1788.
Hon. Paine Wingate	1787–1809.
Benjamin Abbot, A.M., *ex officio*	1791–1838.
Hon. Oliver Peabody, A.M.	1794–1828.
Hon. John Taylor Gilman, LL.D.	1795–1827.
Rev. Joseph Buckminster, D.D.	1801–1812.
Rev. Jesse Appleton, D.D.	1802–1803.
Hon. John Phillips	1802–1820.
Rev. Daniel Dana, D.D.	1809–1843.
Hon. Nathaniel Appleton Haven	1809–1830.

Rev. Jacob Abbot, A.M. . . . . 1812–1834.
Rev. Nathan Parker, D.D. . . . . 1821–1833.
Hon. Jeremiah Smith, LL.D. . . . . . . 1828–1842.
Samuel Hale, A.M. . . . . 1831–1869.
Samuel Dana Bell, A.M. . . . . 1834–1838.
Hon. Daniel Webster, LL.D. . . . . . . 1835–1852.
Rev. Charles Burroughs, D.D. . . . . . 1835–1867.
Benjamin Abbot, LL.D. . . . . 1838–1844.
Gideon Lane Soule, A.M., *ex officio* . . . . 1838–1873.
Hon. James Bell, A.B. . . . . 1842–1852.
Rev. Andrew Preston Peabody, A.M. . . . 1843–
David Wood Gorham, A.B., M.D. . . . . 1844–1873.
Hon. Amos Tuck, A.M. . . . . 1853–1879.
Francis Bowen, A.M. . . . . 1853–1875.
Hon. Jeremiah Smith, A.M. . . . . . . 1868–1874.
Hon. George Silsbee Hale, A.B. 1870–
Albert Cornelius Perkins, A.M., *ex officio* . . 1873–1883.
William Henry Gorham, M.D. . . . . . 1874–1879.
Joseph Burbeen Walker, A.M. 1874–
Rev. Phillips Brooks, D. D. . . . . . . 1875–1880.
Nicholas Emery Soule, A.M., M.D. 1879–
Hon. Charles Henry Bell, A.M. 1879–
John Charles Phillips, A.B. 1881–

Treasurers.

Thomas Odiorne . . . . 1781–1793.
Hon. John Taylor Gilman, LL.D. . . . . 1793–1806.
Hon. Oliver Peabody, A.M. . . . . . . 1806–1828.
Hon. Jeremiah Smith, LL.D. . . . . . . 1828–1842.
Hon. John Kelly, A.M. . . . . 1842–1855.
Joseph Taylor Gilman . . . . 1855–1862.
S. Clarke Buzell . . . . 1862–1880.
Charles Burley 1880–

STATISTICAL AND MISCELLANEOUS. 289

Principals.

William Woodbridge, A.B.	1783–1788.
Benjamin Abbot, LL.D.	1788–1838.
Gideon Lane Soule, LL.D.	1838–1873.
Albert Cornelius Perkins, Ph.D.	1873–1883.

Instructors.

Ebenezer Adams, A.M., Prof. Math. and Nat. Phil.	1808–1809.
Hosea Hildreth, A.M., Prof. Math. and Nat. Phil.	1811–1825.
Rev. Isaac Hurd, A.M., Theol. Instructor	1817–1839.
Gideon Lane Soule, A.M., Prof. Anc. Languages	1822–1838.
John Parker Cleaveland, A.B., Prof. Math. and Nat. Phil.	1825–1826.
Charles C. P. Gale, A.B., Prof. Math. and Nat. Phil.	1826–1827.
Joseph Hale Abbot, A.M., Prof. Math. and Nat. Phil.	1827–1833.
Francis Bowen, A.B., Prof. Math. and Nat. Phil.	1833–1835.
William Henry Shackford, A.B., Prof. Math. and Nat. Phil.	1835–1842.
Henry French, A.B., Instructor in Languages	1836–1840.
Nehemiah Cleaveland, A.M., Prof. Anc. Languages	1840–1841.
Joseph Gibson Hoyt, A.M., Prof. Mathematics	1841–1859.
Richard Wenman Swan, A.B., Prof. Anc. Languages	1842–1851.
Paul Ansel Chadbourne, A.M., Prof. Anc. Languages	1851–1852.
Theodore Tebbets, A.B., Prof. Anc. Languages	1852–1853.
Henry Stedman Nourse, A.B., Prof. Anc. Languages	1853–1855.
George Carleton Sawyer, A.B., Prof. Anc. Languages	1855–1858.
George Albert Wentworth, A.B., Prof. Mathematics	1858–
Bradbury Longfellow Cilley, A.B., Prof. Anc. Languages	1859–
Robert Franklin Pennell, Prof. Latin	1875–1882.

Assistant Instructors.

Joseph Willard, A.B.	1784–1785.
Salmon Chase, A.B.	1785–1786.
Joseph Dana, A.B.	1789–1789.
Daniel Dana, A.B.	1789–1791.

John Phillips Ripley, A.B. . . . . 1791–1791.
Rufus Anderson, A.B. . . . . 1792–1792.
Abiel Abbot, A.B. . . . . 1792–1793.
Charles Coffin, A.B. . . . . 1793–1794.
Joseph Perkins, A.B. . . . . 1794–1795.
Timothy Winn, A.B. . . . . 1795–1796.
Peter Oxenbridge Thacher, A.B. . . . . . . 1796–1797.
Nicholas Emery, A.B. . . . . 1797–1797.
George Wingate, A.B. . . . . 1797–1797.
William Craig, A.B. . . . . 1797–1799.
Samuel Dunn Parker, A.B. . . . . 1799–1800.
Horatio Gates Burnap, A.B. . . . . 1799–1803.
Joseph Stevens Buckminster, A.B. . . . . . 1801–1803.
Samuel Willard, A.B. . . . . 1803–1804.
John Stickney, A.B. . . . . 1804–1805.
Ashur Ware, A.B. . . . . 1804–1805.
Martin Luther Hurlbut, A.B. . . . . 1805–1805.
Nathan Hale, A.B. . . . . 1805–1807.
Jaazaniah Crosby, A.B. . . . . 1806–1807.
Alexander Hill Everett, A.B. . . . . 1806–1807.
Nathaniel Appleton Haven, Jr., A.B. . . . . 1807–1808.
Reuben Washburn, A.B. . . . . 1808–1809.
Nathaniel Whitman, A.B. . . . . 1809–1810.
Nathan Lord, A.B. . . . . 1810–1811.
Jonas Wheeler, A.B. . . . . 1810–1811.
Henry Holton Fuller, A.B. . . . . 1811–1812.
Henry Ware, Jr., A.B. . . . . 1812–1814.
James Walker, A.B. . . . . 1814–1815.
George Goldthwaite Ingersoll, A.B. . . . . 1815–1816.
William Bourne Oliver Peabody, A.B. . . . 1816–1817.
Oliver William Bourne Peabody, A.B. . . . 1817–1818.
Gideon Lane Soule, A.B. . . . . 1818–1819.
Samuel Taylor Gilman, A.B. . . . . 1819–1820.
Charles Lane Folsom, A.B. . . . . 1820–1822.
Jacob Abbot Cram . . . . 1856–1857.
William Francis Bennett Jackson . . . . . . 1857–1857.
Orlando Marcellus Fernald . . . . 1860–1861.

Payson Merrill . . . . 1861–1862.
William Harrington Putnam, A.M. . . . . . 1870–1871.
Robert Franklin Pennell, A. B. . . . . 1871–1875.
Oscar Faulhaber, Ph.D. 1874–
Frederic Timothy Fuller, A.B. . . . . 1875–1878.
James Arthur Tufts, A.B. 1878–
George Lyman Kittredge, A.B. 1883–

Among the records of the Academy there is nothing more interesting than the code of rules which the first Board of Trustees established for the good government of the scholars. It is probable that they were written by the Founder. We give them entire.

LAWS OF THE PHILLIPS EXETER ACADEMY.

1. As the great and important Designs of Education cannot be answered, nor any valuable Improvements be attained without Diligence and Attention they are highly recommended and required of all the Students in this Academy; these therefore will be considered as Virtues which merit the Preceptor's Approbation and Friendship.

2. As Idleness and Inattention will utterly defeat the End of this Institution and hinder all Improvement, as they directly tend to introduce Irregularity and Vice, they are strictly forbidden as a Fault that must be censured, and severely punished if persisted in.

3. Silence and strict Attention to all Instructions are required of every Student, and especially in all Exercises of religious Worship and Instruction. The Students

shall stand erect with **Decency and Order at Recitation** and Prayers, and carefully endeavor to sit decently **in** all such Exercises when they **are** not required to stand.

4. After **Worship is begun they are** not to rise up **to any who** may **enter; all other times** they shall rise and **bow** respectfully to **Gentlemen when** they enter the **Room** and when **they leave it.**

5. Every Student **shall be** exact upon his Attendance upon all the **Exercises of this** Academy. **He** shall **carefully prepare for them,** and not fail **to** sweep, kindle **Fire,** ring the Bell, shut up the Academy, tend the **Fire, &c., &c.,** in his **Turn, and exactly at the** Time, &c.

6. **Each Student shall endeavor to be** supplied with **every Article necessary for** his Studies and Writing, and have these articles in **his** place before Study Time, so **as** to prevent **all** Noise and Borrowing. When he enters the Room, he shall endeavor **to** do it without bold Forwardness and Noise, without incommoding those in their Seat. He shall take his Place without speaking, or moving from it, unless by Permission, which must not be asked or granted, without absolute Necessity. Their Behavior as they go to and from the Academy shall be decent and orderly, especially on the Sabbath. They are **not to** meet at the Academy on Sabbath Evenings before **the** Bell rings **for Prayers.**

7. Every Student shall keep an exact Account of the Lessons studied **and** recited every day, of the Time of Entrance, of the Studies of each Term, of the Time of Absence and Continuance at the Academy and expense

of it. A fair Copy of the Studies of each Term, and a Specimen of his first and last Writing, shall be delivered to the Preceptor at Dismission.

8. All Students are strictly required to be at home on Saturday Evenings and on the Sabbath, also in good Season every other Evening of the Week, to behave with Decency and Order in the Families where they belong and board. Also give an Account of the manner in which they spend their leisure Hours, their Company, &c., whenever the Preceptor requires it, carefully observing his Direction and Advice upon the Subject. They are to use great Care in their Amusements, not to transgress the Bounds of Reason, the Rules of Virtue, Manliness, and Honor, or the Regulation of this Academy.

9. All Gaming, Immorality, Profaneness, and Indecency in Language or Actions, are forbidden in the most positive Terms, and must be severely censured. The contrary Virtues of Neatness and Decency in Person and Dress, in Language and Behavior, are highly recommended and strictly required. As the Character and Usefulnes of Men greatly depend upon amiable and engaging Manners, the Preceptor would highly recommend and strictly require a constant and persevering Attention to the rules of true Honor and Politeness, and a careful Endeavor to express those Principles of unaffected Benevolence by a cheerful Readiness to perform every kind office in their Power, and to do it in the most obliging and becoming Manner. Ever remember that great Favors are diminished, and that small ones greatly

increase, **by the** Manner in which they are conferred. **A** Gift **may** be unkindly bestowed, and a Favor kindly **and** politely **refused.**

10. All Students shall strictly observe and persever**ingly** practise good **Manners and** Civility **to** all; Condescension and Kindness to **those** younger than themselves; Affability and good Manners to their Equals; their Language and Behavior to Superiors should be decent and respectful, never speaking disrespectfully of them **or** their Conduct **when** absent. This rule is carefully **to be observed to all Men** of public Character. These **important** Rules **are** highly recommended and strongly enforced as containing the Sum of Virtue and Benevolence, agreeable to that complete **Rule** of Virtue and **Honor,** "Whatever you can rationally desire others **should do for you,** that do for them in the kindest manner."

11. **Every** Student **shall constantly attend public Worship on** Sabbath both **parts of the Day, and** endeavor **to do** it with **Reverence** and Attention suitable to the Solemnities **of divine Service in the** Temple of God, who is greatly **to** be revered in the Assembly of his adoring Worshipers. They shall carefully observe **a** decent and orderly **Behavior on** Sabbath Evening. **All** noisy Levity and Amusements, **some of** which might **be** allowed on other Evenings, are absolutely forbidden on this. The Preceptor does **not** forbid their visiting **each other** or a virtuous Friend, but in general would recom**mend that** they would tarry at home, **or** spend it regu-

larly in sacred Music, which is a noble and improving Amusement to a virtuous Mind.

12. Every Student shall also repair all Damages done to the Building, Glass, or Furniture of the Academy, whether done by Accident or Design. Any Student who is absent without a sufficient Reason shall pay a Fine of one Shilling Sterling for every Day's Absence, and after a proper Time forfeit his place in the Academy.

13. Every Student who shall break these Laws thro' negligence or design, who shall neglect his Studies and prove disobedient and refractory, shall be subjected to a proper Punishment; and, if persevering to offend, shall be publicly admonished or expelled, as the Nature and Circumstances of the Offence may require, &c., &c. All Students are strictly forbidden to spend their Time at any Tavern, and much more to call for Liquors or join in Company or Diversions with any Persons who do the same.

The following rules, established during the administration of Dr. Soule, are in force to-day.

"No scholar shall enjoy the privileges of this institution, who shall board in any family not licensed by the Trustees." — *Constitution.*

Therefore heads of families, who take students to board, are expected to maintain good order in their houses, to exercise a parental watchfulness over their boarders, and to report to the instructors any instances of disorderly or immoral conduct, that may occur.

Study hours in the evening, during the fall and winter

terms, begin at half-past seven o'clock. During the day, students are not allowed to visit each other's rooms between the hours of recitation.

No student is permitted to spend the night away from his own room; nor, on Saturday evening, to be absent from his lodgings after nine o'clock. All visiting on the Sabbath is prohibited.

It is confidently expected that those who take students to board will see that these regulations are carefully observed.

Agreeably to a vote of the Trustees, no scholar under the age of twenty-one is permitted to incur expense on credit unless authorized by his parent, guardian, their agent, or one of the instructors; and it is the opinion of the Trustees, that parents and guardians ought not to discharge debts contracted without this formality.

No student under the age of twenty-one, after having taken lodgings, shall be permitted to exchange them without permission, first obtained from the Principal, or, in his absence, from one of the Faculty.

For the Faculty,
G. L. SOULE, Principal.

REGULATIONS FOR BOARDING-HOUSES.

"No scholar shall enjoy the privileges of this institution, who shall board in any family not licensed by the Trustees." — *Constitution.*

· Heads of families, who let rooms to students, are required to maintain good order in their houses, and to report to the instructors any instances of disorderly or immoral conduct that may occur.

They shall also report any student who is absent from his room after ten o'clock in the evening.

They shall also report any student who receives visitors on Sunday.

No person who refuses or neglects to comply with these **rules shall** be allowed to receive students into his house.

No student is allowed **to change his boarding-house** without permission.

For the Trustees,
G. L. SOULE, Principal.

Although in this school **the course of** studies **and the** names **of** text-books differ but little from year **to year, yet,** if we compare the curriculum published **at long periods of time, the changes are more marked.**

It will be interesting to compare the selection we have **made from a Catalogue of Dr.** Abbot's time with one **of Dr.** Soule's day, **and both** with one issued during **Dr.** Perkins's administration.

The following course **of** instruction was published **during Dr.** Abbot's administration.

Phillips Exeter Academy.

Candidates for admission must furnish evidence of good **moral character,** studious habits, and good capacities for **improvement. They must give** assurance for themselves, **if of age, otherwise through** their parents **or** guardians, of **their intention to remain** at the Academy, until they shall have completed the usual course of preparation for **College,** — or the course of English education established in this institution.

The time for admission will be at the commencement

of the term **next** succeeding the annual meeting **of the** Trustees **in** August. — Provided, however, that **persons** duly qualified may at any time be admitted to advanced standing, at the discretion of the Instructors.

DEPARTMENT OF LANGUAGES.

This department **comprises** three Classes, exclusive **of** an Advanced Class, **on** the presumption **that** three years **will** usually be **necessary to** prepare **for** College. These classes are so subdivided and arranged, as to give scope and encouragement to industry and talents; but all advancements from **one** class or division to another take **place in consequence of satisfactory examination.**

Those students who may choose to remain **at the Academy** after **completing the course of** preparation for College, with **a view, either to** obtain a more accurate and extensive knowledge of the Latin and Greek classics, **or to enter** College in advanced standing, constitute the Advanced Class.

COURSE ON PREPARATION FOR COLLEGE.

First Year.

Adam's Latin Grammar, Liber Primus, **or a** similar work, Viri Romani, **or** Cæsar's Commentaries, **Latin Prosody**, exercises in reading and making Latin, Ancient and Modern Geography, Virgil, and Arithmetic.

Second Year.

Virgil, Arithmetic, exercises in reading and making Latin continued, **Valpy's** Greek Grammar, **Delectus,** Roman History, Cicero's Select Orations, Dalzel's Collectanea Græca Minora, Greek Testament, English Grammar, and Declamation.

Third Year.

The same Latin and Greek authors in revision, English Grammar and Declamation continued, Sallust, Algebra, exercises in Latin and English translations, and Composition.

Advanced Class.

2. Horatius Flaccus, Titus Livius, Excerpta Latina, parts of Terence's Comedies, Collectanea Græca Majora, Homer's Iliad,— or such Latin and Greek authors as may best comport with the student's future destination; Algebra, Geometry, Adam's Roman Antiquities, and elements of Ancient History.

ENGLISH DEPARTMENT.

Candidates for admission into this department must be at least twelve years of age, well instructed in reading and spelling, familiarly acquainted with Arithmetic through Simple Proportion with the exception of Fractions, with Murray's English Grammar through Syntax, and must be able to parse simple English sentences.

The following is the course of Instruction and Study in the English Department, which, with special exceptions, will comprise three years.

First Year.

English Grammar, including exercises in parsing and analyzing, in the correction of bad English, Punctuation, and Prosody; Arithmetic, Geography, and Algebra through Simple Equations.

Second Year.

English Grammar continued, Geometry, Plane Trigonometry, and its application to Heights and Distances, Mensuration of Superficies and Solids, Elements of Ancient History, Logic, Rhetoric, English Composition, **and** exercises of the Forensic kind.

Third Year.

Surveying, **Navigation, Elements of** Chemistry and Natural Philosophy with experiments, Elements of Modern History, particularly of the United States, Astronomy, Moral and Political Philosophy, with English Composition, Forensics, and Declamation **continued.**

A course of Theological Instruction **is given to the** several classes, and likewise Instruction in **Sacred Music.** Writing is daily **taught in** both **departments by an** *approved master.*

Those who shall have spent at least one year in the department of languages, and have made good improvement, **may enter upon the** course **of** English education **without the** examination prescribed for mere English scholars. **Students** qualified to enter College may **be** allowed the privilege of completing, if able, the course of English education in two years. The same privilege may also be extended to others, whose **superior** improvement shall **appear on** examination **to authorize** such advancement.

At the close of **each** Term **the** several classes of both departments are critically examined **in all the studies** of that Term; those students who are found to excel, are advanced or **otherwise** distinguished; but those who prove materially deficient are prohibited from proceeding **with** their class, until deficiencies are made up.

To those students who honorably complete their Academical course, testimonials are publicly presented by the Principal at the annual Exhibition.

Per order of the Trustees.

BENJAMIN **ABBOT,** *Principal.*

We give here an extract from a Catalogue published in 1850.

Course of Study.

The regular classes are the Preparatory, the Junior, the Middle, the Senior, and the Advanced Classes, — the last composed of such as are expecting to enter College as Sophomores. Provision is made for such as wish to pursue the Extended Course.

PREPARATORY CLASS.
First Term.

LATIN . . Andrews' Lessons. Andrews and Stoddard's Grammar.
RHETORIC . Weld's Grammar and Parsing Exercises. Quackenbos' Composition. Declamations, begun and continued throughout the course.

Second Term.

LATIN . . Andrews' Reader. Arnold's First and Second Latin Book. Exercises in writing Latin, continued throughout the course.
PHYSICS . . Cutter's or Hooker's Physiology and Hygiene.

Third Term.

LATIN . . Viri Romæ.
GEOGRAPHY Worcester's Ancient.
HISTORY . . Worcester's.

JUNIOR CLASS.
First Term.

LATIN . . Cæsar's Commentaries. Dwight's Mythology.
MATHEMATICS Dodd's or Thompson's Arithmetic, begun.

Second Term.

LATIN . . Bucolics of Virgil. Prosody. Cicero's Orations, begun.
GREEK . . Crosby's Grammar and Exercises.
MATHEMATICS Dodd's or Thompson's Arithmetic, completed. Thompson's, Day's, or Greenleaf's Algebra, begun.

Third Term.
LATIN . . Cicero's Orations, to Milo (**Folsom's Ed.**). Arnold's Prose Composition.
GREEK . . Colton's or Jacobs' Reader, begun.
MATHEMATICS Thompson's, Day's, or Greenleaf's Algebra, completed. Peirce's or Smyth's Algebra, begun.

MIDDLE CLASS.
First Term.
LATIN . . Æneid, **to Book V.**
GREEK . . Colton**'s or Jacobs' Reader continued.** Arnold's First **Book.**
MATHEMATICS Peirce**'s or** Smyth's Algebra completed. **Introduction to** Geometry and Science **of Form.**
RHETORIC . **Themes,** begun and continued **throughout the** course.

Second Term.
LATIN . . . Æneid, to Book XI.
GREEK . . Colton's or Jacobs' Reader, completed.
MATHEMATICS Robinson's Geometry, or Davies' Legendre, begun.

Third Term.
LATIN . . . Æneid, completed. **Cicero's Orations, completed.**
GREEK. . . Felton's Reader, begun. Arnold's **Prose** Composition.
MATHEMATICS Robinson's Geometry, or Davies' **Legendre,** completed.

SENIOR CLASS.
First Term.
LATIN . . **Georgics of Virgil.** Conspiracy of Catiline — **Sallust.** Zumpt's Grammar, for reference.
GREEK . . . Felton's Reader, completed. Kuehner's and Buttmann's Grammars, for reference.
MATHEMATICS Robinson's Trigonometry, Plane and Spherical. Day's or Davies' Surveying and Navigation.

Second Term.

LATIN . . . Jugurthine War of **Sallust.** Cicero de Senectute, or the Andria **of Terence.**
GREEK . . Homer's Iliad, Books **VI., XXII., and XXIV.**
MATHEMATICS Day's Mensuration of Planes **and Solids.**

Third Term.

LATIN . . . Cicero and Virgil, reviewed.
GREEK . . Felton's Reader, **reviewed.**
MATHEMATICS Arithmetic and **Algebra, reviewed.**
HISTORY . . Weber's **Outlines.**

ADVANCED CLASS.

First Term.

LATIN . . Tusculan Disputation. Book I. Odes and Epodes of Horace, — Moore's or Schmitz and Zumpt's Ed.
GREEK . . Greek Historians, — Felton's **Selections.**
PHILOSOPHY . Paley's Evidences, continued through the year.
[1]MATHEMATICS Conic Sections, — Robinson's or Bridge's.

Second Term.

LATIN . . . Livy, Books **XXI., and XXII.,** — **Lincoln's or** Schmitz and Zumpt's Ed.
GREEK . . Greek Historians, continued.
[1]PHYSICS . . Natural Philosophy. — Olmsted's.

Third Term.

LATIN . . . Horace and Livy, reviewed.
GREEK . . Greek Historians reviewed.
MATHEMATICS Geometry and Trigonometry, reviewed.
[1]PHYSICS . . Astronomy.—McIntire's or Olmstead's.

N. B. Some of the Text-Books in the foregoing **scheme may be** occasionally changed, but the system of Classification **will be rigidly** adhered to.

[1] Instead of Conic Sections, Natural Philosophy, **and Astronomy,** *German* or *French* **may be taken as a substitute.**

EXTENDED COURSE.

Selections may be made from the following **Books** : —

LATIN . . . Cicero de Amicitia. Tacitus. **Plautus.** Juvenal.
GREEK . . Demosthenes de Corona (Champlin's Ed.). Iliad or Odyssey of Homer. Clouds of Aristophanes (Felton's Ed.). Alcestis of Euripides, Prometheus of Aeschylus (Woolsey's Ed.), and Ajax of Sophocles.
ENGLISH . . The higher Mathematics in **its** application to Mechanics and Civil Engineering ; Bookkeeping ; Agricultural Chemistry ; and other branches of study suited to the various pursuits of active life.

The following is taken from the Catalogue of 1881–82.

Classical Course.

PREPARATORY CLASS.

First Term.

LATIN . . . . . Allen and Greenough's Grammar. Leighton's Latin **Lessons.** Pennell's Latin Subjunctive.
MATHEMATICS . . Wentworth and Hill's Arithmetic.
HISTORY . . . . Barnes's United States.

*Second **Term.***

LATIN . . . . . Grammar and Lessons. Cæsar's Gallic War, Books II., III. Exercises in Writing Latin. Bennett's First Latin Writer.
MATHEMATICS . . Arithmetic, finished.
HISTORY . . . . **Continued.**

Third Term.

LATIN . . . . . Cæsar's Gallic War, Books I., IV., V., VI. Bennett's First Latin Writer to page 116.
MATHEMATICS . . Hill's Geometry for Beginners.
HISTORY . . . . Finished.

JUNIOR CLASS.
First Term.

LATIN	Virgil, Æneid, Books I., II. Bennett's Latin Writer, continued.
GREEK	Goodwin's Grammar. White's Lessons.
MATHEMATICS . .	Wentworth's Elements of Algebra.
ANCIENT HISTORY .	Pennell's Greece.
ANCIENT GEOGRAPHY.	
ENGLISH	Scott.

Second Term.

LATIN	Virgil, Æneid, Books III., IV., V.
GREEK	Grammar and Lessons, continued.
MATHEMATICS . .	Algebra, continued.
ANCIENT HISTORY .	Pennell's Greece, finished.
ANCIENT GEOGRAPHY.	
ENGLISH	Scott.

Third Term.

LATIN	Virgil, Æneid, Book VI. Bennett's First Latin Writer, finished.
GREEK	Anabasis, Book I. Exercises in writing Greek, begun and continued through the course.
MATHEMATICS . .	Algebra, finished.
ANCIENT HISTORY .	Pennell's Rome.
ENGLISH	Irving.

MIDDLE CLASS.
First Term.

LATIN	Virgil, Eclogues. Cicero, Orations against Catiline. Jones's Latin Composition. Writing Latin through the year.
GREEK	Anabasis, Books II., III., IV. Greek Testament.
MATHEMATICS . .	Wentworth's Plane Geometry, Books I., II., III., IV. Wentworth's Geometrical Exercises.

PHYSICS	Arnott's.
ENGLISH	Shakespeare. Thackeray.
HISTORY	Ancient Greece and Rome.

Second Term.

LATIN	Sight Reading. Cæsar's Civil War. Virgil, reviewed.
GREEK	Extracts from Hellenica. Greek Testament.
MATHEMATICS	Plane Geometry finished. Geometrical Exercises.
PHYSICS	Arnott's, to page 165.
HISTORY	Ancient Greece and Rome.
ENGLISH	Addison.

Third Term.

LATIN	Cæsar and Virgil, reviewed.
GREEK	Xenophon at sight.
MATHEMATICS	Arithmetic, Algebra, and Geometry, reviewed.
PHYSICS	Reviewed.
HISTORY	Reviewed.
ENGLISH	Review.

SENIOR CLASS.

First Term.

LATIN	Cicero, Oration for the Poet Archias. Virgil, Æneid VII., VIII., IX., X. Bennett's Latin Writer, Part II.
GREEK	Herodotus, Book VII.
MATHEMATICS	Wentworth's Solid Geometry.
FRENCH	Otto's Grammar. Brette's French Principia, Part II.
GERMAN	Progressive German Course, Macmillan's, Parts I. and II. German Principia, Part II. Eugene Fasnacht, Parts I. and II.
PHYSICS	Arnott's.
ENGLISH	Webster. Themes throughout the year.

Second Term.

LATIN	Virgil, Æneid, XI., XII. Ovid, Selections. Bennett's Latin Writer, Part II.
GREEK	Homer, Books I., II., III.
MATHEMATICS	Wentworth's Plane Trigonometry. Wentworth and Hill's Logarithms.
FRENCH	Reading. Le Français.
GERMAN	Prose Selections.
CHEMISTRY	Nichols's Abridgment of Eliot and Storer.
PHYSICS	Arnott's to Part IV., Section III.
ENGLISH	Webster.

Third Term.

LATIN	Cicero, Defence of Roscius. Bennett's Latin Writer, Part II.
GREEK	Herodotus and Homer at sight.
MATHEMATICS	Halsted's Mensuration.
FRENCH	Prose Selections.
GERMAN	Prose Selections.
CHEMISTRY	Finished.
PHYSICS	Reviewed.
ENGLISH	Burke.
BOTANY	Gray.

NOTE. — The branches above indicated for the first three years are required of all. In the Senior year, some choice of electives will be allowed. The Odes of Horace and two Books of Livy may be read by those who are able to do work in addition to what is included in the course of study for the Senior year.

English Course of Study.

JUNIOR CLASS.

First Term.

MATHEMATICS	Wentworth's Elements of Algebra.
MODERN HISTORY	Barnes's United States. Thalheimer's England.
ENGLISH GRAMMAR	Reed and Kellogg's.
PENMANSHIP	

COMPOSITION	Letter Writing and Elementary **Rhetoric** throughout the year. **Map Drawing** throughout the year.
GEOGRAPHY	**Swinton's** Complete Geography.
ENGLISH	**Scott.**

Second Term.

MATHEMATICS	Algebra, continued.
MODERN HISTORY	United States and English, finished.
ENGLISH GRAMMAR	Continued.
GEOGRAPHY	Continued.
ENGLISH	**Scott.**

Third Term.

MATHEMATICS	Algebra, finished.
HISTORY	European History.
ENGLISH GRAMMAR	Art of Expression.
GEOGRAPHY	Finished.
ENGLISH	Irving.

MIDDLE CLASS.

First Term.

MATHEMATICS	Wentworth's Plane Geometry, Books I., II., III., IV. Wentworth's Geometrical Exercises.
GEOGRAPHY	Maury's Physical.
PHYSICS	Arnott's.
RHETORIC	Kellogg's.
MODERN HISTORY	Selections from Epochs of History.
ASTRONOMY	Ray's.
ENGLISH	Shakespeare, Thackeray.

Second Term.

MATHEMATICS	**Plane** Geometry, finished. Geometrical Exercises.
PHYSICS	Arnott's to page 165.
GEOGRAPHY	Maury's Physical.
RHETORIC	Hill's.
ENGLISH	Addison.

Third Term.

MATHEMATICS . .	Arithmetic, Algebra, and Geometry, reviewed.
MODERN HISTORY .	Selections from Epochs of History.
CONSTITUTION . .	Flanders's Exposition.
PHYSICS	Reviewed.
ANCIENT HISTORY .	Smith's Smaller Scripture.
RHETORIC . . .	Finished. Abbott's How to Write Clearly.
ENGLISH	Reviewed.
PHYSIOLOGY . . .	Hutchinson's.

SENIOR CLASS.
First Term.

MATHEMATICS . .	Wentworth's Solid Geometry.
ENGLISH	Themes.
HISTORY	Barnes's France.
FRENCH	Otto's Grammar. Brette's French Principia, Part II.
GERMAN	Progressive German Course. Macmillan's, Parts I. and II. German Principia, Part II.
PHYSICS . . .	Continued.
MORAL PHILOSOPHY	Peabody's.
ENGLISH	Webster.

Second Term.

MATHEMATICS . .	Wentworth's Plane Trigonometry. Wentworth and Hill's Logarithms.
FRENCH	Reading. Le Français.
GERMAN	Prose Selections.
POLITICAL ECONOMY	Fawcett's.
PHYSICS	Arnott's to Part IV. Sec. III.
CHEMISTRY . . .	Nichols's Abridgment of Eliot and Storer.
ENGLISH	Webster.

Third Term.

MATHEMATICS . .	Halsted's Mensuration.
POLITICAL ECONOMY	Financial Legislation.
LOGIC	Jevons.

ENGLISH LITERATURE.
BOTANY . . . . Continued.
FRENCH . . . . Reading.
GERMAN . . . . Prose Selections.
PHYSICS . . . . Reviewed.
CHEMISTRY . . . Finished.
ENGLISH . . . . Burke.

For many years previous to 1850, there was but little change in the number of students entering the Academy. In the decade from 1850–60, however, there was an increase of over fifty per cent; in the next ten years a still further increase of nearly thirty per cent; and from 1870–80, an increase of over twenty per cent. This is shown by the following table.

Number of Students who entered before 1800	647
" " " " from 1800 to 1810	367
" " " " " 1810 " 1820	441
" " " " " 1820 " 1830	378
" " " " " 1830 " 1840	365
" " " " " 1840 " 1850	358
" " " " " 1850 " 1860	566
" " " " " 1860 " 1870	807
" " " " " 1870 " 1880	983
" " " " " 1880 " 1883	357
Whole number of Students	5,269
No. of Students under Principal Woodbridge (1783–1788)	175
" " " " Abbot (1789–1838)	1,991
" " " " Soule (1839–1873)	2,148
" " " " Perkins (1874–1883)	955
Total	5,269
Number of Students under Dr. Soule both as Instructor and Principal (1823–1873)	2,736

STATISTICAL AND MISCELLANEOUS. 311

The number of students in the school, as well as the number in each of the classes, during the sixteen years succeeding 1866-67, will be found in the table given below. It also gives the number of students in the English Department since its establishment in 1875.

Year.	Advanced Class.	Senior Class.	Middle Class.	Junior Class.	Preparatory Class.	Classical Department.	English Department.	Total.
1866-67	7	35	51	51		144		144
1867-68	7	36	46	48		137		137
1868-69	7	26	56	41		130		130
1869-70		36	51	43		130		130
1870-71	6	62	58	55		181		181
1871-72		52	63	51		166		166
1872-73		57	46	37	22	162		162
1873-74		40	52	46	30	168		168
1874-75		40	34	39	53	166		166
1875-76		36	33	45	68	167	15	182
1876-77		29	52	69	55	182	23	205
1877-78		33	50	76	65	193	31	224
1878-79		33	61	56	62	191	21	212
1879-80		43	57	49	55	176	28	204
1880-81		41	80	58	55	202	32	234
1881-82		36	61	65	49	181	30	211
1882-83		45	55	57	49	167	39	206

Most of **those who** take the English course at Exeter do **so** with the expectation of engaging in mercantile pursuits at the conclusion **of the course.** A few continue their studies at some **technical** school, like the Massachusetts Institute of Technology, but for the most of them school life is **at** an end. Exeter, however, is essentially a college preparatory school, and of those who leave at the end **of** each year about four fifths enter some college. Oberlin and other Western colleges, Princeton and other colleges of the Middle States, Williams, **Amherst,** Yale, Brown, and Dartmouth receive a **few;** **the** remainder go to Harvard. We give here a table **of the** eight principal preparatory schools from which young men actually entered Harvard College from 1867 to 1882 inclusive, and the number that entered each year.

School.	1867.	1868.	1869.	1870.	1871.	1872.	1873.	1874.	1875.	1876.	1877.	1878.	1879.	1880.	1881.	1882.	Total.
The Phillips Exeter Academy	22	23	22	23	25	32	40	25	26	34	18	20	24	25	19	¹23	401
Phillips Academy, Andover	5	2	8	6	3	14	13	9	1	5	8	4	4	4	3	5	94
Adams Academy, Quincy, Ms.							1	5	13	11	9	22	13	13	12	13	112
St. Paul's School, Concord, N H	0	1	3	3	4	2	1	2	4	2	4	2	6	4	4	5	47
St. Mark's School, Southborough, Mass.	2	0	2	1	1	2	0	3	1	2	8	1	2	1	3	5	34
Boston Latin School, Boston	17	9	21	23	18	13	18	12	27	10	21	13	13	23	17	17	272
Roxbury Latin School, "	0	2	5	4	6	9	3	6	11	6	8	10	14	8	14	11	117
Chauncey Hall School, "	7	3	1	4	0	3	4	0	1	1	3	1	5	1	2	3	39

¹ This number would be increased to thirty, and the **other** numbers proportionally, if those who entered **as** special students, or who entered the Law School and other departments of the University, were included.

Good scholars of high character, but of slender means, are seldom or never obliged to leave Exeter for want of money.

The tuition, amounting to but sixty dollars a year, is remitted to every needy student, who may also receive aid from such sources as the Sibley Book Fund, loan funds, monitorships, and scholarships.

To aid worthy students, twenty scholarships, styled "Foundation Scholarships," were established with funds left by the Founder for that purpose. These yield sixty dollars each per year.

In addition to these, there are four other scholarships, viz.: the Bancroft Scholarship, with an income of $140, founded by Hon. George Bancroft; the Hale Scholarship, with an income of $140, founded by Miss Martha Hale, in memory of her father, the late Hon. Samuel Hale; the Gordon Scholarship, with an income of $120, founded by Hon. Nathaniel Gordon; the Burroughs Scholarship, with an income of $70, founded by the late Rev. Charles Burroughs, D. D.

The award of scholarships is made by the Trustees at the end of the fall term, after pupils have had the opportunity by their work in the school to show something of their ability and worth. Such aid is not considered as a charity offering, but as prizes won by the deserving and the industrious.

We give below the names of those who have received the income of these scholarships, from their foundation to the year 1883.

Year.	Bancroft.	Gordon.	Hale.	Burroughs.
1871	G. E. Woodbury.			
1872	C. H. Wiswell.	J. B. Harding.		
1873	E. W. Morse.	W. B. Hill.	E. P. Reed.	
1874	W. B. Hill.	H. P. Amen.	G. H. Burrill.	
1875	T. D. Kenneson.	W. H. Parker.	W. W. Stickney.	
1876	C. E. Atwood. / J. W. Babcock.	W. H. Parker.	W. W. Stickney.	
1877	J. W. Babcock.	G. W. Perkins.	A. A. Wyman.	
1878	O. E. Perry.	I. B. Burgess.	G. W. Perkins.	
1879	I. B. Burgess.	H. Hubbard.	G. W. Sawin.	
1880	W. C. Smith.	G. Jenkins.	J. A. Hill.	J. F. Holland.
1881	J. McQ. Thompson.	C. M. Howard.	C. F. A. Currier.	M. J. Holland.
1882	C. F. A. Currier.	M. J. Holland.	M. W. Cooley.	C. M. Howard.

"Free tuition is given to students to the amount of more than four thousand dollars annually; and assistance in money (by means of scholarships) to the further amount of more than sixteen hundred dollars per year. Moreover, rooms in Abbot Hall, a building erected by the Academy for lodging and boarding students of limited means, are furnished at a nominal rent, so that fifty boys are thus supported at about one half the cost of living at the ordinary boarding-houses. The Trustees believe that no other institution of the kind in the country has approached this Academy in giving substantial aid to young men of poverty and merit."

Generous friends are constantly adding to the beneficiary funds, which within the last ten years have rather more than doubled.

This is shown by the following table: —

Beneficiary Funds.	1872.	1882.
Phillips Charity Fund, for Foundation Scholarships	$20,000.00*	$20,000.00*
Kingman Charity Fund		42,421.43
Sibley Charity Fund, income not yet available .	15,000.00*	32,380.00
Sibley Book Fund	300.00	300.00
Bancroft Scholarship	2,000.00	2,000.00
Hale Scholarship		2,000.00
Gordon Scholarship	2,000.00	2,000.00
Burroughs Scholarship		1,000.00
Total	$39,300.00	$102,101.43

* Approximated.

The students who have received the benefit of the Founder's scholarships have always been known as "Foundationers," or "Foundation Scholars." Unlike the beneficiaries in English schools, they are in no way to be distinguished from the other students at the Academy.

The proportion existing between the two classes in the chief schools of England[1] which admit both, is shown by the following table, which also includes the Phillips Exeter Academy.[2]

[1] From Report of Royal Commissioners in 1862.
[2] 1881-1882.

	Foundationers.	Non-Foundationers.
Eton	70	770
Winchester	70	146
Westminster	40	96
Harrow	32	449
Rugby	61	402
Shrewsbury	26	114
Charterhouse	44	92
Exeter	20	191

The expense of sending a boy through the Phillips Exeter Academy need not be great; in fact, when compared with other schools of the same grade in this country, and with any of the great English schools, Exeter is acknowledged to possess a very great pecuniary advantage. The two chief items of expense at Exeter are for tuition and board. The tuition fees are twenty dollars a term, sixty dollars a year, payable in advance, *but remitted to indigent students.*

The cost of education at Exeter varies of course with each individual student. A few students keep their expenditures within $300, and this can be done without injury to health or suffering of any sort. Fully one half spend less than $500 each, and there are few whose year at Exeter costs them over $800. We append here a table based upon reliable data and careful estimates. It contains four grades of expenditures, and accounts for everything except railroad fares and the expenses of the long vacation. The figures in the last two columns could be lessened by dividing the cost of room and furniture between two students rooming together.

The figures are as follows: —

Items.	Least.	Economical.	Moderate.	Ample.
Tuition			$60	$60
Board	$110*	$110*	190†	‡190 to ‡228
Room and Furniture	15*	25*	80	‡114 to ‡156
Laundry	10	15	25	40
Fuel, Lights, and Service	8	10	15	60
Books and Stationery	8	18	20	30
Society Fees and Subscriptions		5	12	25
Clothing	50	70	100	200
Sundries	20	35	50	100
Total	$221	$288	$552	$819 to $899

* Abbot Hall.   † Gorham Hall.   ‡ Private Family.

THE PRINCIPAL, PROFESSORS, AND INSTRUCTORS.

For several years past there have been six teachers regularly engaged at the Academy; viz. the Principal, three Professors, and two Instructors. At present the Chair of Latin is vacant, a third instructor performing the duties of the regular professor. The salaries paid to the various teachers are as follows: —

Principal (with house) . . . . $3,000 per annum.
Professor of Latin . . . . 2,000 "   "

Professor of **Greek** . . . . $2,000 per annum.
Professor of Mathematics . . . . . . 2,000 "   "
Instructor of English and Latin . . . . 1,500 "   "
Instructor of French and German . . . **900** "   "

One of the above instructors generally teaches sacred music to the chapel choir and any other students who wish to join the class. For this he receives sixty dollars a year, the income of the Gilman Fund.

CHAPTER XVII.

EXETER: ITS PAST AND PRESENT.

THERE are few New England towns of more historic interest than Exeter. It is one of the oldest towns in New Hampshire, having been founded in 1639, by Rev. John Wheelwright, and has furnished many leaders, both in times of peace and of war. The town is located fifty miles from Boston, on the line of the Boston and Maine Railway, and extends along both banks of the Swamscot, where the fresh waters of the Exeter River join the tide-waters of the ocean.

It is indebted for its prosperity to its industrious and enterprising mechanics. Soon after the settlement of Exeter, saw-mills were erected at the falls of the Swamscot, where the water power has now been utilized for about two hundred and forty years, and lumber became an important article of exportation. In early days, when the channel of the river was much deeper, many ships were built; and not a few of the citizens were shipwrights and mariners. Afterward, when timber began to grow scarce, many engaged in the manufacture of saddles, and it is said that this business was more extensive in Exeter than in any other town east of Philadelphia. The large cotton-mill now in operation was completed in 1830. From 1810 to 1840 the business of printing was extensively carried on, and many books were published. The Exeter Machine Works, with the iron and brass foundries, have carried on a large business during the last few years.

After the close of the French war Exeter rapidly increased in wealth and population, so that, at the beginning of the Revolution, it became the headquarters for New Hampshire both in civil and in military affairs. Though some of its citizens had been favored by the government of England, and were personal friends of Governor Wentworth, their love for their country outweighed their personal interests, and when the tocsin of war was sounded, Exeter took its stand on the side of liberty. It then became the capital of the State. The legislature held its sessions there, and the courts were established.

"The structure which has perhaps retained its old-time appearance most perfectly for the past century is the powder-house, situated on the point near the river, on the east side. It was built about 1760, and has apparently undergone little repair since that time. It probably first held military stores destined for the French and Indian War, which, however, terminated before they could have been much needed. A few years later it was opened, no doubt to receive a part of the powder captured by the Provincials in the raid, under Sullivan, upon Fort William and Mary, in Portsmouth harbor, in December, 1774. But as powder without ball hardly met the requirements of the times, the Selectmen of Exeter purchased lead for the 'town stock' from John Emery, and sent for a further supply to Portsmouth, by Theodore Carlton, employed Thomas Gilman to 'run it into bullets,' and finally stored the

leaden missiles in a chest which Peter Folsom made for the purpose, at a cost of three and sixpence. The ammunition was dealt out from time to time to other places which stood in greater need, — very sparingly though, for, notwithstanding Exeter had a powder-mill in 1776, the explosive dust was too precious to be wasted, through a large part of the Revolutionary War. The old powder-house is now somewhat weather-beaten and dilapidated, and perhaps past its usefulness; but we hope it may be spared, on account of the good service it has done in former days. May no vandal hand be laid upon it, but may it be left to the gentle touch of time, and remain a landmark for many years to come!"

The oldest dwelling in Exeter is, doubtless, the house standing on the corner of Water and Franklin Streets, now the residence of Mr. Manley Darling. The main building is constructed like a garrison house, of squared oak logs, and is said to have been used as a protection against the attacks of the Indians. It was in this house that Daniel Webster boarded when a student in the Academy.

The Court House, formerly the meeting-house of the First Parish, was moved across the street, and stood upon the site of the dwelling of the late Joseph Boardman, at the east corner of Front and Court Streets. It was also used as a Town House and State House. The meeting-house of the First Parish stood nearly on the same spot where the present church now stands. The yard around it was then larger, and served as a burying-ground. But all outward traces of the dead are now gone, as a number of years ago the monuments were carefully levelled with the ground and covered with earth, and now the sidewalk passes over a portion of what was formerly the churchyard.

SECOND CONG. CHURCH   FIRST

In 1776 Exeter had only two churches, but within the last century the number has increased to eight. Of these the Episcopal Church was organized through the efforts of a few Academy students, aided by some of the townsfolk.

Exeter is best known to-day as the seat of the classical school which links the name of the town and its well-loved citizen, John Phillips. Although the capital of the State has been removed to Concord, much of the ancient glory of the town still remains; and on account of its healthful climate, its educational advantages, and its accessibility, it is a favorite place of residence throughout the year. Among its most important business enterprises of the present day are its iron foundries and manufactories of steam-heating apparatus, and the cotton-mill to which we have already referred.

In this sketch, which is necessarily brief, it would be impossible to mention the many pleasant features of the old town. Can any Academy student ever forget the Oaks, the Eddy, or Rocky Point, the winding Swamscot, the Great Bay, or the Shoals?

> "Once more on Stratham's wind-swept crest I stand,
> Once more these wooded vales to view expand."

Can any one fail to recall the view from Stratham Bridge, or Kensington Hill, whence can be seen the mountains, raising their pine-clad tops, and the great stretch of ocean, speckled with many a white sail?

The remembrance of such scenes, and of the half-holidays spent at Portsmouth, at Hampton, or at Rye, are dear to every student of Phillips Exeter. The thousands of Exeter students scattered through the various States of the Union can but look back with pleasure to the happy days spent at Exeter, and recall with gratitude the hospitality of the old town.

APPENDIX.

Act of Incorporation.

STATE OF NEW HAMPSHIRE. In the year of our Lord one thousand seven hundred and eighty-one. An Act to incorporate an Academy in the town of Exeter by the name of THE PHILLIPS EXETER ACADEMY. Act of General Court.
Name: The Phillips Exeter Academy.

WHEREAS the education of youth has ever been considered by the wise and good as an object of the highest consequence to the safety and happiness of a people, as at an early period in life the mind easily receives and retains impressions and is most susceptible of the rudiments of useful knowledge, and whereas the Honorable John Phillips, of Exeter, in the county of Rockingham, Esquire, is desirous of giving to Trustees hereinafter to be appointed certain lands and personal estate to be by said Trustees forever appropriated and expended for the support of a public free school or Academy in the town of Exeter, and whereas the execution of such an important design will be attended with very great embarrassments unless by an act of incorporation said Trustees and their successors shall be authorized to commence and prosecute actions at law, and transact such other matters in a corporate capacity as the interests of said Academy shall require, — Be it therefore enacted by the Council and House of Representatives in General Assembly convened and by the authority of the same, that there be and hereby is established, in the town of Exeter and county

Purposes of founding.

Phillips endowment.

of Rockingham, an **Academy by the name of** the Phillips Exeter Academy, for the purpose of promoting piety and
Curriculum. virtue, **and for the** education **of** youth **in the** English, **Latin,** and Greek languages, **in** writing, arithmetic, music, **and the art** of speaking, practical geometry, logic, and geography, **and** such other **of the** liberal arts and sciences **or languages** as opportunity **may hereafter** permit, and **as the** Trustees hereinafter **provided shall direct.**

And be it further **enacted** by the authority afore-
Original said, that the honorable **John** Phillips, Esquire, Daniel
Trustees. Tilton, **Esquire, Thomas** Odiorne, Esquire, and **Benjamin** Thurston, **Gentlemen, all of Exeter aforesaid, John Pickering, of Portsmouth, Esquire,** and the **Rev. David** MacCluer, **of Northampton, Clerk, all in the** county of Rockingham **and** State of **New Hampshire, and the Honorable** Samuel Phillips, **Jr., of Andover, in** the county **of Essex** and **Commonwealth of Massach**usetts, Esquire, be and they hereby are nominated and appointed Trus-
Incorporate tees **of said Academy, and they hereby are incorporated**
and legal ti- **into a body politic by the name of the Trustees of the**
tle: the Trus- Phillips **Exeter Academy, and that they and their suc-**
tees of the
Phillips Exe- cessors **shall be and continue a body politic and** corporate
ter Academy. **by the** same name **forever. And be it further** enacted by **the** authority aforesaid, **that the said Trustees** and their
Seal. successors shall **have one common seal, which** they may **make** use of in **any cause** of business that relates to the **said** office of Trustees of said Academy; and they shall have power and **authority** to break, change, and renew the said seal from **time to time, as they** shall see fit; and
May sue and **that they may** sue **and be sued in** all actions, real and per-
be sued. **sonal and mixed,** and **prosecute** and **defend** the same to **final judgment** and execution, by the name of the Trustees **of the Phillips** Exeter Academy. And be it further enacted **by the** authority aforesaid, that the said John Phillips, Esquire, and others, the Trustees aforesaid, the longest

livers and survivors of them, and their heirs, successors, be the true and sole visitors, Trustees, and governors of the said Academy in perpetual succession forever, to be continued in the way and manner hereinafter specified, with full power and authority to elect such officers of the said Academy as they shall judge necessary and convenient, and to make and ordain such laws, orders, and rules for the good government of said Academy as to them, the said Trustees, governors, and visitors aforesaid, and their successors, shall from time to time, according to the various occasions and circumstances, seem most fit and requisite. All which shall be observed by the officers, scholars, and servants of the Academy, upon the penalties therein contained. Provided notwithstanding, that the said rules, laws, and orders be noways contrary to the laws of this State. Be it further enacted by the authority aforesaid, that the number of said Trustees and their successors shall not at any one time be more than seven nor less than four; four of whom shall constitute a quorum for transacting business, and the major part of the members present at any legal meeting shall decide all questions that shall come before them, except in the instances hereinafter excepted. That the principal Instructor, for the time being, shall ever be one of the said Trustees; that a major part shall be laymen and reputable freeholders. Also that all elections of the said Trustees shall be so governed in future that major part of them shall consist of men who are not inhabitants of the town where the Academy is situated. And to perpetuate the successors of said Trustees, Be it further enacted by the authority aforesaid, that as often as one or more of the Trustees of said Academy shall die, or resign, or in the judgment of the major part of the other Trustees be rendered, by age or otherwise, incapable of discharging the duties of his office, then and so often the

In perpetuity.

Powers.

Number of Trustees.

Quorum.

Principal, Trustee ex officio.

Non-resident Trustees.

328 THE PHILLIPS EXETER ACADEMY.

Vacancies in Board.

Trustees surviving and remaining, or the major part of them, shall elect one or more persons to supply the vacancy or vacancies so happening. And be it further enacted by the authority aforesaid, that the Trustees aforesaid and their successors, be, and they hereby are,

Endowments.

rendered capable in law to take and receive by gift, grant, devise, bequest, or otherwise, any lands, tenements, or other estate, real and personal, provided that the annual income of the said real estate shall not exceed the sum of five hundred pound, and the annual income of the said personal estate shall not exceed the sum of two thousand pounds,[1] both sums to be valued in silver at the rate of six shillings and eight pence by the ounce. To have and to hold the same to them, the said Trustees and their successors, on such terms and under such conditions and limitations as may be expressed in any deed or instrument of conveyance which shall be made to them, provided always that neither the said Trustees nor their successors shall ever hereafter receive any grant or donation the conditions whereof shall require them or any others concerned to act in any respect counter to the

Deeds, binding if signed by four Trustees.

design of the first Grantor. And all deeds and instruments which the said Trustees shall make, when made in the name of said Trustees, and signed and delivered by four of the said Trustees at least, and sealed with their common seal, shall bind the said Trustees and their successors, and be valid in law. And be it further enacted by the authority aforesaid, that if it shall hereafter be judged, upon mature and impartial considerations of all circumstances by two thirds of all the Trustees, that for good and substantial reasons, which at this time do not exist, the true design of this institution will be better

Power of removing Academy.

promoted by removing the Academy from the place where it is founded, it shall be in the power of the said Trustees

[1] This restriction should, and probably will, be repealed.

APPENDIX.

to remove it accordingly, and to establish it in such other place within the State as they shall judge to be best calculated for carrying into effectual execution the intentions of the Founder. And whereas the said institution may be of very great and general advantage to this State, and deserves every encouragement, Be it therefore enacted by the authority aforesaid, that all the lands, tenements, and personal estate that shall be given to said Trustees for the use of the said Academy shall be, and hereby are, forever exempted from all taxes whatsoever. <small>Exemption from taxation.</small>

State of New Hampshire in the House of Representatives, March 30, 1871. The foregoing bill having been read a third time,

Voted, that it pass to be enacted. Sent up for concurrence.

JOHN LANGDON, *Speaker*.

In Council, the 3d of April, 1781. This Bill having been read the third time,

Voted, the same be enacted.

W. WEARE, *President*.
SAM. BROOKS, *Recorder*.

Copy examined by JOSEPH PEARSON, *D. Sec'y*.

Received and recorded 11th March, 1782.

Copy of the Act of General Court, recorded in Office of Registry of Deeds (Exeter, N. H.), Book 113, page 507.

GEO. W. WESTON, *Register of Deeds*.

Sept. 17, 1881.

Constitution.

Preamble.

WHEN we reflect upon **the grand design of** the great **Parent of the** universe in **the** creation of mankind; and the improvements of which **the** mind is capable, both in **knowledge and** virtue; **as well as upon the** prevalence **of ignorance and vice, disorder and wickedness, and** upon **the direct tendency and certain issue of such a course** of **things, such reflection must occasion in thoughtful minds an earnest solicitude to find the source of these evils and their remedy. And small acquaintance with the qualities of young minds,** how **susceptible and tenacious they are of impressions,** evidences **that the time of** youth is the **important period,** on the improvement or neglect of **which depends** the most weighty consequences to individuals **themselves, and** the community.

Reasons for founding Academy.

A serious consideration of these things, and an observation **of the growing** neglect of youth, must excite a painful **anxiety for the event**; and may well determine those whom **their Heavenly** Benefactor **hath blessed** with **an** ability therefore to promote **and encourage public** free schools **or** Academies **for** the purpose of instructing youth not **only in** the English and Latin grammar, writing, arithmetic, and those sciences wherein they are commonly **taught,** but more especially to learn them the great end **and real** business of **living.** Earnestly wishing that such **institutions** may grow and flourish, that the advantages **of them may** be extensive and lasting, that their usefulness **may be** so manifest as to lead the way to other establishments **on the** same principles, and that they may finally prove eminent means of advancing the interest of **the** Great Redeemer. To His patronage and blessing **may all friends** to learning and religion most humbly **commit them.**

To ALL PEOPLE to whom these presents shall come, Greeting: Whereas the General Assembly of the State of New Hampshire did by their Act, on the third day of April, Anno Domini 1781, Incorporate an Academy in the town of Exeter and county of Rockingham, by the name of the Phillips Exeter Academy, for the purposes of promoting piety and virtue, and for the education of youth as is in said Act directed. And whereas by said Act all the lands, tenements, and personal estate that shall be given to Trustees for the use of said Academy are and shall be forever exempted from all taxes whatsoever, — {Name: The Phillips Exeter Academy.}

Therefore, in consideration of the great importance of the design mentioned, and of the powers, privileges, and immunities in and by said Act granted, and for the sole purposes of promoting piety, virtue, and useful literature, I, John Phillips, of Exeter aforesaid, Esquire, have granted, and with most humble thanks to the Lord and Giver of all things for the opportunity, ability, and disposition by Him given, do by these presents most cheerfully grant to the Trustees of the said Phillips Exeter Academy nominated and appointed by said Act, and to their successors in that Trust, all my right, title, and interest in and unto the real estate described as followeth: — {Conveys to the Trustees 3,200 acres of land, and other property.}

[He then describes the various tracts of land, — 3,200 acres or more in all, — the saw-mill rights, and other property conveyed, and continuing: —]

Provided, however, that any mortgaged land, how long soever the time for payment has been elapsed, may be redeemed by the mortgagee's payment, at a time the Trustees shall judge reasonable, such sum or sums of money as shall appear to them justly and righteously due on their respective mortgages. To have and to hold the granted premises with all their appurtenances to the said Trustees of the said Phillips Exeter Academy, and to their successors in said Trust, for the use and purposes {Outstanding mortgages.}

and upon the Trust hereinafter mentioned, on such terms and conditions as the first Grantor has a legal right to express in the deed or instrument of conveyance by him made: and which are the necessary or beneficial standing regulations forming the Constitution of this Academy, and ever to be considered as essentially and inseparably connected with this Grant, being as follows, viz.:—

<small>Conditions of grant.</small>

<small>Regulations forming Constitution of the Academy.</small>

The first Instructor shall be nominated and appointed by the Founder. The Trustees, or a major part of them, shall meet once a year at the Phillips Exeter Academy; their first meeting shall be on the 18th day of December, A. D. 1781, when they shall determine on the time for holding the annual meeting, which may be altered as they shall hereafter find most convenient.

<small>Meeting of Trustees.</small>

A President, Clerk, and Treasurer shall be annually chosen, who shall officiate till their places are supplied by a new election, and no member shall sustain the office of Clerk and Treasurer at the same time. An Instructor shall not be chosen President, and upon the decease of a President, Clerk, or Treasurer, another shall be chosen in his room at the next annual meeting.

<small>Officers.</small>

The President shall call special meetings upon the application of any three of the Trustees; or upon the concurrence of any two of them in sentiment with him on occasion of such meeting; and upon the decease of the President a special meeting shall be called by any three of the Trustees. All notifications for special meetings shall express the business to be transacted if convenient, and be given at least one month previous to such meeting if not incompatible with the welfare of the Academy. And when a special meeting shall be called for the appointment of an instructor, or to transact other business of material consequence, information shall be given by leaving a written notification at the house of each Trustee, or in such other way as that the President

<small>Special meetings.</small>

or members notifying shall have good reason to believe that each member has received the notice. The Clerk shall record all votes of the Trustees, inserting the names of those present at every meeting. He shall keep a fair record of every donation, with the name of each benefactor, of the purpose, if expressed, to which it is constitutionally appropriated, and of all expenditures of them. And a true copy of the whole shall be taken and kept in the Academy, to be open for the perusal of all men. And if he shall be absent at any meeting of the Trustees another shall be appointed to serve in his room during such absence. *Clerk. Records open to all men.*

The Treasurer shall, previous to his receiving the interest of the Academy into his hands, give bond for the faithful discharge of his office, in such sum as the Trustees shall direct, with sufficient sureties to the Trustees, which bond shall express the use both in the obligatory part and in the condition; he shall give duplicate receipts for all moneys received, countersigned by one of the Trustees, one to the donor, the other to be lodged with such member as the Trustees shall from time to time direct; and the Trustees shall take such other measures as they shall judge requisite to make the Treasurer accountable and effectually to secure the interest of the Academy. The Trustees shall let or rent out personal or real estate, or make sale and purchases of lands, and improve the property of the Academy as they shall judge will best serve its interest without diminishing the Fund. Whereas the success of this institution much depends under Providence on a discreet appointment of its instructors, and the human mind is liable to imperceptible bias, it is required that when a candidate for election is so near akin to any member of the Trust as a first-cousin, such member shall not sit in determining the election. No person shall be *Treasurer. Investments. Instructors. Appointment.*

chosen as a principal instructor unless he be a member of a church of Christ, in complete standing, whose sentiments are similar to those hereinafter expressed, and will lead him to inculcate the doctrines and perform the duties required in this Constitution; also of exemplary manners, of good natural abilities and literary acquirements, of a natural aptitude for instruction and government; a good acquaintance with human nature is also much to be desired, and in the appointment of any instructor regard shall be had to qualifications only, without preference of friend or kindred, place or birth, education or residence. The Trustees shall make a contract with instructors as to salary, before their entrance upon office; and when the number of scholars shall require more instructors than the Principal, it will be expected that persons of ability who reap some advantage by this institution will cheerfully assist in supporting the additional, so that poor children of promising genius may be introduced, and members who may need some special aid may have it afforded them. It shall be the duty of the Trustees to inquire into the conduct of the instructors, and if they or either of them be found justly chargeable with such misconduct, neglect of duty, or incapacity as the said Trustees shall judge renders them or either of them unfit to continue in office, they shall remove them or either of them so chargeable.

As the welfare of the Academy will be greatly promoted by the students being conversant with persons of good character only, no scholar may enjoy the privileges of this Institution who shall board in any family which is not licensed by the Trustees. And applications will be in vain where the daily worship of God and good government is not said to be maintained. And in order to preserve this Seminary from the baneful influence of the

incorrigibly vicious, the Trustees shall determine for **what
reasons a** scholar shall be expelled, and the manner in **which the sentence** shall be administered. *Expulsion.*

The Trustees at their annual meetings shall visit the Seminary and examine into **the proficiencies of the** scholars, examine and adjust all **accounts** relative to the Seminary, and make any further rules **and orders which** they find **necessary and conformable to this Constitution.** The principal **instructor may not sit in** determining matter wherein he is particularly **interested.** Extravagant entertainments shall be **discountenanced and economy recommended** by Trustees and instructors. **Ap-plications for admission of** scholars are to be made to **the principal instructor,** and the rules and orders the instructors may make for **the** good government of the scholars shall be subject to the examination, amendment, or discontinuance of the Trustees. *Duties of Trustees. Economy recommended. Admission.*

It shall ever be considered as a principal duty of the instructors to regulate the temper, to enlarge the minds and form the morals of the youth **committed to their care.** They are to give special attention to **the health of the** scholars, and ever to urge the importance of an **habit of** industry. **For these** purposes **they may encourage the** scholars to perform some **manual labor, such as gardening, or the like, so far as is consistent** with cleanliness and the **inclinations of their parents; and** the fruit of their labor **shall be applied, at the** discretion of the **Trustees,** for procuring **a Library,** or in some other way **increasing the** usefulness of this Seminary. But above all it is expected that **the** attention of instructors to the disposition of **the** minds and morals of the youth under **their charge will** exceed every other care, **well considering that though** goodness without knowledge as it respects **others is weak and feeble,** yet knowledge without goodness is dangerous, **and that** both united **form** the noblest character **and lay** *Duties of Instructors.*

Instructors must especially teach morality.

the surest foundation of usefulness to mankind. It is therefore required that they most attentively and **vigorously guard** against the earliest irregularities; that they frequently delineate in their natural colors the deformity and **odiousness** of vice, and **the beauty and** amiableness of virtue; that they spare **no** pains to convince them of the numberless and indispensable obligations to abhor and avoid the former, and **to love** and practise the latter; of **the** several great duties they owe to God, their country, their parents, their neighbors, and themselves; that they critically and constantly observe **the** variety **of** their natural tempers, and solicitously endeavor to bring them **under such** discipline as may tend most effectually to promote **their** own satisfaction **and the** happiness of others; that **they** early **inure them to** contemplate the several connections and various scenes incident to human life, furnishing such general maxims of conduct as may **best enable them to** pass through all with care, reputation, **and comfort. And** whereas many of the students of this **Academy may be** devoted to the sacred work of the **Gospel ministry, therefore** that the **true** and fundamental principles of **the Christian** religion may be cultivated, established, and perpetuated in the Christian Church, so **far as** this institution **may have influence, it** shall be the **duty of** the instructors, as the age and capacity of the **scholars** will admit, **to** teach them the principles of natural religion, as **the being** of a God, and his perfections, **his** universal providence and perfect government, of the natural and moral **world, and obligations to** duty resulting from them. Also **to teach** them doctrines of revealed religion as they are contained in the sacred scriptures of divine authority, being given by inspiration of God, the doctrine of the Father, the Word, and the Holy Ghost, particularly the doctrine of Christ as true God, the only begotten of the Father, with all the truths they declare

Religious instruction.

Doctrines.

relative to his office of Mediator and work of redemption and salvation from the state of sin, guilt, and depravity of nature man has fallen into; the necessity of atonement by the blood of Jesus Christ, and of regeneration by the spirit of God; the doctrine of repentance towards God and of faith in our Lord Jesus Christ considered as duties and gifts of God's grace; and the doctrine of justification by the free grace of God, through the redemption that is in Jesus Christ, whose righteousness in his obedience unto death is the only ground and reason of the sinner's pardon and acceptance as righteous in the sight of God. The doctrine also of the Christian progressive sanctification in dying unto sin and living unto God, in new obedience to all the commandments of Christ proceeding from Gospel motives and views supremely to the glory of God; and the doctrines of the resurrection from the dead and of the great and final judgment, with its consequences of happiness to the righteous and misery to the wicked.

These, and all the doctrines and duties of our holy Christian religion, nothing founded on human authority, will be proved by Scripture testimony. And whereas the most wholesome precepts without frequent repetitions may prove ineffectual, it is further required of the instructors that they not only urge and re-urge, but continue from day to day to impress these instructions; and let them ever remember that the design of this institution can never be answered without their persevering, incessant attention to this duty. Protestants only shall ever be concerned in the Trust or Instruction of this Seminary; and they, having severally approved the Constitution, their government and instructions conformably thereto must appear steady, cordial, and vigorous. *Protestants alone eligible as instructors.*

The election of the officers of this Academy shall be by ballot only; and it shall ever be equally open to youth *Election of officers.*

of requisite qualifications from every quarter, provided that none be admitted till, in common parlance, **they can read** English well, excepting such particular members as the Trustees may hereafter license. And in order to prevent a perversion of the **true** intent of this foundation, it is again declared that **the first** and principal design of **this** institution is the promoting virtue and true piety; **useful** knowledge in **the order** before referred to (in the Act of Incorporation) **being subservient thereto.** And I hereby reserve to myself, during any part of my **natural** life, the full **right to** make any special rules **for the perpetual** government **of** this Academy which **shall be** equally binding on those **whom they may concern with any** clause **in these regulations, provided no such rule** shall be subversive of **the true** intent of this foundation. **I also reserve** a right to appoint one person to succeed me **in the Trust** after my decease or resignation, to whom shall be **transferred** the same right of appointment, and to his successors in the said Trust forever. The foregoing regulations, forming the Constitution of the Phillips Exeter **Academy,** shall ever be read **by the President** for the time being **at the annual meetings of** the Trustees of said Academy, **that they and their** successors may be fully acquainted **with, and in all future time** be reminded of their **duty.**

And considering them as true to their Trust, I, the said John Phillips, for myself and my heirs, executors, and administrators, **do** hereby covenant, grant, and agree to and with the **said Trustees and** their successors, that I will **warrant and defend** the before granted premises to them **forever** against **the** lawful claims and demands of any **person** or persons whomsoever holding from, by, or under me. Likewise Elizabeth, my wife, doth hereby **freely and** voluntarily relinquish all right of dower and **power of** thirds in the premises. In witness whereof, we have hereunto set our hands and seals, the seventeenth day of May, **Anno** Domini one thousand seven hundred and **eighty-one.**   Date. May 17, 1781.

Signed, sealed, and delivered in presence of
P. White.
Jacob Abbot.
}   JOHN PHILLIPS.   [seal.]
      ELIZABETH PHILLIPS. [seal.]

Rockingham ss., January 9, 1782.

John Phillips, Esquire, and Elizabeth, his wife, owned this instrument to be their free act and deed.

        Before me,   Phillips **White,** *J. Peace.*

Received and recorded, **11th March, 1782.**

                     Saml. Brooks, *Rdr.*

The foregoing is the copy **of a record from** Rockingham **Registry** of Deeds, in Exeter, **N. H.,** Book 113, page 499.

           Attest:

               Geo. W. Weston, *Register.*

REUNION.

A SONG WRITTEN BY DR. HENRY WARE, JR., AND SUNG AT
THE ABBOT FESTIVAL.

TUNE: — *Sandy and Jenny.*

From the highways and byways of manhood we come,
And gather like children about an old home;
We return from life's weariness, tumult, and pain,
Rejoiced in our hearts to be schoolboys again.

The Senator comes from the hall of debate;
The Governor steps from the high chair of state;
The Judge leaves the bench to the law's wise delay,
Rejoiced to be schoolboys again for a day.

The parson his pulpit has left unsupplied;
The doctor has put his old sulky aside;
The lawyer his client has turned from the door,
And all are at Exeter, — schoolboys once more.

O, glad to our eyes are these dear scenes displayed,
The Halls where we studied, the fields where we strayed;
There is change, — there is change; but we will not deplore,
Enough that we feel ourselves schoolboys once more.

Enough that once more our old master we meet,
The same as of yore when we sat at his feet;
Let us place on his brow every laurel we've won,
And show that each pupil is also a son.

And when to the harsh scenes of life we return,
Our hearts with the glow of this meeting shall burn;
Its calm light shall cheer till earth's school-time is o'er,
And prepare us in Heaven for one meeting more.

THE PHILLIPS EXETER ACADEMY.

BUILT, 1794. — BURNED, 1870.

BY PROF. JOHN B. L. SOULE.

ALAS! those dear old classic halls,
  Where all the Muses sat,
More loved than old Dardanian walls,
  Amo, amas, amat.
How have the flames that laid them low
  New flames within us lit,
And set our bosoms all aglow,
  Uro, uris, urit.

There all the victories were won,
  Heroic and divine;
There Cæsar crossed the Rubicon,
  And Xerxes chained the brine:
There Juno raised her dire alarms,
  And Jove 'mid thunders sat;
And men and gods were up in arms,
  Pugno, pugnas, pugnat.

When he, our reverend Abbot, came
  Upon the dais to sit,
How rose we at the whispered name,
  Surgo, surgis, surgit;
And at his passing presence all
  Stood still with lifted hat,
Then furious kicked the groaning ball,
  Calco, calcas, calcat.

And then to free his patient flock,
  At every close of day
He turned him to the gray old clock,
  And bowed his head to pray;

And to the monitor who tried
  Our wayward steps to keep,
The old, diurnal question plied, —
  "*Whose turn is it to sweep?*"

Again that question seems along
  On every breeze to come,
To every ear of all the throng
  Exoniensium;
The ashes from our temple seat
  "Whose turn to sweep is it?"
A thousand hands the task shall greet,
  Verro, verris, verrit.

Leave mount and valley, hill and plain,
  And every calling quit;
And run with all your might and main,
  Curro, curris, currit;
Let none with tardy step delay,
  Whatever he is at,
But push with all his strength away,
  Pulso, pulsas, pulsat.

From high and by way, far and wide,
  Let all the builders come,
And do good service side by side,
  Bonus, bona, bonum;
With rapid strokes build strong and high
  The everlasting stone,
Τύπτω, τύπτω, τύπτοιμι,
  Τύπτε, τύπτειν, τύπτων.

SCHOOL DAYS AT EXETER.[1]

A POEM READ AT THE DEDICATION OF THE NEW ACADEMY BUILDING, BY HON. GEORGE S. HALE.

The young Iulus, midst the Trojan fire,
With steps unequal, followed his great sire;
His wanderings o'er, the patriotic boy
Helped to build up another greater Troy.

With steps unequal though we follow those
Whose wide-spread fame each proud alumnus knows,
Who made the glory of the days gone by,
And moved conspicuous in the Nation's eye, —

Perchance our second Troy shall bear our fame
To future ages, with some greater name, —
Our Hector by some Cæsar be outdone,
And Webster's glory find some greater son.

Dear are the memories of the ancient shrine;
Who is not proud to say, "And these were mine"?
The morning greetings in the noisy Hall,
The jovial crowd that chased the flying ball,

The rare events, when boyish hands set free
Clapped for a bride or birth with eager glee,
The hour reluctant, given to the broom,
When Smith Secundus swept the Latin room,

The happy wanderings when spring was new,
The happy holidays that swiftly flew,
The Record, which we feared yet longed to see,
That told our parents what their boys might be.

[1] Used through the courtesy of Hon. Charles H. Bell.

But hours there are that graver **thoughts employ,**
Signs of the man fast growing **in the boy,** —
The hours of study and the thoughts of fame
Stirred by the memory of some honored **name.**

For some the counting of the scanty store,
The anxious question **where to look for more;**
How best to spare a father's weary toil,
And constant struggle with th' ungrateful soil.

O, may these walls we dedicate anew
Still to the memory of **the past be true,**
And sons, succeeding sires, still hold
The lengthening chain that binds the young and old, —

Still learn **the** lessons that their fathers **learned,**
With brighter honors than **their fathers earned,**
And crown the latter house their **fathers raise**
With glory greater than in former **days!**

DEDICATION SONG.

WRITTEN BY C. H. B. SNOW, ESQ., AND SUNG AT THE
"SOULE FESTIVAL."

TUNE: — *Old Hundred.*

Like mists **the** intervening years
 Roll up, exhale, and pass **away;**
And once again the sun appears
 That gilded boyhood's opening day.
Touched by its rays, each bygone scene
 Starts forth in outlines clear and **bright,**
And all the Past, in fadeless **green,**
 Is bathed once more **in morning light.**

These walls, that grateful hands have reared,
  Like dreams dissolve and fade away;
We see, to every heart endeared,
  The structure of an earlier day,
Beneath whose roof our youth was spent,
  Where first we tasted learning's spring,
To which, where'er our steps have bent,
  Our hearts, untravelled, ever cling.

With honors crowned, and length of days,
  Soothed with the solace age should shed,
The approving conscience, general praise,
  We hail our venerated head.
Our loving hands with haste displace
  Whate'er disguise these years may lend,
And still to memory's eye his face
  Unchanged we greet, our guide and friend.

Dear Home! This day, from every side,
  Come wanderers from land and sea,
Long tossed on Time's tempestuous tide,
  Thy children hastening back to thee.
Thy arms receive them as of yore;
  Thy blessing, like a holy strain,
Shall sanctify this favored hour,
  And bring back boyhood once again.

ORDER OF EXERCISES.

[August, 1808?]

Music.

1. Salutatory Address in Latin.
   E. Everett.
2. "The Country Schoolmaster."
   C. Brown.
3. Extract from the "Good-Natured Man."
   J. Heath, J. E. Abbot, S. B. Ladd, C. Thorndike.
4. Extract from "Hamlet."
   D. Williams, H. Smith, E. Haskell.
5. "The Painter."
   J. H. Duncan.
6. Extract from "Andria."
   T. R. Sewall, J. Fellows.
7. Extract from "Indigence and Nobleness of Mind."
   S. B. Ladd, E. F. Paige, J. W. Peirce, S. Woodbury.
8. Inconsistent Expectation.
   E. Blanchard.
9. Parallel of Dryden and Pope.
   E. A. White.
10. "Military Academy."
    J. Lane, B. Hanson, T. A. Deblois, G. Lamson, E. Kimball, E. Everett.
11. "Mahomet's Prohibition."
    J. W. Peirce.
12. Extract from "The Earl of Warwick."
    B. T. Pickman, D. Williams.

APPENDIX. 347

13. Intermediate Address in Latin, on Learning.
                H. SMITH.
14. Extract from " Who wants a Guinea ? "
    E. EVERETT, F. E. HUTCHINGS, J. E. ABBOT.
15. Dialogue in Greek.
     E. BLANCHARD, E. HASKELL, N. H. CARTER.
16. " Immortality of the Soul."
                B. BATES.
17. Extract from " Alfonso."
  B. T. PICKMAN, W. REED, J. LITTLE, D. WILLIAMS, H. SMITH.
18. An Oration against Philip.
                E. F. PAIGE.
19. Extract from " School of Reform."
  W. REED, S. WOODBURY, F. E. HUTCHINGS, N. H. CARTER, J. W. PEIRCE.
20. Valedictory Address.
                B. T. PICKMAN.

MUSIC.

N. B. The Names of Performers in the several Dialogues are placed in the order in which they first speak.

ORDER OF **EXERCISES**

FOR

EXHIBITION AT PHILLIPS EXETER ACADEMY,

AUGUST 20, 1835.

The Speakers in the Dialogues, &c. will speak in the order of their names.

MUSIC.

1. Salutatory **Oration in** Latin.
    EDMUND B. WHITMAN, **East Bridgewater, Mass.**
2. **Translations from the Latin, by**
    FRANCIS B. HAYES, South Berwick, Me.
    NATHANIEL B. BAKER, Concord.
3. Comparative Influence of *Forms of Government* and *Systems of Education* on National Character.
    WILLIAM **HENDERSON,** Dover.
    THOMAS CLEMENTS, **Dover.**
4. Greek Dialogue. (*Selected.*)
    WILLIAM P. **HILL, Concord.**
    CHARLES JARVIS, **Weathersfield,** Vt.
    GEORGE N. EASTMAN, Farmington.
5. Arnold and Pausanias.
    HORATIO MERRILL, Brownfield, Me.
    WALTER H. TENNEY, Concord.
6. Personal Exertion necessary to Success.
    EZEKIEL GILMAN, Exeter.
7. Translations from the Latin, by
    EDMUND CHADWICK, Dover.
    HENRY C. WHITMAN, Billerica, Mass.
8. **Latin Poem.** Albæ Excidium.
    JOHN B. L. SOULE, Freeport, Me.

9. Comparative Value of Civil and Military Services, as exemplified in the Lives of Washington and Marshall.
     WILLIAM H. LOW, Dover.
     GEORGE T. UPHAM, Portsmouth.

10. English Dialogue. (*Selected.*)
     JAMES W. BROWN, Framingham, Mass.
     HENRY C. WHITMAN.

11. Hospitality of the Ancients.
     BERNARD B. WHITTEMORE, Peterborough.

12. English Poem. The Indian Assault.
     NATHANIEL H. MORISON, Peterborough.

13. Translations from the Greek, by
     WILLIAM B. PORTER, Newburyport, Mass.
     FRANCIS P. HURD, Exeter.

14. Poverty.
     EDMUND CHADWICK.

15. English Dialogue. (*Selected.*)
     JOSEPH L. LEACH, Concord.
     NICHOLAS A. CLARKE, Exeter.
     EDMUND B. WHITMAN.
     JOHN B. L. SOULE.
     FREDERICK MORRILL, Brentwood.
     FRANCIS E. PARKER, Portsmouth.
     GEORGE HOBART, East Bridgewater, Ms.

16. Onward.
     JAMES W. BROWN.

17. The Reformation.
     WILLIAM C. TENNEY, New-Market.

18. Valedictory Address.
     NICHOLAS A. CLARKE.

MUSIC.

ODE. — BY NATHANIEL M. MORISON.

INDEX.

INDEX.

Abbot, Abiel, assistant instructor at Exeter Academy, 17.

Abbot, Benjamin, second Principal of Academy, 16; enters the Phillips Academy at Andover, 18; his studies and schoolmates, 18; graduates from Harvard College, 19; instructor in Exeter Academy, 19; chosen Preceptor of Exeter Academy, 19, 77; his qualifications as a teacher and his interest in his work, 19, 20; his benignity of character, 20, 21; pleasant reminiscences of, by former pupils, 21-25; his pride in the Academy, 24; extract from the North American Review concerning, 25-27; resigns his position as Principal, 27, 80; the Festival in honor of, 27-33, 80; the Abbot Scholarship founded at Cambridge in honor of, 32; the portrait of, presented to Exeter Academy, 32; death of, 34, 81; some biographical notes of, 34; his grave at Exeter, 35; summary of his principalship of Exeter Academy, 35, 36; resolutions adopted by the Board of Trustees at his death, 81; reminiscence of, by A. S. Packard, 228, 229.

Abbot, Charles Benjamin, some account of, 34 (*note*).

Abbot, Elizabeth Perkins, some account of, 34 (*note*).

Abbot, George, some account of the family of, 16, 17.

Abbot, Hannah Tracy Emery, the first wife of Benjamin, 34.

Abbot, John, name borne for five generations, 16.

Abbot, John, Professor and Librarian at Bowdoin College, 17.

Abbot, John Emery, some account of, 34 (*note*).

Abbot, Mary Perkins, the second wife of Benjamin, 34; death of, 35.

Act of Incorporation of Exeter Academy, 325-329.

Adams, Ebenezer, first Professor of Mathematics and Natural Philosophy at Exeter Academy, 19.

Athletic Association, the, its organization, 269, 270; how maintained and conducted, 270, 271.

Bancroft, George, endows a scholarship at Exeter Academy, 83, 156; presides at the centennial celebration of Exeter Academy, 86; biographical sketch of, 154-156.

Boat Club, the, its organization, 267, 268; how maintained and conducted, 269; its ensign, 269.

Bowen, Francis, biographical sketch of, 195-197.

Buckminster, Rev. Joseph, elected Professor of Divinity at Exeter Academy, 77, 133; biographical sketch of, 179-181.

Burroughs, Charles, biographical sketch of, 217, 218.

Butler, Hon. Benjamin F., biographical sketch of, 158-162.

INDEX.

Cambridge, Harvard College established at, 4; first printing-press in America at, 4; first Bible in Indian tongue printed at, 4.

Cass, Lewis, biographical sketch of, 142–145.

Chadbourne, Paul Ansel, biographical sketch of, 181–184.

Chadwick, Edmund, reminiscence of Benjamin F. Butler by, 159.

Christian Fraternity, the, origin **of,** 249; its founders, 249 (*note*); its officers and its meetings, 250.

Cilley, Bradbury Longfellow, biographical sketch of, 200, **201.**

Cleaveland, John P., biographical sketch of, 187, **188.**

Cogswell, Joseph **Greene, biographi**cal sketch of, **171.**

Constitution of **the** Founder of Exeter Academy, **330–339.**

Copeland, William E., reminiscence by, of school life at Exeter in **1855,** 240–244.

Cunningham, Frank H., speech by, at the anniversary of the Christian **Fraternity,** 251, 252.

Dartmouth College, established by royal grant, 7 (*note*).

Dearborn, Colonel Henry, 77.

Dummer Academy, established at Byfield, Mass., 5.

Dunbar, Charles **F., biographical** sketch of, 171.

Emery, Nicholas, assistant tutor at Exeter Academy, 132.

Everett, Alexander Hill, biographical sketch of, 188, **189.**

Everett, Edward, biographical sketch of, 139–142.

Exeter, brief sketch of, 319–324; its early settlement and location, 319; its principal industries, 319, 320, 323; its active part in the Revolution, 320–322; its principal buildings of interest, 320, 322–324; its beautiful scenery, 323, 324.

Exonian, the, its origin, 272; **censor**ship exercised by the Faculty **over,** 274; its financial prosperity, **275,** 276; its editors, 276–279; miscellaneous remarks on, 279, 280.

Faulhaber, Oscar, **biographical sketch** of, 201.

Gideon Lane Soule Literary Society, the, its motto, **263;** its organization, 264; **its** officers, past and present, 264–267; programme of its meetings, 264, 267; its **growth** and prosperity, 265–267.

Gilman, John Taylor, Treasurer **of** Exeter Academy, 71; President **of** the Board of Trustees of Exeter Academy, 79.

Gilman, Nicholas, his bequest to Exeter Academy, 73, 79; anecdote of, by George Kent, 225.

Golden Branch Society, the, its motto, 252, **255;** its object, 253, 262; origin of, 253, 254; original members of, 254 (*note*); its meetings, 255, 262; extract from the inaugural address of one of its Presidents, 216; the cause of ill-feeling **among** non-members, 256, 257; the office of critic, and how abolished, 258, 259; its library, 259; list of lecturers at **its** anniversaries, 260; its roll of membership since its organization, **261.**

Gordon, Nathaniel, founds a scholarship at Exeter Academy, 84.

Hale, Hon. George S., poem by, 344, 345.

Hale, John Parker, biographical sketch of, 145–147.

Hale, Martha, founds a scholarship at Exeter Academy, 84.

Hale, Nathan, biographical sketch of, 194, 195.

Harvard College, established at Cambridge, Mass., 4.

Harvard, John, the early patron of Harvard College, 4.

INDEX. 355

Haven, Nathan A., Jr., biographical sketch of, 163, 164.
Hildreth, Hosea, teacher at Exeter Academy, 42, 193; biographical sketch of, 192, 193.
Hildreth, Richard, biographical sketch of, 156, 157.
Hoyt, Joseph Gibson, a summary of the characteristics of Benjamin Abbot by, 25–27; biographical sketch of, 173–179; early life and struggle for an education, 173; his professional life, 174; his efforts in behalf of the town of Exeter, 174, 175; his death, 174; his success as a teacher, 175, 176; his literary ability, 176; anecdotes of, 176, 177; eulogy on, by Sylvester Waterhouse, 178.
Hurd, Isaac C., elected Theological Instructor at Exeter Academy, 79, 194; biographical sketch of, 194.
Incorporation, Act of, for the Exeter Academy, 325–329.
Kent, George, reminiscences of school life at Exeter in 1808, 220–225.
Kingman, Jeremiah, biographical sketch of, 203–311; his early youth and education, 203, 204; his interest in the work of education, 204; his bequest to Exeter Academy and Dartmouth College, 205; his public and social life, 205, 206; his devotion to study in later years, 206, 207; his rare argumentative ability, 207, 208; anecdotes of, 209; characteristics of, 210.
Kittredge, George Lyman, biographical sketch of, 202.
Lincoln, Hon. Robert T., anecdote of Dr. Soule by, 57; biographical sketch of, 149, 150.
Lord, Nathan, biographical sketch of, 190.
Lyman, Theodore, biographical sketch of, 171.

Massachusetts Colony, early provisions for education in, 3, 4.
Mather, Cotton, his epitaph on Samuel Phillips, 89.
McClure, Rev. David, discourse by, at the opening of Exeter Academy, 8; oration by, at the dedication of the Academy building and the installation of the first Preceptor, 9; one of the first Trustees of the Academy, 326.
Morison, Rev. John H., anecdote of Dr. Soule by, 51–53.
Moulton, William P., reminiscence of Benjamin F. Butler by, 159.
Odlin, Woodbridge, 74; founds the Odlin Professorship at Exeter Academy, 85, 214; biographical sketch of, 213, 214.
Orders of Exercises, 346–350.
Packard, Alpheus Spring, Professor at Bowdoin College, 42, 166; biographical sketch of, 166, 167; reminiscences of school life at Exeter in 1811, 226–235.
Palfrey, Dr. John G., presides at the Soule Festival, 60; biographical sketch of, 162, 163.
Peabody, Dr. A. P., President of the Board of Trustees of Phillips Exeter Academy, 45, 219; extract from a speech by, on the resignation of Dr. Soule, 45, 57; high tribute paid to Dr. Soule by, 57; biographical sketch of, 218, 219.
Peabody, General Nathaniel, anecdote of, by George Kent, 224.
Peabody, Oliver W. B., biographical sketch of, 191, 192.
Peabody, William B. O., biographical sketch of, 191.
Pearson, Eliphalet, a friend and schoolmate of Judge Samuel Phillips, 5; his efforts for the establishment of the Phillips Academy at Andover, 7; teacher at the Phillips Academy at Andover, 18.

INDEX.

Pennell, Robert Franklin, anecdote of, 126; biographical sketch of, 198, 199.

Perkins, **Albert** Cornelius, fourth Principal **of** the Phillips Exeter Academy, 67, 84; some account of, 67, 68; resigns his position as Principal, 67, 86.

Phillips, Christopher, genealogical table **of the** family of, 105.

Phillips, Elizabeth, her gift to the Phillips Exeter Academy, 72, 101.

Phillips, George, Rev., ancestor of the founder of Phillips Exeter Academy, 3 ; some account of, 87–**89**; brief sketch of the family of, 87–90, 105.

Phillips, John (*a*), 105.

Phillips, John (*b*), 105.

Phillips, John (*c*), 105.

Phillips, John (*d*), one of the founders of the Phillips Academy at Andover, 6, 96; founds the Phillips Exeter Academy, 7; letter from, **to Judge** Samuel Phillips, regarding the opening of the Phillips Exeter Academy, 8; birth of, 90; some account of his early life, 90, 91; invited to become pastor of the Second **Church** in Exeter, 91; retires from **the** ministry and enters business, **91**; his thrift and economy, 92 ; his home at Exeter, 93; anecdote of, by Wendell Phillips, 94; his zeal **and activity** during the Revolution, 95 **; retires** from business, 95; his interest **in** the advancement of education, 96 ; receives the degree of LL. D. from **Dartmouth** College, 96; his various gifts **to the** Phillips Academy **at** Andover, **97**; a letter from, **to** Judge Samuel Phillips, regarding the incorporation of Exeter Academy, 99 ; his interest in Exeter Academy, 100 ; married life of 101; his death, 78, 101, 102 ; disposition of his fortune after his death, 102 ; his grave, 103 ; high tribute paid to the memory of, by Josiah Quincy, 103, 104; fac-simile of his handwriting, 103, 105.

Phillips, John C., 105.

Phillips, Jonathan, 105.

Phillips, Mary Ann, **105.**

Phillips, Samuel (*a*), **preacher at Row-**ley, 89, 105.

Phillips, Samuel (*b*), **goldsmith at** Salem, 89, 105.

Phillips, Samuel (*c*), pastor of Second Church at Andover, Mass., **5**; some account of, 90, 105.

Phillips, Samuel (*d*), Judge, **enters** Dummer Academy, 5 ; the originator of our American Academy system, 5 ; Taylor's memoir of, 5 ; graduates from Harvard College, 5 ; his marriage, 5 ; prominent part taken by, in the struggle of the Colonies for independence, 6 ; the idea of establishing an Academy conceived by, 6 ; a letter from, to John Phillips, favoring the founding of Exeter Academy, 98; Lieut.-Governor of Massachusetts, 105.

Phillips, Samuel (*e*), one **of the** founders of the Phillips **Academy** at Andover, Mass., 7, 105.

Phillips, Sarah, 101.

Phillips, Wendell, 105 ; address by, at the Soule Festival, 61-63.

Phillips, William (*a*), 105.

Phillips, William (*b*), 105.

Phillips, William (*c*), 105.

Phillips, William (*d*), **benefactor of** Exeter Academy, 74, 105.

Phillips Academy at Andover, constitution of, drawn up and signed, 7, 96; incorporation of, 7, 96.

Phillips Exeter Academy, the, first hundred years of, 1 ; honorable record of its pupils, 2 ; how it originated, 2 ; Founder's Day and its celebration, 3 ; its act of incorporation

INDEX.

signed, 7, **76, 100**; powers granted by its act **of** incorporation, 7, 121; first meeting of its Board of Trustees, **7**, **76**; first Academy building erected, **8, 77,** 106; opening of the school, **how** delayed, 8; Benjamin Thurston named as first Preceptor of, 8; the school opened, 8, 77; formal dedication of **its** building and installation of William Woodbridge as first Preceptor, 9, **77, 100**; account of the opening ceremonies of, 13, 14; **the first** period of, under William Woodbridge, 15; summary of the first period of, 15; the second period of, under Benjamin Abbot, 16–19; prosperity of, during the second period, 19; summary of the second period of, 35, **36**; instructors at, during the second period, 36; the third period of, under **Dr.** Soule, 37-67; gift of John Langdon Sibley to, 64-66; summary of the third period of, 66, 67; instructors at, during the third period, **67;** distinguished **pupils at,** during **the** third period, 67; **the** fourth period of, under **Albert** Cornelius Perkins, 67, 68; financial history of, **69–70; the** original endowment **of, 69, 70;** charity fund merged **into general fund** of, 73; chronological summary of, 76-86; second **Academy** building erected, 78, **107; second** Academy building enlarged, **79, 108;** limitation of number of students at, 80; **some** account of Abbot Hall, 82, 116; second Academy building destroyed by fire, 83, 109; subscription to rebuild the Academy building, 84, 110, 111; third Academy building erected, 84, 112; dedication of the third Academy building, 84, 112; some **account of** Gorham Hall, 84, 117; **description** of the third Academy building, 113-116; list **of** portraits and busts belonging **to, 117– 120;** government of, how **vested,** 121; terms of its constitution, **122, 123;** its Trustees and their duties, **122, 123**; duties of its instructors, **123; the** Faculty and its office, 124; monitors **and** their duties, 124, 125; punishment, how inflicted, 125; 126; biographical sketches of distinguished pupils of, 128, 172; biographical sketches of its instructors, **173–202; biographical** sketches **of its benefactors and** Trustees, **203–220;** reminiscences and anecdotes of, 220–247; **some** account of the societies **of, 248– 271;** sports and games at, **281– 286**; tables of records for **football, base ball, and boating at,** 285, 286; table of athletic tournaments at, 286; list of its officers since its foundation, 287, 288; list of its teachers, 289–291; its laws **and** regulations, 291 - 297; regulations for boarding-houses, 296, 297; course **of** instruction at, under Dr. Abbot, 297 – 300 ; course **of** instruction at, under Dr. Soule, **301–304;** course of instruction for **1881–82,** 304–310; **table showing** increase in the number **of its pupils** from its **foundation to 1883, 310**; table showing **the** number **of** students in the **different** departments of, from 1866 to 1883, 311; **table** showing **how it** compares **with other** schools in the number of pupils sent to Harvard College, **312**; sources of aid for needy students at, 313; list of recipients of its scholarships, 314; table showing the proportion between Foundationers and Non-Foundationers at different schools, 316; its beneficiary funds, and their increase, 316; estimate of expenses

at, 316, 317; salaries of its teachers, 317, 318; Act of Incorporation of, 323-329; the Constitution of, **330-339**; poems commemorative **of,** 340-345; order of exercises at two of its anniversaries, 346-349.
Poems commemorative of Exeter Academy, 340-345.
Prescott, Benjamin F., **biographical sketch of,** 147-149; his birth, **147; his course at** Exeter Academy, **148;** graduates from Dartmouth College, 148; admitted to **the bar** in New Hampshire, 148; **his public life, 148.**
Quincy, Josiah, an early pupil at the Phillips Academy **at** Andover, 18; a reminiscence of **his** school **life,** 18; toast offered **by, at the Abbot** Festival, 31; **high** tribute paid by, to the memory **of John** Phillips, 102, 103.
Ringe, Aunt, reminiscence **of, 244-246.**
Saltonstall, Hon. Leverett, his bequest **to Exeter** Academy, 73, 165; **biographical** sketch of, 165, 166.
Saltonstall, Sir Richard, one of the early settlers **of** Watertown, Massachusetts, **3.**
Seligman, Jesse, **his gift to Exeter** Academy, 113.
Sibley, Dr. Jonathan, **his gift to** Exeter Academy, 65, **83.**
Sibley, John Langdon, **his connection** with the library **at** Harvard College, 64, 211, 212, 213; speech by, at the Soule Festival, 64-66; his gift to Exeter Academy, 64-66, 83, 212; biographical sketch of, 211-213.
Smith, **Jeremiah, teacher at the** Phillips Academy at Andover, **18,** 215; extract from speech by, at the Abbot Festival, 30, 215; biographical sketch of, 214-216.

Snow, C. H. B., verses by, **sung at** the Soule festival, 345, 346.
Soule, George, **37;** some account of the family of, **38.**
Soule, Gideon Lane, his high commendation of Benjamin Abbot, 27; the third Principal of Exeter Academy, 37; **his early** educational advantages, **39, 42;** his birth and **birthplace, 39, 40;** his pre-eminence **in both** scholarship and sports, **41;** anecdote of, 41; nervous temperament **of,** 41; begins his classical studies, 42; enters **Exeter** Academy, **42; enters** Bowdoin College, **42; his high** rank **at** both school **and college,** 42, **43;** graduates from **Bowdoin** College, 43; appointed assistant instructor at Exeter Academy, 43; **enters the Andover** Theological Seminary, 43; **his** further studies at Bowdoin College, after graduation, 43; appointed Professor of Ancient Languages **at** Exeter Academy, **44,** 79; **becomes** Principal of the **Academy,** 44, 81; some account **of the** family of, 44; receives the **degree** of LL. D. from Harvard **College, 44;** semi-centennial festival in honor of, **45, 59-66,** 84; **resigns his position as** Principal, 45, **84; receives the** title of "Principal Emeritus," 44; his interest in **the** Academy after resignation, 45; his gradual failure in health and mental powers, 46; death of, 46, 85; funeral of, 46; the physical characteristics of, 46; how he was led to prepare for college, 47-50; his joyous disposition, 50; popularity of, among his pupils, 51; his good influence upon the morals of his pupils, 50, 51; anecdote of, by Rev. John H. Morison, 51-53; his eminent qualifications as a disciplinarian,

53, 56; anecdote of, by George T.
Tilden, 53-55; high tribute paid
to, by Dr. Peabody, 57; anecdote
of his method of conducting recitations, 57; his after-school talks
with his pupils, 58; his interest in
the town and townspeople of Exeter, 58; his grief at the destruction
of the second Academy building,
110; anecdote of, 247.

Soule, John B. L., reminiscence of
Benjamin Abbot by, 21, 23, 24;
his verses on the loss of the second Academy building, 111, 342,
343.

Soule, Moses, Deacon, 38.

Soule, Moses, reminiscences of school
life at Exeter in 1822, 235-239.

Sparks, Jared, widow of, 111; biographical sketch of, 151-154; is
placed on the "Foundation" list
at Exeter Academy, 151-153; his
early efforts to obtain an education,
152, 221; high praise of, by Dr.
Abbot, 153, 154; outline of his
life and labors, 154,

Sparks, William E., reminiscence of
the Phillips Exeter Academy by,
107.

Stebbins, Rev. Horatio, orator at the
centennial celebration of the Phillips Exeter Academy, 86.

Thacher, Peter O., biographical
sketch of, 197, 198.

Thurston, Benjamin, suggested as
first Preceptor of Exeter Academy,
8; as temporary instructor hears
first lesson recited in the Academy, 9; his address at the installation of William Woodbridge as
first Preceptor of the Academy,
9, 10; one of the first Trustees,
326.

Tilden, George T., anecdote of Dr.
Soule by, 53-56.

Tuck, Amos, biographical sketch of,
216.

Tufts, James Arthur, biographical
sketch of, 201, 202.

Walker, James, teacher at Exeter
Academy, 42, 186, 187; biographical sketch of, 186, 187.

Ware, Jr., Henry, teacher at the
Phillips Exeter Academy, 42, 184;
biographical sketch of, 184-186;
song by, sung at the Abbot
Festival, 341.

Washington, Bushrod, biographical
sketch of, 170.

Waterhouse, Prof. Sylvester, anecdote of Lewis Cass by, 143; biographical sketch of, 167-170;
testimony of regard from his former pupils at Washington University, 168, 169; his public life, 169;
his literary productions, 169, 170;
eulogy on J. G. Hoyt by, 178.

Webster, Abigail Eastman, 129.

Webster, Daniel, presides at the
Abbot Festival, 29, 138; elected a
Trustee of Exeter Academy, 80,
135, 139; biographical sketch of,
129-139; his birth and early youth,
129; his father decides to give
him a college education, 129, 130;
enters Exeter Academy, 130; anecdote of, 130, 131; his superiority
in scholarship at Exeter, 132, 133;
his earliest efforts and failure at
declamation, 133; enters Dartmouth College, 134; the development of his oratorical powers, 134;
his success at college, 134; anecdote of, by Edmund Chadwick,
135; sends his son Edward to
Exeter, 137; extract from a letter
to his son at Exeter, 137; a letter
to the pupils of Exeter Academy,
139; death of, 139; his last words,
139.

Webster, Ebenezer, 129.

Wentworth, Prof. George A., 84;
biographical sketch of, 200; anecdotes of, 246, 247.

Wheelwright, John, founder of the town of Exeter, 38, 219.
Whitman, Judge H. C., his reminiscences of Benjamin Abbot, 21.
Winkley, Henry, his gift to Exeter Academy, 74, 85.
Wood, Rev. Samuel, prepares Daniel Webster for Dartmouth College, 134.
Woodbridge, Rev. Ashbel, 15.
Woodbridge, William, installed a first Preceptor of Exeter Academy, 9; his address at his installation, 10–13; biographical notice of, 15: resigns his position as Preceptor, 15, 77.
Wyman, Jeffries, biographical sketch of, 172.

University Press: John Wilson & Son, Cambridge.

www.ingramcontent.com/pod-product-compliance
Lightning Source LLC
Chambersburg PA
CBHW032027220426
43664CB00006B/394